JON S T QUAH

CURBING
CORRUPTION
IN ASIA

A Comparative
Study of Six
Countries

EASTERN UNIVERSITIES PRESS
by Marshall Cavendish

© 2003 Times Media Private Limited

First published 2003
by Times Media Private Limited
(Academic Publishing) under the imprint
Eastern Universities Press
by Marshall Cavendish

Times Centre, 1 New Industrial Road,
Singapore 536196
Fax: (65) 6284 9772
E-mail: tap@tpl.com.sg
Online Book Store:
http://www.timesacademic.com

Printed by Vine Graphic Pte Ltd, Singapore
on non-acidic paper

National Library Board (Singapore)
Cataloguing in Publication Data
Quah, Jon S. T.
Curbing Corruption in Asia: A Comparative
Study of Six Countries / Jon S.T. Quah. – Singapore:
Eastern Universities Press, 2003.

p. cm.
ISBN: 981-210-215-9

1. Misconduct in office – Asia.
2. Political corruption – Asia.
3. Political corruption – Asia – Prevention.
I. Title.

JQ29.5
364.1323095 — dc21
SLS2003009304

London • New York • Beijing • Shanghai
• Bangkok • Kuala Lumpur • Singapore

Table of Contents

Chapter 8

List of Tables

Foreword

A current scandal in China dubbed *Heishao* or Black Whistle involves the matter of alleged bribing of soccer referees.[1] Before soccer was privatised, referees received about five cents a game and sometimes bath coupons as a bonus. Now the going rate is about $7,300 a game. If teams fail to pay, it is rumoured that referees throw games to those who do. The Chinese Soccer Association that governs the professional sport has investigated but has not taken any action because of lack of evidence. The owner of Zhejiang Lucheng based in Hangzhou blew the whistle after his team lost several important games. He maintained that only after he got into the business that he discovered giving money to referees was standard operating procedure. Soccer fans do not believe that anything will be done to change this practice which would not have come to light had the owner's team won its matches. Now, he is subject himself for possible prosecution for his charges. Meantime, presumably the practice of bribing referees and fixing games continues as part of the corruption that has become common in post-Mao China.[2]

If there is any doubt about this, the presence of so many Chinese high rollers, including notorious gangster Liu Yong, in the gambling city of Las Vegas in Nevada in the United States is further evidence of the spread of this disease.[3] Their open gambling raises questions about the source of their huge bets, how come the Chinese and American authorities allow their frequent trips, and who suffers when they lose so much money which does not actually belong to them but is being laundered for Chinese organisations. Like casinos in North and South Korea, Australia and the Philippines, several Las Vegas casinos have offices in Beijing to organise groups of high stakes gamblers (or "whales" as they are known in the business) and provide assistance to them for obtaining entry visas. Even though many risk being refused visas and possible prosecution on their return, much of the money they bet is known to have been embezzled from China and smuggling. To get around visa requirements (which ask for proof of financial resources and source of money) and Chinese restrictions on currency export and customs regulations, many set up bogus companies, submit fake documents and bribe customs officials to put bags of money on board their planes. Banned in 1949, gambling and prostitution have returned since the 1980s, together with government organised "research" teams whose itinerary somehow often includes Las Vegas and other gambling resorts in the United States and elsewhere in Asia.

These relatively petty scandals show how studies of corruption are at the same time both enticing and intriguing on the one hand, and off-putting and distasteful on the other because they reveal flaws in human nature. They are enticing and intriguing because they stir people's curiosity about who is corrupt and corrupted, what they do and what impact they have on everybody else. Despite progress in civilised behaviour over the centuries and successes in combating and confining much wrongdoing, corruption persists, takes novel forms and seems impervious to attempts to rid society of this scourge. Unless relentless pressure is maintained, corruption reappears, assumes more sophisticated guises and re-establishes itself in ways that prove harder to tackle.

THE CHALLENGE TO INVESTIGATION

The fact that corruption is disreputable does not make its investigation inviting. Indeed, there may well be dangers to the whistleblowers and the investigators should they find out too much, reveal too much and expose themselves to the vengeance of the corrupt and their collaborators. To start with, corruption by its very nature is secretive, hidden, closed, and the corrupt combine in a common vow of silence to protect themselves against exposure. To penetrate corrupt circles, investigators take risks; if they become known, they may be killed or otherwise effectively silenced by threats to their loved ones. They may have to flee and hide to avoid personal injury, unable for the time being to live normal lives until the danger recedes. They may not know at the outset where their investigations may lead them and what they may uncover, who may be involved and how powerful and well connected the latter might be, sufficient enough to prevent any further discoveries. Indeed, the mischief done to investigators is so well known that it is often fictionalised in books and films to disguise reality and protect others from being harmed. The truth can be stranger or less believable than fiction.

The more corrupt the society and the more corrupt the powerful within it, the more dangerous it is to embark and persist in investigation, research and reporting. Few societies take kindly to anyone revealing their failings and shortcomings, certainly not to exposures of corrupt practices in their midst. The penalties for breaking taboos sheltering corruption can be quite harsh and exacting, not necessarily because the corrupt rule but because the rulers want to preserve their front of integrity and assure the ruled that wrongdoing is rare and exceptional i.e., not the rule. Bad eggs do exist and fail to be detected in time but their infrequent occurrence only proves how trustworthy the whole system is and how reliable it is. Better if exposures should be confined to the inner circle who know how to handle such things behind closed doors to limit any damage to credibility that might otherwise occur. It is in the public's interest that the public be kept unaware of internal wrongdoing, lest people become too alarmed, too suspicious, too questioning, and too cynical.

Indeed, corruption may be so shielded that the only way to get to know about it is to indulge or participate oneself, that is, to become corrupt in order to expose corruption. One may have to dirty one's hands to get access to the corrupt to be able to expose what is really going on so that the innocent public is protected and avoids becoming victim. This is the classic dilemma of many a potential whistleblower. Even when clean, there is always the nagging possibility that the whistleblowers too are guilty of the same misconduct and that maybe they know even more than they are prepared to reveal; they might be covering up far worse or protecting themselves or falsely accusing others of their own misdeeds. Unsuspected corruption too often comes to light this way not just through honest whistleblowers who cannot go along with what they see around them but also through guilt-ridden participants who can no longer live with their secrets. There is no guarantee as to who will be given the benefit of any doubt. Whistleblowers too, can find themselves shouting to deaf ears and viewed merely as disgruntled trouble-makers or opportunistic publicity seekers or just touched in the head and making it all up.

If these were not difficulties enough, there is the obvious fact that every society, every regime, every country has its own particular way of doing things—different political, economic and legal systems, different attitudes to wrongdoing and corruption, different values and priorities as to what should be done and what can be ignored. As reported by Transparency International headquartered in Berlin, at one extreme are those so indulgent and permissive, it matters not what is said because little is likely to be done. There is not much point writing about corruption because it is so endemic, so embedded and so expected, i.e., so institutionalised, that few are likely to take any notice other than to see that such information is suppressed and the purveyors are stopped in their tracks. They engage in "constructive deceit" and the pretence that all is well in their world although to outsiders the contrary is the case. The less, therefore, that outsiders know, the better for all concerned for the less outsiders are likely to interfere and stir things up, being misinformed or malicious or hypercritical. Thus, their accounts must be distortions or fabrications, certainly unreliable and suspect, and without credibility. At the other extreme, there are those, admittedly few and far between, so intolerant of corruption that they encourage whistleblowers and complainants, embark on investigations, follow up on suspicions to see whether there is any truth at all in allegations of wrongdoing, and take measures to root out offenders and adopt reforms to minimise any recurrence. Where between these extremes, any specific society fits is a matter of guesswork although Transparency International and the World Bank are trying to provide some accurate measures. Nevertheless, it is conceded by all that the ingenuity of the unscrupulous often outwits preventive measures so that the fight against corruption is endless, intricate and handicapped by the need to protect and preserve other precious social values of which the unscrupulous can take advantage to continue their corrupt practices.

SCARCITY, MORALITY AND POWER

What is unique about corruption is that it occurs at the convergence of scarcity, morality and power (or position). If there were so much abundance in the world that all human needs could be met and all human desires fulfilled, there would be little point to be corrupt. Corruption occurs just because the opposite applies: the world is beset with scarcity. Demand often far exceeds supply. Economic rent can be extracted and the consequences of going without may be so catastrophic that people will pay whatever price (not just in monetary terms) is being asked and morality can be thrown to the winds when sheer survival is at stake. So much has to do with circumstances. The rich can afford to be honest; the desperately poor cannot, not when it comes to personal security, reputation, privilege, collective services, position or wherever there is fierce and bitter competition and access is restricted. Even so, wealth is no guarantee of morality because wealth in itself can promote greed or expectations of similar success in matters unrelated to wealth. Nonetheless, reducing scarcity should reduce corruption or the need for corruption and this can be achieved by reducing common expectations (or limiting the public show of privilege), increasing the availability wherever possible of that which is scarce through increased supply, and ensuring greater and more equitable access for all to what is available.

But scarcity is only one part of the equation. There is little evidence to prove that the rich are more honest or moral than anyone else. On the other hand, there is telling proof that even in the most desperate circumstances, not everyone turns on everybody else. The poor retain their honesty under trying conditions, at least with their peers although sorely tempted to cheat those who they consider their exploiters. They seem to have an inherent sense of fair play. Hence the democratic belief that while human beings may be imperfect, on the whole they can be trusted to do the right thing, that right thing being the religious and ideological golden rule: "Don't do to others what you would not want them to do to you" which is simple and easily understood by everyone. If everyone practised or lived by the golden rule, then corruption would be much diminished. But for all kinds of reasons, they only follow it selectively or they fail to see where it applies in their daily lives. Beliefs differ. Morals differ. Values differ. Priorities differ. Where one person sees right, another sees wrong. Where one sees innocent gesture, another sees intimidation.

Yet, when it comes to identifying what constitutes corrupt practices, there is surprising universal agreement although there is difference of opinion about some specific forms of corruption such as institutionalised gift-giving and about the degree of tolerance allowed for instance to feather-bedding. What probably most defines corruption and distinguishes it from incompetence or ignorance or inexperience is motivation. Those who indulge do not participate out of ignorance; they know what they do and they know that what they do is not approved: it is considered wrong for being against prevailing norms, morality, expected behaviour, sense of right, just action. They persist in their wrongdoing, perhaps out of fear, perhaps with guilty conscience, perhaps they see no alternative but to go along, perhaps they believe that what they do is for the best, not for themselves personally but to advance some noble cause, some national advantage, some party goal. Whatever the motivation, they can excuse themselves and justify their wrongdoing.

Differences in attitude toward corruption depend much on whether one is on the receiving end or not, which in turn depends on power or position. People without power or position rarely gain from corrupt practices; on the contrary, they are usually the exploited and helpless, its victims whether or not they are aware of being the greatest losers. Lord Acton is rightly remembered for his dictum: "Power corrupts; absolute power corrupts absolutely". While his emphasis was meant to be on the second part of the sentence, that the holders of absolute power come to believe themselves beyond human accountability other than history's judgment, the first part of his sentence hits home to everyone. What is the point of having power if one does not benefit from it? There seems to be an overwhelming impulse or temptation to use one's power to advantage and to deny its fruits to anyone who does not possess it. That is what power is all about. If one does not use it, then one will quickly lose it and its advantages. History records what terrible misdeeds have been done by people in power. Hence, civilised societies have tried to erect many safeguards around the exercise of power to prevent its abuse and misuse. How much corruption prevails depends largely on the effectiveness of such safeguards.

The major key is the integrity of the legal system and legal enforcement. The rule of law is meaningless without honest independent judges and professional police. With those firmly in place, everyone else had better beware and think again about committing corrupt acts lest these authorities find out what is occurring and will take the necessary actions in their relentless pursuit of wrongdoers. If there is one place to start combating corruption, it is here. Fearless judges can override all others, enforce the law and protect basic human rights against false accusations. Honest police cannot be bought, will not make deals, will not turn a blind eye and will follow up complaints to sort fact from fiction. Likewise, honest prison guards do not allow their charges to escape or conduct business from their prison or make deals to allow a pleasant if not profitable sojourn there. Knowing that once caught and proven guilty, the corrupt cannot escape punishment or gain from their misdeeds helps to prevent outrageous acts of corruption and even minor acts put them in jeopardy.

CORRUPTION IN ASIAN COUNTRIES

The six country studies in this book illustrate all these points. They try to let the facts speak for themselves without embellishment or distortion. None is compromising or fearful of stepping on too many toes. Underlying them is the clear realisation that one of the major challenges to the further progress and development of much of Asia is institutionalised corruption where corrupt practices have become or remain standard operating procedure at least for the initiated and accepted by the inner circle of participants who greatly benefit thereby: indeed so much so that corrupt practices do not raise many eyebrows or evoke much open discussion. Anyone who does not join in and remains aloof is considered odd, suspect and untrustworthy and something of a sucker. Obviously, this institutionalised corruption is a deviation from what others assume to be the case, a distortion that has become habitual and self-perpetuating, and even a perversion from what outsiders understand obtains. It might take quite minor, unimportant and even highly efficient forms of conducting public business than otherwise might be the case, and therefore not worth bothering about. But, alas too often, it degenerates into major, important and expensive forms to all those who do not participate, who are being deceived, cheated and defrauded by what amounts to hollow governance where little is what it appears. Eventually, if the rot goes too far, institutionalised corruption like outrageous forms of personal corruption that it incorporates can be catastrophic for everyone, for it eventually ends up in military defeat, civil revolt, economic collapse, endemic violence and communal strife.

In this, corruption in Asia fits a common pattern experienced around the world; it does not differ that much from official behaviour elsewhere outside Western Europe, North America and the wealthier countries in the Commonwealth. What these six countries compellingly illustrate is that although corruption is difficult to tackle, it can be done successfully with political will, public support, administrative determination, legal enforcement and civic conscientiousness. In some countries, the circumstances are favourable whereas in others the task is still overwhelming.

For instance, the detailed accounts of the current situation in India and South Korea sound very familiar, even though neither country was included in the classic study undertaken some 40 years ago by a Dutch sociologist whose main concern then was Indonesia.[4] Several Asian countries were however part of the study 20 years later undertaken by Ledivina Carino and colleagues.[5] Over the past forty or so years in India[6] and South Korea,[7] little seems to have changed compared with Hong Kong[8] and particularly with Singapore where every effort has been made to stamp out official corruption as Professor Quah has previously recorded.[9]

Now that Hong Kong has become part of China, it remains to be seen which will make the greater impact on the other as far as anti-corruption efforts are concerned. The situation in the Philippines has changed. As this book records, a new stand is being taken against institutional corruption in that country. Even the democratically elected President Estrada has been forced to step down for his alleged misdeeds in office although this can be interpreted as the kleptocracy ridding itself of an upstart populist. In contrast, the situation in Mongolia appears not to have changed significantly if at all. Without benchmarks it is difficult to know because until recently it was part of the Soviet Union and inaccessible to outside study. Professor Quah's analysis is in line with what is now known about other former Asian members of the Soviet Union east of the Urals, if not with most of the countries that were dominated by the Soviet Union and ruled by communism. The facts as recorded and related about the country studies speak for themselves and hardly need further analysis or speculation. However, they do open several new and innovative paths to further research about each country and why they differ from each other.

How different is corruption in general in Asia from other countries outside the region? Not much at all from the rest of the world outside democratic Western Europe, North America and the wealthier members of the Commonwealth that rank relatively clean on the annual Transparency International Corruption

Perceptions Index that attempts to assess the perceived extent of reputed corrupt practices. The region seems to follow much the same patterns as elsewhere although there are interesting variations among even neighbouring countries. Some countries seem incapable of warding off foreign sources of corruption while others have much more to worry about from domestic sources. Some export their reputation of corruption through expatriates who cause trouble for their newly adopted countries by acting as illegal conduits while others find their emigrants adapt quite quickly to prevailing practices elsewhere and leave any former links to the underworld or organised crime or black economy behind. One exception appears to be the export from South East Asia of home grown narcotics and rare items found only in the region but much in demand in the rest of the world; again, their availability differs much between countries and while some countries try to stamp out any such trade, others turn a blind eye or actually indulge in illegal international smuggling from which they benefit. In this, such countries resemble the narco-democracies in Latin America and the narcotics exporters of the Middle East, all of which without oil fare badly.

The implication is clear. Corruption thwarts progress. The very circumstances that give rise to widespread corruption are handicapping enough in themselves but the virulence of corrupt practices makes the implementation of progressive developmental measures even more difficult. Outsiders are put off and are reluctant to get involved in any risky investments if they believe they will be denied any fruits there-from or they are required to share too much with undeserving insiders who contribute very little and take no risk themselves. Insiders secrete their returns and salt what they can away either overseas or in conspicuous consumption at home, neither contributing much to real national development. The rewards are distorting, going from the truly deserving to the undeserving, thereby setting the wrong example, giving the wrong message and undermining incentives to change. This is not to say that nothing gets done and nothing changes. Things do get done but at a price and too often are greatly overpriced, and the things that get done are not necessarily those that need doing the most and can give the best returns. Changes occur but are very much self-selected, gradual, unthreatening to the corrupt, and unavoidable. Where the corrupt rule and hold all the cards, who can stand up to them, who can take them on, who would want to beat them at their own game? To resist requires a different mindset, one that may not be appreciated by the majority let alone by the minority as long as every person believes, rightly or wrongly, that more can be gained by going along than by standing up, i.e., every man for himself and the devil take the hindmost which is hardly the way to national development. After many years of ignoring corruption, the international community has at last admitted that it is more dysfunctional than functional to making a better future for humanity. There is just too much evidence that cannot be excused away. Yes, progress has been made but without so much corruption, so much more might have been achieved.

HELP IS AT HAND

This recent change of international heart has meant that corruption is now seen as an obstacle to global as well as national development. International organisations are now trying to make up for their puny efforts in the past when they either ignored corruption altogether and even protected corrupt practices as being entrepreneurial or merely paid lip service to combating it without really doing much about it even in their midst. To some extent, in their haste they are rediscovering the wheel so to speak. In the past 40 years, corruption has been taken seriously by others less well placed and connected. Professor Quah has long been an example of a serious scholar of corruption who has been bold enough to investigate the phenomenon and to publish his findings. He has been a member of a global network of people and organisations who have been exposing corruption to anyone who would listen and who have been evaluating efforts to combat corrupt practices. After all, corruption is almost as old as governance itself and attempts to put it on a better path go back as least as far. In this respect, there is little new under the sun. But, finally, their initiatives are being rediscovered and the taboos that have surrounded the subject have been broken almost all over the world so that knowledge is now freely available to anyone who wants to tackle corruption.

Pride of place must fall to the non-governmental organisation, Transparency International, established in 1993 by former World Bank official Peter Eigen, whose attempts to establish an anti-corruption programme within had been stifled. Headquartered in Berlin, Transparency International (TI) operates through its many national chapters that act as its driving force to combat both domestic and international corruption, mostly bribery, by raising public awareness about its damaging effects ("undermines good government, fundamentally distorts public policy, leads to the misallocation of resources, harms the private sector and private sector development and particularly hurts the poor"), advocating policy reform, working toward the implementation of multilateral conventions and monitoring compliance by governments, corporations and banks. TI is an international network of like-minded individuals and organisations that uses its connections to support anti-corruption campaigns and to educate the public through mass media exposure of wrongdoing. Most influential has been its annual publication of its Corruption Perceptions Index based on surveys of the perception of corruption that rates more than a hundred countries from the least corrupt (usually the Scandinavian countries together with some Commonwealth countries) to the most corrupt (usually West African and some Asian countries).

TI has begun to publish a Bribe-Payers Index which surveys the propensity of countries to pay bribes for business. Its new Global Corruption Report is an annual survey of corruption as exposed by the world's mass media and a mine of information about what has been done to reduce corrupt practices, updates on international conventions like the OECD Anti-Bribery Convention, special reports on topics such as money laundering, and a fairly complete bibliography on corruption.[10] Its Source Book, the largest and most inclusive of its publications, discusses different aspects of corruption and anti-corruption measures in detail and in effect constitutes an updated handbook.[11] TI has become possibly the major anti-corruption organisation by taking over the International Anti-Corruption Conferences that preceded its establishment and by sub-contracting with other international organisations their anti-corruption campaigns. Paradoxically, where once TI's founder struggled in vain to convince the World Bank to recognise corruption and do something about it, the World Bank now funds TI to conduct much of its anti-corruption work. Such has been the revolution in the World Bank's thinking.

Until the early 1990s, the World Bank had been reluctant to confront the issue of corruption; indeed, the word had rarely been employed in any World Bank document although it was an obvious fact of life in its dealings with countries and alas, as Peter Eigen had tried to point out, all too often a way of life in many countries which borrowed from the bank. The turnaround can be dated from its two reports on governance in 1992 and 1994, a change in its Director, and his announcement at the 1996 Annual Meeting that it would offer assistance to member countries for anti-corruption programmes. Wolfenson said:

> [W]e need to deal with the cancer of corruption. In country after country, people are demanding action on this issue. They know that corruption diverts resources from the poor to the rich, increases the cost of running businesses, distorts public expenditures, and deters foreign investors. They also know that corruption erodes the constituency for aid programs and humanitarian relief. And we know that corruption is a major barrier to sound and equitable development.... Working with our partners, the World Bank Group will help any of our member countries to implement programs to discourage corrupt practices.[12]

Since then, the World Bank has overhauled its own procedures to reduce the possibilities of corrupt dealings, it has strengthened its internal affairs investigations to uncover corruption within, it has invested more in discovering the nature of corruption and effective strategies to combat it and has embarked on a programme to assist member countries combat their own corruption, particularly bribery, extortion, and fraud.[13] Today, the World Bank openly admits that corruption is a major barrier to sustainable and equitable development and that an anti-corruption strategy is essential for political, social and economic development. It is working on the details of daily operating practices not just in its own dealings with member countries but also on the latter's financial and commercial dealings with allcomers, particularly looking at public accountability, transparency, civil society participation, competition, power-sharing, and public sector management. The World Bank's sister organisation, the International Monetary Fund, has not been far behind in its quest to curb worldwide corruption in trade, commerce and banking. Since 1997, IMF staff must consider corruption and accountability issues in dealing with borrowing countries according to guidelines designed to eliminate opportunities for rent seeking, corruption and fraudulent activity.

Actually the Organisation for Economic Cooperation and Development (OECD) had beaten the World Bank and Transparency International. It placed corruption on its agenda in 1989 to fight corruption in international business and to help level the competitive playing field for companies in the international market. But it was not until 1997 that it agreed to the Anti-Bribery Convention (Convention on Combating Bribery of Foreign Officials in International Business Transactions) that went into effect in 1999 to criminalise transnational bribery. Since then, most OECD countries have altered their laws accordingly, revoking the tax deductibility of bribes for example, and have strengthened their ability to enforce the law and identify loop-holes. In addition, its Public Management Committee (PUMA) assists governments in detecting, investigating, prosecuting and penalising official misconduct and corruption and promotes ethics in government.[14] A joint initiative between the OECD and the European Union led in 1992 to the establishment of the Support for Improvement in Governance and Management (SIGMA) to advise countries in Central and Eastern Europe to improve their public administration, including anti-corruption measures.[15] The OECD in partnership with the U.S. Agency for International Development (AID) provide the Anti-Corruption Network for Transition Economies (ACN) to bring together government, private sector and civil society participants to promote reforms that foster integrity, transparency and ethics. Independently, the U.S. AID's Center for Democracy and Governance has issued a handbook on fighting corruption to assist its missions to develop strategic responses to official corruption.[16]

Before all of these got into the act, the United Nations had employed its various units dealing with governance and public administration and economics to look into corruption and these were later joined by the United Nations Center for International Crime Prevention and its 1999 Global Programme Against Corruption and the United Nations Development Programme.[17] So the list could be lengthened of all the international bodies, banks, management consulting firms, universities, research institutions and private organisations such as the Journalists Against Corruption (funded by the Center for International Private Enterprise in Washington, D.C.) which have been plugging away to draw attention to corruption and to find ways of combating it and establishing international standards for public ethical conduct.[18] All publish and share their findings and information on the internet. No more is there any lack of knowledge. No more can corruption be excused. What is alas missing is how the corrupt defuse all these initiatives and bend the anti-corruption measures to their advantage. Rarely can be found any assessment of anti-corruption strategies over any lengthy period of time. Most claim immediate successes and have to be taken at their word. Actually, more is expectation than result and what seems to work in the short run fades away in time and the old corrupt practices return in different, more sophisticated guises.

The corrupt turn out to be resilient and also so politically powerful that they capture the anti-corruption agencies and derail them. Once the initial fanfare is over, wily operators ensure that they are hamstrung by lack of resources, jurisdiction disputes, virulent criticism of incompetence and infringement of civil rights, plants and stooges, need for secrecy, need to avoid national disgrace and personal embarrassment, and deliberate sabotage. Unless the pressure is maintained, corruption is likely to escape effective remedy or return in more virulent form. The battles may be won but the war never ceases no matter how many victories are scored. As international organisations are finding out, the horse can be led to the stream but cannot be made to drink.

This obvious truth has been well illustrated in recent years. Transparency International's annual reports continue to cite country after country, case after case where hardly anything seems to change despite visits of international advisers, several national conferences, new anti-corruption campaigns and official reports claiming success in combating corrupt practices. While much attention is given to official corruption, worse scandals take place in the private sector and among leading business corporations, illustrating lax ethical standards among all sections of society, the leading professions, particularly in law, accounting and medicine, and with the apparent connivance of the very organisations established to ensure fair practices and upright behaviour in governance. Awareness of the dysfunctions of corruption and immorality has been raised, action stirred and more publicity given to scandals but the challenge to contain and reduce corruption remains just as difficult as it has always been, perhaps even more difficult despite new investigative techniques and technology. In short, public officials are far from being alone in misusing entrusted power for private gain. Every public institution is at risk. The will to tackle corruption remains weak, smothered by layers of secrecy, indifference, self-indictment and indecision. In too many countries, corruption thrives openly and unashamedly. Public disenchantment, media publicity and organisational transparency are all very well but political and business leaders are still wary if not unwilling of grasping the nettle. Professor Jon Quah's comparative study of anti-corruption strategies in six Asian countries reveals little that is not already known but clearly it calls for strong, effective action now, not just polite, inoffensive talk to prevent corruption from getting completely out of hand.

Gerald E. Caiden
Professor of Public Administration
University of Southern California

ENDNOTES

1   Ching-Ching Ni, "Bribery Scandal Kicks Up a Controversy in Chinese Soccer", *Los Angeles Times*, 7 April 2002, p. A3.

2   Stephen K. Ma, "The Culture of Corruption in Post-Mao China". In Gerald E. Caiden, O.P. Dwivedi, and Joseph Jabbra (eds.), *Where Corruption Lives*, Bloomfield: Kumarian Press, 2001, pp. 145-158.

3   John Pomfret, "China's High Rollers Flock to Las Vegas", *The Washington Post National Weekly Edition*, 1-7 April 2002, p. 17.

4   W.F. Wertheim, "Sociological Aspects of Corruption in Southeast Asia", In his *East-West Parallels*. The Hague: W. van Hoeve, 1964, pp. 103-131.

5   Ledivina V. Carino, (ed.), *Bureaucratic Corruption in Asia: Causes, Consequences and Controls*. Quezon City: JMC Press and College of Public Administration, University of the Philippines, 1986.

6   Samuel Paul, "Corruption in India: Who Will Bell the Cat?" *Asian Journal of Political Science*, Vol. 6, No. 1 (June 1998), pp. 1-15.

7   Young Jong Kim, *Bureaucratic Corruption: The Case of Korea*, 4th ed. Seoul: Chomyung Press, 1994.

8   Bertrand de Speville, *Hong Kong: Policy Initiatives Against Corruption*. Paris: Organisation for Economic Cooperation and Development, 1997.

9   Jon S.T. Quah, *Administrative and Legal Measures for Combatting Bureaucratic Corruption in Singapore*. Singapore: Department of Political Science, University of Singapore Occasional Paper No. 34, 1978; and Jon S.T. Quah, "Singapore's Experience in Curbing Corruption". In Arnold J. Heidenheimer, Michael Johnston and Victor T. LeVine (eds.), *Political Corruption: A Handbook*. New Brunswick: Transaction Publishers, 1989, pp. 841-853.

10   Robin Hodess (ed.), *Global Corruption Report 2001*. Berlin: Transparency International, 2001.

11   Jeremy Pope, *TI Source Book 2000, Confronting Corruption: The Elements of a National Integrity System*. Berlin: Transparency International, 2000.

12   John Wolfenson, "Address at the Opening Session of the World Bank/ IMF Annual Meeting", in Washington, D.C., on 1 October 1996.

13   Cheryl Gray and Daniel Kaufmann, "Corruption and Development". *Finance and Development*, Vol. 35, No. 1 (1998), pp. 7-10.

14   Organisation for Economic Cooperation and Development, "Principles for Managing Ethics in the Public Service". *PUMA Policy Brief* No. 4. Paris: OECD, 1998; and Organisation for Economic Cooperation and Development, *Reinforcing Ethics in the Public Sector.* Paris: OECD, 2000.

15   Bart Edes, "Promoting Integrity in the Public Service: the Contribution of the OECD". Paper presented at the Milan International Conference on "Responding to the Challenge of Corruption". Paris: SIGMA, OECD, 1999; and Organisation for Economic Cooperation and Development, *Corruption in the Public Sector.* Paris: OECD, 1999.

16   Phyllis Dininio, *USAID Handbook on Fighting Corruption.* Washington, D.C.: Center for Democracy and Governance, 1998.

17   United Nations Development Programme, *Fighting Corruption to Improve Governance.* New York: Management Development and Governance Division, UNDP, 1999.

18   Terry Cooper and Diane Yoder, "Public Management Ethics Standards in a Transitional World ". *Public Integrity*, Vol. 4, No. 4 (2002), pp. 333-352.

Preface

My research interest in corruption dates back to 1977, when I was invited to participate in a comparative study of seven Asian countries which was funded by the International Development Research Centre (IDRC) of Canada. The countries involved in the project were Hong Kong, Malaysia, Nepal, the Philippines, Singapore, South Korea and Thailand. This IDRC project was entitled "Negative Bureaucratic Behaviour in Asian Countries" even though corruption was the actual subject of research. At that time, 26 years ago, it was not politically correct to use the term "corruption" in the research project title in order to obtain research funding.

Looking back now, it is indeed remarkable that the research project was initiated by Professor Raul P. de Guzman, who was then Dean of the College of Public Administration, University of the Philippines, and the project coordinator. It is also remarkable that the project involving seven country research teams was completed and resulted in many publications.[1] I am grateful to Raul for inviting me to participate in the project as part of the Singapore team[2] and for our subsequent association in various projects.

From my initial interest in corruption in Singapore, I extended my interest to the other original four members of the Association of Southeast Asian Nations (ASEAN)–Indonesia, Malaysia, the Philippines and Thailand[3]–and subsequently to Hong Kong,[4] South Korea,[5] Mongolia,[6] and India.[7] Since 1998, I have also participated in many conferences and workshops on corruption and governance issues organised by the Asian Development Bank, the Organisation for Economic Cooperation and Development, the United Nations Development Programme, and the World Bank.

During January to June 2000, I began teaching PS3221 Corruption and Governance in Asian Countries to students at the Department of Political Science, National University of Singapore (NUS). I taught this module again during January-June 2001, January-June 2002 and January-June 2003.[8] I am very grateful to the many students from Singapore and Malaysia and the exchange students from Canada, Germany, Hong Kong, Japan, and the United States for their interest in these modules and their feedback on my analysis of the anti-corruption strategies in the ten Asian countries.[9]

I was invited by Professor Tan Chwee Huat to teach MHR6008 Corruption in the Asia Pacific to his graduate students enrolled in the Master of Human Resources at the NUS Faculty of Business Administration from September to November 2000. I am also grateful to Professor Yuzo Yabuno of the Faculty of Law at Kyushu University for inviting me to conduct an intensive three-day seminar on Combating Corruption in Asian Countries for his graduate students from December 3-5, 2001 in Fukuoka, Japan. Finally, I would like to thank Dr Peter Larmour, Director of Graduate Studies in Development Administration at the National Centre for Development Studies, Australian National University for inviting me to give two seminars on corruption in Asian countries for his Corruption and Anti-Corruption Course in August 2002.

This book examines how corruption is controlled in six Asian countries, namely, Hong Kong, India, Mongolia, the Philippines, Singapore and South Korea. These countries have been selected because of my familiarity with them and because they illustrate between them three patterns of corruption control in Asian countries. Pattern 1 is demonstrated by Mongolia, which has anti-corruption laws but no independent agency. India and the Philippines are examples of Pattern 2 as they have many anti-corruption laws and anti-corruption agencies. Pattern 3 refers to the implementation of anti-corruption legislation by an independent anti-corruption agency and is best exemplified by Singapore and Hong Kong. South Korea has moved from Pattern 1 to Pattern 3 with the formation of the Korean Independent Commission Against Corruption in January 2002.

I would like to take this opportunity to thank all those who have helped me in the writing of this book. First, I would like to acknowledge my intellectual debt to the late Professor Malcolm B. Parsons and the late Professor Donald P. Warwick. Malcolm Parsons was the Chairman of my doctoral dissertation committee at the Department of Government, Florida State University. He introduced me to the fascinating field of comparative public administration through his interesting seminars on bureaucracy. I met Don Warwick during my first sabbatical leave as a Harvard-Yenching Fellow at Harvard University from September 1979 to May 1980. Don allowed me to audit his graduate seminar on policy implementation at Harvard and in 1985, we jointly taught a public policy course when he was Visiting Professor at the NUS Department of Political Science. I will always remember Don for his kindness and assistance during my two subsequent sabbatical stints at Harvard from August 1993 to March 1994 and from July to September 1997.

Professor Gerald E. Caiden of the University of Southern California has been a very good friend for more than two decades. We became friends through our mutual interest in administrative reform and bureaucratic corruption.[10] I am very grateful to him for his friendship, intellectual support and for writing the foreword to this book.

Professor Fred W. Riggs of the University of Hawaii has also been an inspiration to me since I read his book, *Administration in Developing Countries*,[11] in 1968 as a student for my public administration course at the University of Singapore. I have met Fred subsequently on many occasions at conferences in the United States and elsewhere. I would like to thank him for his friendship and warm encouragement for my research.

My favourite book on corruption is Leslie H. Palmier's *The Control of Bureaucratic Corruption: Case Studies in Asia* as it is the first attempt to compare systematically the anti-corruption strategies in three Asian countries: Hong Kong, India and Indonesia.[12] I am grateful to Leslie for presenting me with a signed copy of his book when it was published in 1985. I have learnt a great deal from his comparative analysis of the three countries.

Professor Krishna K. Tummala of Kansas State University has also been a good friend since 1982, when he invited me to contribute the chapter on Singapore for his book, *Administrative Systems Abroad*.[13]

We have collaborated on many projects since then and I am grateful to him for sharing his knowledge and insights on corruption in India with me. I would like to thank him for inviting me to contribute an article on corruption in Asian countries for the Symposium on "Comparative Study and the Section on International and Comparative Administration".[14]

I am grateful to Ms Pauline Tamesis of the United Nations Development Programme (UNDP) in New York for inviting me to participate as the Lead Consultant for the UNDP Mission to Mongolia to develop a National Anti-Corruption Plan for the Mongolian Government from September to November 1998. I would also like to thank Dr Robert Beschel and Dr Salvatore Shiavo-Campo for inviting me to participate in several workshops on corruption and governance organised by the Asian Development Bank in Manila.

I would also like to take this opportunity to thank the National University of Singapore for sponsoring my various sabbatical stints at Harvard University, University of California at Berkeley, Stanford University, and the Australian National University (ANU). It was during my last sabbatical leave at the National Centre for Development Studies at the ANU from August to December 2002 that I completed this book.

I wish to thank Mr Mew Yew Hwa, former General Manager of Federal Publications, and the Managing Editor, Mr Anthony Thomas, for facilitating the publication of this book.

Finally, I am most grateful to my wife and best friend, Dr Stella R. Quah, Associate Professor of Sociology at NUS for her love, encouragement and intellectual support for my research on corruption in Asian countries. Without her assistance and moral support, it would not have been possible for me to write and complete this book. As a small token of my gratitude, I have dedicated this book to her.

Jon S.T. Quah
Singapore
February 2003

ENDNOTES

1   See for example: Ledivina V. Carino (ed.), *Bureaucratic Corruption in Asia: Causes, Consequences and Control* (Quezon City: JMC Press and College of Public Administration, University of the Philippines, 1986); Rance P. L. Lee (ed.), *Corruption and Its Control in Hong Kong* (Hong Kong: The Chinese University Press, 1981); *Philippine Journal of Public Administration*, Vol. 23, Nos. 3-4 (July-October 1979) is a special issue containing seven articles on graft and corruption in the Philippines; Jon S. T. Quah, *Administrative and Legal Measures for Combatting Bureaucratic Corruption in Singapore* (Singapore: Department of Political Science, University of Singapore, Occasional Paper No. 34, 1978); Jon S. T. Quah, "Police Corruption in Singapore: An Analysis of Its Forms, Extent and Causes", *Singapore Police Journal*, Vol. 10, No. 1 (January 1979), pp. 7-43; Jon S. T. Quah, "Singapore's Experience in Curbing Corruption", in Arnold J. Heidenheimer, Michael Johnston and Victor T. LeVine (eds.), *Political Corruption: A Handbook* (New Brunswick: Transaction Publishers, 1989), pp. 841-853; Suek Hong Oh, "The Counter-Corruption Campaign of the Korean Government (1975-1977): Administrative Anti-Corruption Measures of the *Seojungshaeshin*", in Bun Woong Kim and Wha Joon Rho (eds.), *Korean Public Bureaucracy* (Seoul: Kyobo Publishing, 1982), pp. 322-344; Thinapan Nakata, "Corruption in the Thai Bureaucracy: A Survey of Public Officials and General Citizenry's Attitudes", *Thai Journal of Development Administration*, Vol. 17 (July 1977), pp. 355-405; and Thinapan Nakata, "Corruption in the Thai Bureaucracy: Who Gets What, How and Why in its Public Expenditures", *Thai Journal of Development Administration*, Vol. 18 (January 1978), pp. 102-128.

2   The other members of the Singapore team were Dr Seah Chee Meow from the then Department of Political Science, University of Singapore; and Dr Tan Chwee Huat from the Faculty of Business Administration, University of Singapore.

3   Jon S. T. Quah, "Bureaucratic Corruption in the ASEAN Countries: A Comparative Analysis of Their Anti-Corruption Strategies", *Journal of Southeast Asian Studies*, Vol. 13, No. 1 (March 1982), pp. 153-177; and Jon S.T. Quah, "Tackling Bureaucratic Corruption: The ASEAN Experience", in Gerald E. Caiden and Heinrich Siedentopf (eds.), *Strategies for Administrative Reform* (Lexington: D.C. Heath and Company, 1982), pp. 109-121.

4   Jon S. T. Quah, "Controlling Corruption in City-States: A Comparative Study of Hong Kong and Singapore", *Crime, Law and Social Change*, Vol. 22 (1995), pp. 391-414.

5   Jon S. T. Quah, "Combating Corruption in South Korea and Thailand", in Andreas Schedler, Larry Diamond, and Marc F. Plattner (eds.), *The Self-Restraining State: Power and Accountability in New Democracies* (Boulder: Lynne Rienner Publishers, 1999), pp. 245-256; and Jon S.T. Quah, "Singapore's Anti-Corruption Strategy: Some Lessons for South Korea", *Korean Corruption Studies Review*, Vol. 4 (December 1999), pp. 173-193.

6   Jon S. T. Quah, *Combating Corruption in Mongolia: Problems and Prospects* (Singapore: Department of Political Science, National University of Singapore, Working Paper No. 22, July 1999).

7   Jon S. T. Quah, "Combating Corruption in India: Some Suggestions for Reform", in Stephen Howes, Ashok Lahiri and Nicholas Stern (eds.), *Fiscal and Governance Reform in India's States: Proceedings of the 2000 India States' Reform Forum* (New Delhi: Macmillan India, forthcoming).

8   This module was renamed PS3216B Corruption and Governance in Asia from January-June 2002.

9   The 10 countries covered in these modules are: China, Hong Kong, India, Indonesia, Malaysia, Mongolia, the Philippines, Singapore, South Korea, and Thailand.

10   See Gerald E. Caiden, *Administrative Reform* (London: Penguin Press, 1969); Gerald E. Caiden, *Administrative Reform Comes of Age* (Berlin: Walter de Gruyter, 1991); Gerald E. Caiden and Naomi J. Caiden, "Administrative Corruption", *Public Administration Review*, Vol. 37, No. 3 (May/June 1977), pp. 301-309; Gerald E. Caiden, "Toward a General Theory of Official Corruption", *Asian Journal of Public Administration*, Vol. 10, No. 1 (June 1988), pp. 3-26; Gerald E. Caiden, "Undermining Good Governance: Corruption and Democracy", *Asian Journal of Political Science*, Vol. 5, No. 2 (December 1997), pp. 1-22; Gerald E. Caiden, "Dealing with Administrative Corruption", in Terry L. Cooper (ed.), *Handbook of Administrative Ethics*, 2nd ed. (New York: Marcel Dekker, 2001), pp. 429-455; and Gerald E. Caiden, O.P. Dwivedi and Joseph Jabbra (eds.), *Where Corruption Lives* (Bloomfield: Kumarian Press, 2001).

11   Fred W. Riggs, *Administration in Developing Countries* (Boston: Houghton Mifflin, 1964).

12   Leslie H. Palmier, *The Control of Bureaucratic Corruption: Case Studies in Asia* (New Delhi: Allied Publishers, 1985).

13   Jon S. T. Quah, "The Public Bureaucracy and National Development in Singapore", in Krishna K. Tummala (ed.), *Administrative Systems Abroad* (Lanham: University Press of America, 1982), pp. 42-75.

14   Jon S.T. Quah, "Corruption in Asian Countries: Can It Be Minimized?" *Public Administration Review*, Vol. 59, No. 6 (November/December 1999), pp. 483-494.

CHAPTER **1**

Corruption: Causes and Control Patterns

INTRODUCTION

Corruption is a serious problem in many Asian countries today, judging from the many press reports and exposés of corruption scandals in these countries in recent years. In its cover story on "Corruption: The Asian Lubricant" in September 1974, the *Far Eastern Economic Review* (FEER) observed: "With pathetically few exceptions, the countries in this region are so riddled with corruption that the paying of 'tea money' has become almost a way of life." Nearly 23 years later, in another cover story on "Corruption: Reform's Dark Side" in the March 20, 1997 issue of the FEER, Aparisim Ghosh *et al.* wrote:

> Looking back on the Year of the Rat [1996] some time in the future, historians may well marvel at how much Asian newsprint and television time was devoted to reports and discussions on corruption in government. From Pakistan to Japan, corruption was the year's biggest story.[1]

Beginning from 1995, the Berlin-based non-government organisation, Transparency International (TI), has published an annual Corruption Perceptions Index (CPI) based on the perceptions of selected groups of businessmen, risk analysts, and the general public, on the extent of corruption in many countries. The sample size of TI's CPI has increased from 41 in 1995 to 102 in 2002. Table 1.1 below shows the ranking and scores of the various Asian countries on the CPI from 1995-2002. From Table 1.1, Singapore is perceived as the least corrupt country and Indonesia is perceived as the most corrupt country in Asia. Table 1.2 shows the Political and Economic Risk Consultancy's (PERC) ranking of 12 Asian countries. PERC's ranking generally confirms the CPI's ranking as Singapore is also

1

ranked as the least corrupt Asian country and Indonesia is ranked as the most corrupt Asian country except in 1996 and 2001.

TABLE 1.1 RANKING AND SCORES* OF ASIAN COUNTRIES**
ON THE CORRUPTION PERCEPTIONS INDEX, 1995-2002

Country	1995	1996	1997	1998	1999	2000	2001	2002
Singapore	3 (9.26)	7 (8.80)	9 (8.66)	7 (9.1)	7 (9.1)	6 (9.1)	4 (9.2)	5 (9.30)
Hong Kong	17(7.12)	18(7.01)	18(7.28)	16(7.8)	15(7.7)	15(7.7)	14(7.9)	14(8.20)
Japan	20(6.72)	17(7.05)	21(6.57)	25(5.8)	25(6.0)	23(6.4)	21(7.1)	20(7.10)
Taiwan	25(5.08)	29(4.98)	31(5.02)	29(5.3)	28(5.6)	28(5.5)	27(5.9)	29(5.60)
Malaysia	23(5.28)	26(5.32)	32(5.01)	29(5.3)	32(5.1)	36(4.8)	36(5.0)	33(4.90)
S. Korea	27(4.29)	27(5.02)	34(4.29)	43(4.2)	50(3.8)	48(4.0)	42(4.2)	40(4.50)
Thailand	34(2.79)	37(3.33)	39(3.06)	61(3.0)	68(3.2)	60(3.2)	61(3.2)	64(3.20)
Philippines	36(2.77)	44(2.69)	40(3.05)	55(3.3)	54(3.6)	69(2.8)	65(2.9)	77(2.60)
China	40(2.16)	50(2.43)	41(2.88)	52(3.5)	58(3.4)	63(3.1)	57(3.5)	59(3.50)
India	35(2.78)	46(2.63)	45(2.75)	66(2.9)	72(2.9)	69(2.8)	71(2.7)	71(2.70)
Pakistan	39(2.25)	53(1.00)	48(2.53)	71(2.7)	87(2.2)	NA	79(2.3)	77(2.60)
Vietnam	NA***	NA	43(2.79)	74(2.5)	75(2.6)	76(2.5)	75(2.6)	85(2.40)
Indonesia	41(1.94)	45(2.65)	46(2.72)	80(2.0)	96(1.7)	85(1.7)	88(1.9)	96(1.90)
Sample size	41	54	52	85	99	90	91	102

*   The score ranges from 0 (most corrupt) to 10 (least corrupt). The scores are indicated within brackets.

**   Bangladesh and Mongolia are excluded from the above table as Bangladesh participated only in the 1996, 2001 and 2002 CPI while Mongolia was involved in the 1999 CPI only. Bangladesh was ranked 51st position with a score of 2.29 in the 1996 CPI. Its ranking deteriorated considerably in the 2001 CPI as it was ranked last among the 91 countries surveyed with the lowest score of 0.40. In the 2002 CPI, Bangladesh was ranked last among the 102 countries surveyed with a score of 1.20. Mongolia was ranked 43rd position with a score of 4.30 in the 1999 CPI.

***   Not available.

Source: Compiled from Transparency International's Corruption Perceptions Index from 1995-2002. See http://www.transparency.org

Finally, in January 2001, the PricewaterhouseCoopers (PwC) Endowment for the Study of Transparency and Sustainability launched the Opacity Index as "a new measure of the effects of 'opacity' on the cost

2

and availability of capital" in 35 countries. The Opacity Index is based on surveys conducted with chief financial officers (CFOs) based in the countries, equity analysts familiar with the countries, and bankers and PwC employees in the countries. The sample size for each country was 35 respondents (20 CFOs, five equity analysts, five bankers, and five PwC employees). The Index provides data on these five dimensions which affect capital markets: corruption, legal system, economic policies, accounting standards and practices, and regulatory regime.[2] Table 1.3 below provides the scores of the Opacity Index for the 10 Asian countries included in the survey and shows that Singapore and Hong Kong are the most transparent while China and Indonesia are the most opaque Asian countries.

TABLE 1.2 RANKING OF 12 ASIAN COUNTRIES BY THE POLITICAL ECONOMIC RISK CONSULTANCY, 1995-2001

Country	1995	1996	1997	1998	1999	2000	2001	Average
Singapore	1 (1.20)	1 (1.09)	1 (1.05)	1 (1.43)	1 (1.55)	1 (0.71)	1 (0.83)	1 (1.12)
Hong Kong	3 (2.80)	3 (2.79)	2 (3.03)	2 (2.74)	2 (4.06)	2 (2.49)	3 (3.77)	2.42 (3.09)
Japan	2 (2.00)	2 (1.93)	3 (4.60)	3 (5.00)	3 (4.25)	3 (3.90)	2 (2.50)	2.57 (3.45)
Malaysia	6 (4.60)	4 (5.00)	4 (5.80)	5 (5.38)	6 (7.50)	4 (5.50)	4 (6.00)	4.71 (5.68)
Taiwan	5 (4.20)	6 (5.53)	5 (5.96)	4 (5.20)	5 (6.92)	5 (6.89)	4 (6.00)	4.85 (5.81)
South Korea	4 (4.00)	5 (5.16)	8 (7.71)	7 (7.12)	8 (8.20)	7 (8.33)	6 (7.00)	6.42 (6.78)
Philippines	8 (6.60)	9 (6.95)	6 (6.50)	8 (7.17)	4 (6.71)	8 (8.67)	9 (9.00)	7.42 (7.37)
Thailand	7 (5.90)	7 6.55)	7 (7.49)	11 (8.29)	7 (7.57)	6 (8.20)	8 (8.55)	7.57 (7.50)
China	10 (7.30)	12 (8.00)	10 (8.06)	6 (6.97)	10 (9.00)	9 (9.11)	7 (7.88)	9.14 (8.04)
Vietnam	NA	11(7.78)	9 (8.00)	10(8.25)	9 (8.50)	10(9.20)	12(9.75)	10.16 (8.58)
India	9 (7.00)	8 (6.86)	11(8.20)	9 (7.40)	11(9.17)	11(9.50)	11(9.67)	10(8.25)
Indonesia	10(7.30)	10(7.69)	12(8.67)	12(8.95)	12(9.91)	12(9.88)	11(9.67)	11.28 (8.86)
Sample size	11	12	12	12	12	12	12	NA

Source: PERC, "Corruption in Asia in 2001". See http://www.asiarisk.com/lib10.html

CORRUPTION AS A GROWTH INDUSTRY

Ronald Wraith and Edgar Simpkins published their pioneering book, *Corruption in Developing Countries*, in 1963, when it was quite difficult to do research on such a sensitive topic. In spite of the book's title, Wraith and Simpkins confined their analysis to Britain and Nigeria because of their familiarity with these countries.[3] However, their moralistic approach of viewing corruption as an immoral activity with negative consequences for those individuals involved and the society is not useful as their approach is subjective and they have not provided relevant evidence for the negative effects of corruption.

In 1968, the Swedish economist, Gunnar Myrdal, observed that corruption was "almost taboo as a research topic" and was "rarely mentioned in scholarly discussions of the problems of government and planning". He attributed the research taboo on corruption to "diplomacy in research" which avoided such embarrassing questions as corruption by "ignoring the problems of attitudes and institutions". He illustrated how the taboo could be broken by discussing the "folklore", causes and anti-corruption campaigns in South Asian countries.[4]

TABLE 1.3 THE OPACITY INDEX AND SCORES*
FOR 10 ASIAN COUNTRIES, 2001

Country	Corruption	Legal System	Economic Policies	Accounting Standards	Regulatory Regime	O-Factor
Singapore	13	32	42	38	23	29
Hong Kong	25	55	49	53	42	45
Japan	22	72	72	81	53	60
Taiwan	45	70	71	56	61	61
Pakistan	48	66	81	62	54	62
India	55	68	59	79	58	64
Thailand	55	65	70	78	66	67
South Korea	48	79	76	90	73	73
Indonesia	70	86	82	68	69	75
China	62	100	87	86	100	87

* The scores are from 0 (uniformly and perfectly transparent conditions) to 150 (uniformly and perfectly opaque conditions).

Source: PricewaterhouseCoopers, "The Opacity Index", in Robin Hodess (ed.), *Global Corruption Report 2001* (Berlin: Transparency International, 2001), p. 278.

Fortunately, this research taboo on corruption in Asian countries no longer exists given the many case studies on this topic in recent years. Indeed, in contrast to the dearth of such research in the 1960s, research on Asian corruption has mushroomed into a growth industry since the 1990s.[5] Moreover, since the end of the Cold War the number of news stories on corruption in the *Economist*, the *Financial Times* and the *New York Times* "quadrupled between 1984 and 1995".[6] This "global corruption epidemic" is the result of two trends: the emergence of civil societies and the disclosure of corruption scandals in many countries, and the trend towards democracy and markets, which has paradoxically "increased both the opportunities for graft and the likelihood of exposure".[7]

THE MEANING OF CORRUPTION

Before proceeding further, it is necessary to define "corruption" given the plethora of definitions and the various meanings given to it. For example, Gerald E. Caiden has identified the 20 "most commonly recognised" forms of corruption.[8] Similarly, Michael L. Hager has described the "great variety of sins" of corruption in his analysis of corruption in India by referring to the 34 types of corrupt practices reported by the Central Vigilance Commission from 1964-1966.[9] Perhaps the most useful way of classifying the many contemporary social science definitions of corruption is Arnold J. Heidenheimer's threefold classification of public-office-centred, market-centred, and public-interest-centred definitions.[10]

Public-office-centred definitions of corruption focus on the concept of the public office and describe corruption in terms of the deviations from the norms binding upon its incumbents. The best example of a public-office-centred definition is that provided by Joseph S. Nye, who defined corruption as

> … behaviour which deviates from the normal duties of a public role because of private-regarding (family, close private clique), pecuniary or status gains; or violates rules against the exercise of certain types of private-regarding influence. This includes such behaviour as bribery (use of reward to pervert the judgement of a

5

person in a position of trust); nepotism (bestowal or patronage by reason of ascriptive relationship rather than merit); and misappropriation (illegal appropriation of public resources for private-regarding influence).[11]

While Nye's definition is useful, it should be noted that in those countries where corruption is a way of life, corrupt behaviour is not viewed as deviant as it is practised by the majority of the population.

In contrast, market-centred definitions of corruption shift the emphasis from the public office to the market. Jacob van Klaveren has provided the following market-centred definition of corruption:

> A corrupt civil servant who regards his public office as a business, the income of which he will ... seek to maximise. The office then becomes a "maximising unit." The size of his income depends ... upon the market situation and his talents for finding the point of maximal gain on the public's demand curve.[12]

The third type of definition views corruption as an erosion of public interest. Rejecting the public-office-centred definition as being too narrow and the market-centred definition as being too broad, Carl Friedrich recommended the use of the public-interest-centred definition instead. He has defined corruption thus:

> The pattern of corruption can be said to exist whenever a powerholder who is charged with doing certain things, i.e., who is a responsible functionary or officeholder, is by monetary or other rewards not legally provided for, induced to take actions which favour whoever provides the rewards and thereby does damage to the public and its interests.[13]

However, the problem with the above definition is that the concept of public interest is itself vague and not defined at all.

For this study, a public-office-centred definition of corruption will be used as it is more relevant and useful than the market-centred and public-interest-centred definitions. The United Nations Development Programme (UNDP) has defined corruption as "the misuse of public power, office or authority for private benefit— through bribery, extortion, influence peddling, nepotism, fraud, speed money or embezzlement".[14] This definition not only identifies the major forms of corruption but is also applicable to both the public and private sectors.

There are two important distinctions which must be noted. First, is corruption a fact of life or a way of life?[15] Corruption is a fact of life in a country when cases of corruption are the exception rather than the rule, and are examples of individual rather than systemic corruption. Conversely, corruption is a way of life in a country when it is rampant, occurs at all levels, and is the norm rather than the exception.

Second, is corruption grand or petty in nature? Grand corruption refers to corruption by political leaders and senior civil servants, and usually involves "large, international bribes and 'hidden' overseas bank accounts".[16] George Moody-Stuart has defined grand corruption as "the misuse of public power by heads of state, ministers and top officials for private, pecuniary profit".[17] On the other hand, petty or "survival" corruption is practised by underpaid junior civil servants who demand bribes from the people to expedite their applications or perform other favours. For example, as discussed in Chapter 4, many civil servants in the Philippines are paid "starvation" wages and resort to petty corruption to supplement their incomes. While grand corruption causes more damage than petty corruption, this does not mean that nothing should be done to minimise petty corruption. Indeed, an anti-corruption strategy is only effective if it is able to curb *both* grand and petty corruption simultaneously in the country.

Having defined corruption, we can proceed to identify its causes as a prelude to analysing the three patterns of corruption control in Asian countries.

CAUSES OF CORRUPTION

Under what conditions does corruption thrive? What are the factors which induce individual civil servants or political leaders to commit corrupt acts? Conversely, what prevents or discourages individuals from being corrupt? An individual is more likely to commit a corrupt act if he or she (1) is paid a low or inadequate salary; (2) is exposed to ample opportunities for corruption; and (3) perceives corruption to be a low risk, high reward activity. In other words, corruption thrives when the individuals concerned receive meagre salaries, have ample opportunities to be corrupt, and are unlikely to be caught and not severely punished even if they are caught.

In his comparative study of the control of bureaucratic corruption in Hong Kong, India and Indonesia, Leslie Palmier had identified three factors as important causes of corruption: *opportunities* (which depended on the extent of involvement of civil servants in the administration or control of lucrative activities), *salaries* and *policing* (the probability of detection and punishment). Palmier's hypothesis is:

> [B]ureaucratic corruption seems to depend not on any one of the [three] factors identified, but rather on the *balance* between them. At one extreme, *with few opportunities, good salaries, and effective policing, corruption will be minimal;* at the other, *with many opportunities, poor salaries, and weak policing, it will be considerable.*[18]

Thus, following Palmier's hypothesis, an effective anti-corruption strategy should reduce or remove the opportunities for corruption, raise the salaries of civil servants and political leaders, and ensure a high degree of policing.

Low Salaries

Palmier has identified low salaries as an important cause of corruption. "If the official is not to be tempted into corruption and disaffection, clearly there is an obligation on the government to provide or at least allow such benefits as will ensure his loyalty; one might call it an implicit contract".[19] Thus, "adequate pay" becomes "an essential ingredient in reform".[20] Similarly, Mauro has argued that "when civil service pay is too low, civil servants may be obliged to use their positions to collect bribes as a way of making ends meet, particularly when the expected cost of being caught is low".[21]

In Indonesia, corruption was a serious problem during the Dutch colonial period as the salaries of the Dutch East India Company's personnel were inadequate. Clive Day observed that these personnel "were underpaid and exposed to every temptation that was offered by the combination of a weak native organisation, extraordinary opportunities in trade, and an almost complete absence of checks from home or in Java".[22] Corruption became endemic during President Sukarno's rule because his "disastrously inflationary budgets eroded civil service salaries to the point where people simply could not live on them and where financial accountability virtually collapsed because of administrative deterioration".[23] In 1969, Theodore M. Smith conducted a survey of regional civil servants in Indonesia and found that "there is not a single official who can live by his government income alone" as the "official income amounts to approximately half of [his] essential monthly needs".[24] A more recent survey on corruption in Indonesia of 2,300 respondents (650 public officials, 1,250 households and 400 business enterprises) found that low salaries were identified as the most important cause of corruption by 51.4% of the public officials, 36.5% of the business enterprises, and 35.5% of the households.[25]

Mongolia is another country where the low salaries of its civil servants and political leaders contribute to corruption. As shown in Chapter 2, the monthly salary of the President is US$71. A teacher's average monthly salary is between US$28 to US$32, so it is not surprising that many teachers have gone on strike to demand higher wages. Finally, judges earn between US$33 to US$51 per month and one-third of them are homeless.

In South Korea, Meredith Woo-Cummings has recommended that civil service salaries, which constitute only 70% of private sector wages, should be raised to reduce corruption.[26] In the same vein, Jun and Yoon have suggested that it is unrealistic to expect South Korean civil servants "to show dedication without providing adequate remuneration and changing the administrative culture".[27]

In the case of Thailand, Kasem Suwanagul found that the low salaries of civil servants during the post-war period contributed to more bureaucratic corruption as their low salaries were insufficient to meet inflation and below those offered in the private sector.[28] Recently, Thailand's police chief, General Sant Sarutanond, admitted that Thai policemen "are undereducated and underpaid and that is the reason why they are corrupt". According to him, commissioned police officers should be receiving a monthly salary of 20,000 baht (S$850) to meet their expenses in the large cities, but they are actually getting a starting monthly salary of 6,000 baht (S$260).[29]

Corruption began in the Philippines during the Spanish colonial period, when corruption prevailed as the civil servants were poorly paid and had many opportunities for corruption.[30] In contrast, the bureaucracy was less corrupt during the American colonial period as "the bureaucrats received higher salaries and corrupt officials were promptly prosecuted".[31] Finally, in his analysis of the consequences of low salaries on the prestige of the Philippine Civil Service, Padilla found that civil servants supplemented their low wages by vending within the office, holding a second job, teaching part-time, practising their profession after office hours, engaging in research and consultancy projects, and resorting to petty corrupt practices.[32]

In Singapore, the most important cause of police corruption during the colonial period was the low salaries of the members of the Singapore Police Force (SPF), especially those in the lower ranks. This factor was also said to be the reason behind the SPF's inefficiency and its inability to recruit suitably qualified personnel.[33] Given the low salaries of the policemen, it was not surprising that the *Straits Times* commented: "It is at once evident that the native constables and the European police of the Inspector class are so underpaid that scandals are unavoidable".[34]

To sum up, "if bureaucrats are paid a high enough wage, even a small chance of losing their jobs would discourage them from being corrupt". On the other hand, if the real salary of civil servants decreases drastically, "even the most rigidly honest bureaucrats will be tempted to go beyond the law to preserve their standard of living".[35]

Ample Opportunities for Corruption

The scope of public administration has grown and the role of the public bureaucracy in national development has become more important with the advent of the modern administrative state.[36] The expanding role of the public bureaucracy in national development has increased the opportunities for administrative discretion and corruption as "regulations governing access to goods and services can be exploited by civil servants in extracting 'rents' from groups vying for access to such goods and services".[37] Hong Kong is a good example, where "the necessity for the government to regulate, control and prohibit certain activities" increased the opportunities for corruption in the "areas of construction, import and export, health, hygiene, safety, prostitution, gambling, drugs, markets and stalls, immigration and emigration".[38]

In Indonesia, Donald P. Warwick has introduced the interesting distinction made by civil servants between "wet" and "dry" agencies, depending on their budget and access to the public. According to him:

> "wet" agencies ... are generous with honoraria, allowances, service on committees, boards, and development projects, and, recently, opportunities for foreign training. They are departments that deal in money, planning, banking, or public enterprises. "Dry" agencies are those doing traditional administrative work. Perceptions of unfairness about benefits not only reduce staff morale, but lead to the feeling that illegal compensation is a fair way to even out staff benefits across agencies.[39]

In other words, "wet" agencies like the customs, immigration, internal revenue and police will provide more opportunities for corruption than "dry" agencies like research and administrative departments which do not interact directly with the public. Indeed, as "dry" agencies have reduced opportunities for corruption, "being posted to a dry position is about the worst fate any official could fear".[40]

Radius Prawiro, Co-ordinating Economics Minister in Indonesia in 1989-1993, identified the tax office and customs service as the most lucrative of the "wet" government agencies.

11

Before the 1983 Income Tax Law, there were 48 tax rates for individuals and 10 for corporations. As the pre-1983 tax system was "entirely inaccessible to modern accounting practices", Prawiro observed that "the only way for tax-payers to determine their tax obligations was by visiting the tax office and reviewing their financial data with a tax officer". As the taxpayer could negotiate his tax assessment with the tax officer, it was not surprising that "a job as a tax collector was one of the surest roads to riches in the government bureaucracy".[41] Similarly, customs officers had abundant opportunities for "supplemental income" since "Indonesia's customs service had become a law unto itself according to which the entire trade process was readily manipulated to serve the interests of a retinue of customs officials".[42]

The Knapp Commission Report on Police Corruption identified three factors which influenced the opportunities for corruption among police officers in New York City. First, the branch of the department to which an officer was assigned is important as a plainclothesman would have more and different opportunities than an uniformed policeman. Second, the area to which an officer was assigned not only influenced the opportunities for corrupt behaviour but also the major sources of corruption payments. For example, in New York City, some precincts in Harlem provided more opportunities for corruption than Central Park. Finally, the officer's assignment determined the amount and type of graft available to him as an officer in a patrol car would have more opportunities to be corrupt than his counterpart on guard duty.[43]

The Corruption Prevention Department (CPD) of Hong Kong's Independent Commission Against Corruption (ICAC) identified four "more pernicious and prevalent" factors which increase opportunities for corruption. The first factor is delay, which "provides both the opportunity to extort a bribe and the incentive to offer one, and is also an inevitable consequence of bureaucratic processes". Second, insufficient publicity "leads the public to believe that individual public servants have the authority to decide whether a particular law shall be enforced or who shall benefit from a public service, so creating a situation ripe for exploitation". The third factor providing opportunities for corruption is excessive discretion, which often results from "a well-intended delegation of authority in order to expedite business". The fourth and most important factor was the lack of supervision or accountability, especially of junior officers who operate away from an office. As supervisors are usually preoccupied with other administrative duties which require their presence in their comfortable offices, they are reluctant to visit their junior officers in the field and resort to supervision through correspondence. To minimise the lack of supervision or accountability of junior officers, the CPD recommended that "all supervisory officers should spend sufficient time with their staff and in the field, to gain their own insight into the problems within their area of responsibility and conditions on the ground".[44]

Low Risk of Detection and Punishment

As corruption is an illegal activity in all countries, those individuals found guilty of corrupt offences should be punished accordingly. However, in reality, the probability of detection and punishment of corrupt offences varies in the different Asian countries. Corruption thrives in those Asian countries where the public perceives it to be a "low risk, high reward" activity as corrupt offenders are unlikely to be detected and punished. On the other hand, corruption is not a serious problem in those Asian countries where corruption is perceived as a "high risk, low reward" activity as those involved in corrupt behaviour are likely to be caught and severely punished.

An important cause of the pervasive corruption in the former Soviet Union before its collapse was the lack of fear of punishment among the corrupt officials. Indeed, cases of high-level corruption in the Soviet Union were seldom subject to punishment because the regime was "permissive towards its ruling elite". Syed Hussein Alatas contends that the "involvement of the highest leadership in turn causes permissiveness towards corruption" which is "the greatest cause of its perpetuation".[45]

13

Similarly, even though bribery exceeding 100,000 yuan (US$12,000) is a capital offence in China, the death penalty has not been imposed until recently on senior party officials found guilty of accepting bribes exceeding this amount. For example, the former Beijing party chief, Chen Xitong, became the highest ranking Chinese Communist Party member to be jailed for corruption when he was sentenced to 16 years imprisonment for graft of 555,000 yuan and dereliction of duty on July 31, 1998. It should be noted that Chen's sentence is lenient as more junior party cadres have been given life imprisonment or the death penalty for corruption involving smaller sums of over 100,000 yuan.[46] In other words, senior party officials can "short-circuit corruption investigations by appealing to their protectors in the party hierarchy".[47]

However, former Premier Zhu Rongji had recently waged a crusade against corrupt officials and on March 5, 2000, he informed party delegates at the National People's Congress that: "All major cases, no matter which department or who is involved, must be thoroughly investigated, and corrupt officials must be brought to justice".[48] To reinforce Zhu's message, Hu Changqing, Deputy Governor of Jiangxi province, was the highest ranking public official to be executed three days later on March 8 for corruption involving 5.44 million yuan between May 1995 and August 1999.[49] Similarly, Li Chenglong, Deputy Mayor of Guigang City, was executed on April 23, 2000 for taking US$478,500 worth of bribes.[50] Zhu's commitment to minimising corruption among senior party officials has improved China's ranking on both Transparency International's CPI and PERC's ranking. Table 1.1 shows that China's ranking on the CPI has improved from 63rd position in 2000 to 59th position in 2002. Similarly, as can be seen from Table 1.2, China's ranking by PERC has also improved from 9th position in 2000 to 7th position in 2001.

The final example is provided by Bangladesh, which was ranked the most corrupt country in the world in the 2001 and 2002 CPI. This is not surprising as corruption has been institutionalised in the public service in Bangladesh during the last 25 years.[51] According to

14

Mohammad Mohabbat Khan, Bangladesh's high level of corruption can be attributed to these four factors:

> First, bureaucrats involved in corrupt practices in most cases do not lose their jobs. Very rarely they are dismissed from service on charges pertaining to corruption. Still rarely they are sent to prison for misusing public funds. They have never been compelled to return to the state their ill-gotten wealth. Second, the law-enforcing officials including police personnel are extremely corrupt. They are happy to share the booty with other corrupt bureaucrats. Third, the people have a tendency not only to tolerate corruption but to show respect to those bureaucrats who made fortune through dubious means. ... Fourth, it is easier for a citizen to get quick service because he has already "paid" the bureaucrat rather than wait for his turn.[52]

For the population in a country to perceive corruption as a "high risk, low reward" activity, the incumbent government must publicise through the mass media the detection of corrupt behaviour among civil servants and politicians and their punishment according to the law if they are found guilty. Accordingly, Leslie Palmier has stressed the crucial role of the communications media, which reduces corruption by exposing it as corruption "thrives in secrecy, and withers in the light".[53]

If the media emphasises the harmful effects of corruption and publicises the punishment of public officials for their corrupt offences, such negative publicity can serve as an effective deterrent against corruption. In this connection, Lee Kuan Yew, Singapore's former prime minister, contended in 1987 that "the strongest deterrent is in a public opinion which censures and condemns corrupt persons, in other words, in attitudes which make corruption so unacceptable that the stigma of corruption cannot be washed away by serving a prison sentence".[54] Conversely, those governments which "shackle the media" as in Indonesia under President Suharto or in India during the Emergency of the 1970s, "are in effect encouraging the corrupt".[55]

Thus, while Palmier's analysis of the causes of corruption is not exhaustive, he has nevertheless convincingly argued that corruption thrives in those Asian countries which (1) pay its civil servants and political leaders low salaries; (2) expose them to ample opportunities for corruption; and (3) are unlikely to detect and punish those public officials involved in corrupt behaviour.

PATTERNS OF CORRUPTION CONTROL IN ASIAN COUNTRIES

There are three patterns of corruption control in Asian countries depending on the anti-corruption measures employed. The first pattern occurs when there are anti-corruption laws but no specific agency to implement these laws. The best example of Pattern 1 can be found in Mongolia, which has the Law on Anti-Corruption and three provisions restricting bribery in the Criminal Code. However, there is no special anti-corruption agency as the task of curbing corruption is shared between the police, the General Prosecutor's Office, and the courts.

The second pattern of corruption control involves the combination of anti-corruption laws and several anti-corruption agencies. This pattern can be found in both democratic and communist countries. In the case of India, the Prevention of Corruption Act is implemented by the Central Bureau of Investigation, the Central Vigilance Commission, the state anti-corruption bureaux and the state vigilance commissions. The Philippines has the most anti-corruption measures in Asia as it has established seven laws and 13 anti-corruption agencies since the 1950s.

In China, the anti-corruption laws are implemented by three agencies, depending on the sector. The Supreme People's Procuratorate was re-established in 1978 to combat corruption in the judicial sector. For the administrative sector, the Ministry of Supervision was re-established in 1986 to curb corruption in the civil service. The Central Disciplinary Inspection Committee was formed in 1978 to check corruption among the members of the Chinese Communist Party.[56]

The third pattern of corruption control involves the impartial implementation of comprehensive anti-corruption laws by a specific anti-corruption agency. In Singapore, the Prevention of Corruption Act is implemented by the Corrupt Practices Investigation Bureau, which was formed in October 1952 to take over the function of corruption control from the Anti-Corruption Branch in the Singapore Police Force. Similarly, in Hong Kong, the Independent Commission Against Corruption (ICAC) was established in February 1974 to implement the ICAC Ordinance and Prevention of Bribery Ordinance.

Malaysia, Thailand and South Korea have also adopted the third pattern of corruption control, but these countries have been less effective than Singapore and Hong Kong. In Malaysia, the Anti-Corruption Agency (ACA) was established on October 1, 1967 with three major functions: (1) to investigate and prosecute offences under the Prevention of Corruption Act of 1961; (2) to introduce preventive measures against corruption in the civil service and statutory boards; and (3) to investigate disciplinary complaints against civil servants.[57]

The ACA was initially staffed with seconded police officers who were not trained to investigate corruption offences. Furthermore, these police officers were reluctant to investigate corrupt practices in the police force and other departments where they might be posted to in future.[58] These initial teething problems were resolved by the ACA's reorganisation in 1968. However, more recently, the ACA has been criticised for not investigating corruption cases involving "big fish" impartially as the November 1998 to April 1999 corruption trial[59] and conviction of former Deputy Prime Minister Anwar Ibrahim showed that other "big fish" have not been similarly targeted, and the ACA, which has not been known for its swift action in investigating "big fish", has "acted with alacrity in pursuing corruption allegations against Anwar Ibrahim".[60]

In Thailand, the Counter Corruption Commission (CCC) was created in February 1975 with the enactment of the Counter Corruption Act.[61] However, the CCC was ineffective for three reasons. First, the CCC's task of curbing corruption was handicapped by the tolerant Thai attitude towards corruption, which was not viewed to be against the public's interest.[62] Second, the CCC encountered difficulty in performing its role because of the constant conflict between the Cabinet and the bureaucracy.[63] Finally, and most importantly, the CCC was viewed by its critics as a "paper tiger" without real teeth, as "it could only send reports to the prime minister and Cabinet" since it lacked "direct authority to punish public officials".[64] The promulgation of the "People's Constitution" on October 11, 1997 led to the replacement of the ineffective CCC by the National Counter Corruption Commission in November 1999.[65]

In South Korea, the Anti-Corruption Act (ACA) was established on July 24, 2001 and the Korean Independent Commission Against Corruption (KICAC) was formed in January 2002. Thus, South Korea became the most recent Asian country to adopt the third pattern of corruption control. President Park Chung Hee created the Board of Audit and Inspection (BAI) in 1963 to provide a check on the economic bureaucracy and its functions included the investigation of corrupt offences by civil servants. In March 1975, Park initiated the *Seojungshaeshin* (General Administration Reform) Movement to curb corruption in the civil service. However, the BAI remained unchanged until President Kim Young Sam strengthened it in 1993 and formed the Commission for the Prevention of Corruption to assist the BAI's chairman. South Korea's anti-corruption strategy was further strengthened by the comprehensive anti-corruption reforms introduced by President Kim Dae Jung in 1999, which has culminated in the introduction of the ACA and the formation of the KICAC. In short, the evolution of South Korea's anti-corruption strategy, which has changed from Pattern 1 (1963-2001) to Pattern 3 from 2002, demonstrates that it is possible for a country to improve its efforts in curbing corruption if the incumbent government has the political will to do so. Table 1.4 below provides details of the anti-corruption laws and agencies in nine Asian countries according to the three patterns of corruption control.

AIM AND ORGANISATION OF BOOK

During 1993-1997, corruption was "transformed from a predominantly national or regional preoccupation to an issue of global revolutionary force." Indeed, corruption has emerged in the 1990s as "a truly global political issue eliciting a global political response".[66] Consequently, many international organisations like the Asian Development Bank, the Organisation for Economic Co-operation and Development, Transparency International, the United Nations, and the World Bank have organised conferences, symposia and workshops on various aspects of corruption to enable the participants from many countries to share and learn the best practices in fighting corruption round the world.

TABLE 1.4 PATTERNS OF CORRUPTION CONTROL IN ASIAN COUNTRIES

Pattern and Country	Anti-Corruption Laws	Anti-Corruption Agencies
Pattern 1: Mongolia	Law of Anti-Corruption 1996	None
Pattern 2: China	Criminal Law of 1979	Supreme People's Procuratorate Ministry of Supervision Central Disciplinary Inspection Committee
Pattern 2 : India	Prevention of Corruption Act 1947	Central Bureau of Investigation Central Vigilance Commission State anti-corruption bureaux State vigilance organisations
Pattern 2: Philippines	Republic Act of 1960 and Presidential Decrees	Special Anti-Graft Court Ombudsman Presidential Commission on Good Government Presidential Commission against Graft and Corruption
Pattern 3: Singapore	Prevention of Corruption Act 1960	Corrupt Practices Investigation Bureau
Pattern 3: Hong Kong	ICAC Ordinance of 1974 Prevention of Bribery Ordinance	Independent Commission Against Corruption
Pattern 3: Malaysia	Anti-Corruption Act, 1997	Anti-Corruption Agency
Pattern 3: Thailand	Organic Act on Counter Corruption, 1999	National Counter Corruption Commission
Pattern 3: South Korea	Anti-Corruption Act, 2001	Korean Independent Commission Against Corruption

19

In 1964, Nathaniel H. Leff contended that bureaucratic corruption had positive effects and contributed to economic development by providing the incentive for entrepreneurs to mobilise the bureaucracy, by reducing uncertainty and increasing investment, by promoting innovation, by introducing competition into the economy, and by providing a safeguard against the losses of bad economic policy.[67] However, more recent studies have shown that corruption has toxic rather than tonic effects.[68] More specifically, the report on *Human Development in South Asia 1999* concluded that:

> Corruption is one of the most damaging consequences of poor governance. It undermines investment and economic growth, decreases the resources available for human development goals, deepens the extent of poverty, subverts the judicial system, and undermines the legitimacy of the state. In fact, when corruption becomes entrenched, it can devastate the entire economic, political, and social fabric of a country. ... corruption breeds corruption—and a failure to combat it effectively can lead to an era of entrenched corruption.[69]

With the globalisation of corruption and its harmful effects, it is important to account for the different levels of corruption in Asian countries. Why is corruption a serious problem in India, Mongolia, the Philippines and South Korea? On the other hand, why have Singapore and Hong Kong been able to minimise corruption? Is minimising corruption in India, Mongolia, the Philippines and South Korea an impossible dream? The aim of this book is to answer these questions by comparing how these six Asian countries have dealt with the problem of corruption.

More specifically, this book analyses the three patterns of corruption control in Hong Kong, India, Mongolia, the Philippines, Singapore, and South Korea. These countries are selected for analysis because of the author's knowledge of their anti-corruption strategies. Chapter 2 analyses Mongolia's anti-corruption strategy as an example of the first pattern of corruption control. Chapters 3 and 4 deal respectively with the anti-corruption strategies in India and the Philippines, which illustrate the second pattern of corruption control.

The third pattern of corruption control is best illustrated by the anti-corruption strategies of Singapore and Hong Kong, which are also the least corrupt countries in Asia. The experiences of these city-states in curbing corruption are discussed in Chapters 5 and 6 respectively. The case of South Korea is described in Chapter 7, which shows that it is possible for a country to improve its anti-corruption strategy by changing from the first pattern to the third pattern of corruption control.

The anti-corruption strategies in these six countries are discussed using a common framework to facilitate comparative analysis. Each of the six country chapters begins with a description of the salient aspects of the country's policy context, namely, its geography, economy, demography and political system. The extent of corruption in the country is then analysed, including the identification of the major causes of corruption. Following this, the main features of the country's anti-corruption strategy are described in terms of the anti-corruption measures employed. In the final section of each chapter, the effectiveness of the country's anti-corruption strategy is evaluated in terms of its ranking and scores on Transparency International's Corruption Perceptions Index.

Chapter 8 concludes the book by discussing the importance of the policy context in influencing the extent of corruption in a country as well as the ability of its government to curb corruption. The three patterns of corruption control are compared in terms of their effectiveness. While Pattern 3 is more effective than Patterns 1 and 2, not all the countries which have adopted Pattern 3 have been equally successful in minimising corruption. Finally, the features of an effective anti-corruption strategy are identified and the question of whether such a strategy can be transferred to other countries is discussed.

ENDNOTES

1   Aparisim Ghosh *et al.* "Corruption: Reform's Dark Side", *Far Eastern Economic Review*, March 20, 1997, p. 18.

2   PricewaterhouseCoopers, "The Opacity Index", in Robin Hodess (ed.), *Global Corruption Report 2001* (Berlin: Transparency International, 2001), p. 276.

3   Ronald Wraith and Edgar Simpkins, *Corruption in Developing Countries* (London: George Allen and Unwin, 1963), p. 9.

4   Gunnar Myrdal, "Corruption as a Hindrance to Modernization in South Asia", in Arnold J. Heidenheimer, Michael Johnston and Victor T. LeVine (eds.), *Political Corruption: A Handbook* (New Brunswick: Transaction Publishers, 1989), pp. 406-416.

5   For examples of such research, see Ting Gong, *The Politics of Corruption in Contemporary China: An Analysis of Policy Outcomes* (Westport: Praeger, 1994); Julia Kwong, *The Political Economy of Corruption in China* (Armonk: M.E. Sharpe, 1997); T. Wing Lo, *Corruption and Politics in Hong Kong and China* (Buckingham: Open University Press, 1993); S.S. Gill, *The Pathology of Corruption* (New Delhi: HarperCollins Publishers India, 1998); S. Guhan and S. Paul (eds.), *Corruption in India: Agenda for Action* (New Delhi: Vision Books, 1997); C. Mitra, *The Corrupt Society: The Criminalization of India from Independence to the 1990s* (New Delhi: Penguin Books India, 1998); V. Pavarala, *Interpreting Corruption: Elite Perspectives in India* (New Delhi: Sage Publications, 1996); C.P. Srivastava, *Corruption: India's Enemy Within* (New Delhi: Macmillan India, 2001); Richard Holloway (ed.), *Stealing From the People: 16 Studies on Corruption in Indonesia*, Books 1-4 (Jakarta: Aksara Foundation, 2002); Kee-Chul Hwang, "Administrative Corruption in the Republic of Korea", (Ph.D. dissertation, University of Southern California, 1996); Young-Jong Kim, *Bureaucratic Corruption: The Case of Korea* 4th edition (Seoul: Chomyung Press, 1994); David C. Kang, *Crony Capitalism: Corruption and Development in South Korea and the Philippines* (Cambridge: Cambridge University Press, 2002); Yvonne T. Chua, *Robbed: An Investigation of Corruption in Philippine Education* (Metro Manila: Philippine Center for Investigative Journalism, 1999); Sheila S. Coronel (ed.), *Pork and Other Perks: Corruption and Governance in the Philippines* (Metro Manila: Philippine Center for Investigative Journalism, 1998); C.F. Hofilena, *News for Sale: The Corruption of the Philippine Media* (Metro Manila: Center for Investigative Journalism and the Center for Media Freedom and Responsibility, 1998); Jon S.T. Quah, "Combating Corruption in Singapore: What Can Be Learned?" *Journal of Contingencies and Crisis Management*, Vol. 9, No. 1 (March 2001), pp. 29-35; Pasuk Phongpaichit and Sungsidh Piriyarangsan, *Corruption and Democracy in Thailand* 2nd editon (Bangkok: Silkworm Books, 1996); Jon S.T. Quah, *Comparing Anti-Corruption Measures in Asian Countries* (Singapore: Centre for Advanced Studies, National University of Singapore, CAS Research Paper Series No. 13, November 1999); and *Combating Corruption in Asian and Pacific Economies* (Manila: Asian Development Bank, 2000).

6   Robert S. Leiken, "Controlling the Global Corruption Epidemic", *Foreign Policy*, Vol. 105 (Winter 1996/1997), p. 58.

7   Ibid., p. 58.

8   Gerald E. Caiden, "Toward a General Theory of Official Corruption", *Asian Journal of Public Administration*, Vol. 10, No. 1 (June 1988), p. 5, Table 1.

9   Michael L. Hager, "Bureaucratic Corruption in India: Legal Control of Maladministration", *Comparative Political Studies*, Vol. 6, No. 2 (July 1973), pp. 200-201.

10   Arnold J. Heidenheimer, "Terms, Concepts, and Definitions: An Introduction", in Heidenheimer, Johnston and LeVine (eds.), *Political Corruption*, pp. 8-11.

11   Joseph S. Nye, "Corruption and Political Development", *American Political Science Review*, Vol. 6 (June 1967), p. 419.

12   Jacob van Klaveren, "The Concept of Corruption", in Heideheimer, Johnston and LeVine (eds.), *Political Corruption*, p. 26.

13   Carl J. Friedrich, "Corruption Concepts in Historical Perspective", in Heidenheimer, Johnson and LeVine (eds.), *Political Handbook*, p. 15.

14   UNDP, *Fighting Corruption to Improve Governance* (New York: UNDP, 1999), p. 7.

15   This useful distinction was introduced by Gerald E. Caiden in his article, "Public Maladministration and Bureaucratic Corruption", *Hong Kong Journal of Public Administration*, Vol. 3, No. 1 (June 1981), pp. 58-62.

16   Jeremy Pope, *Confronting Corruption: The Elements of a National Integrity System* (Berlin: Transparency International, 2000), p. xix.

17   George Moody-Stuart, *Grand Corruption: How Business Bribes Damage Developing Countries* (Oxford: WorldView Publishing, 1997), p. 2.

18   Leslie Palmier, *The Control of Bureaucratic Corruption: Case Studies in Asia* (New Delhi: Allied Publishers, 1985), pp. 271-272, emphasis added.

19   Ibid., p. 2.

20   Ibid., p. 6.

21   Paulo Mauro, *Why Worry about Corruption?* (Washington, D.C.: International Monetary Fund, 1997), p. 5.

22   Clive Day, *The Dutch in Java* (Kuala Lumpur: Oxford University Press, 1966), pp. 100-103.

23   J.A.C. Mackie, "The Commission of Four report on Corruption", *Bulletin of Indonesian Economic Studies*, Vol. 6, No. 3 (1970), pp. 87-88.

24   Theodore M. Smith, "Corruption, Tradition and Change", *Indonesia*, No. 11 (April 1970), pp. 28-29.

25   *A National Survey of Corruption in Indonesia* (Jakarta: Partnership for Governance Reform, Final Report, December 2001), p. 39, Figure G1.

26   Meredith Woo-Cummings, "Developmental Bureaucracy in Comparative Perspective: The Evolution of the Korean Civil Service", in Hyung-Ki Kim, *et al.*, *The Japanese Civil Service and Economic Development: Catalysts of Change* (Oxford: Clarendon Press, 1995), pp. 455-456.

27   Jong S. Jun and Jae Poong Yoon, "Korean Public Administration at a Crossroads: Culture, Development and Change", in Ahmed S. Huque *et al.* (eds.), *Public Administration in the NICs: Challenges and Accomplishments* (Basingstoke: Macmillan Press, 1996), p. 107.

28 Kasem Suwanagul, "The Civil Service of Thailand", (Ph.D. dissertation, New York University, 1962), pp. 79-80.

29 "Police chief admits: Yes, Thai cops are corrupt, what do you expect"? *Straits Times* (Singapore), June 5, 2002, p. A5.

30 Onofre D. Corpuz, *The Bureaucracy in the Philippines* (Quezon City: Institute of Public Administration, University of the Philippines, 1957), p. 129.

31 Jon S.T. Quah, "Bureaucratic Corruption in the ASEAN Countries: A Comparative Analysis of Their Anti-Corruption Strategy", *Journal of Southeast Asian Studies*, Vol. 13, No. 1 (March 1983), p. 159.

32 Perfecto L. Padilla, "Low Salary Grades, Income-Augmentation Schemes and the Merit Principle", in Proserpina Domingo Tapales and Nestor N. Pilar (eds.), *Public Administration by the Year 2000: Looking Back into Future* (Quezon City: College of Public Administration, University of the Philippines, 1995), pp. 195-202 and 206.

33 Jon S.T. Quah, "Police Corruption in Singapore: An Analysis of its Forms, Extent and Causes", *Singapore Police Journal*, Vol. 10, No. 1 (January 1979), p. 28.

34 *Straits Times*, October 4, 1887, quoted in ibid., p. 29.

35 Abhijit Banerjee, "Can Anything Be Done About Corruption?" in M.G. Quilbria and J. Malcolm Dowling (eds.), *Current Issues in Economic Development: An Asian Perspective* (Hong Kong: Oxford University Press for the Asian Development Bank, 1996), p. 110.

36 Gerald E. Caiden, *The Dynamics of Public Administration: Guidelines to Current Transformations in Theory and Practice* (Hinsdale: Dryden Press, 1971), pp. 23-24.

37 David J. Gould and Jose A. Amaro-Reyes, *The Effects of Corruption on Administrative Performance: Illustrations from Developing Countries* (Washington, D.C.: World Bank Staff Working Papers No. 580, 1983), p. 17.

38 Bertrand de Speville, *Hong Kong: Policy Initiatives Against Corruption* (Paris: Organisation for Economic Co-operation and Development, 1997), p. 14.

39 Donald P. Warwick, "The Effectiveness of the Indonesian Civil Service", *Southeast Asian Journal of Social Science*, Vol. 15, No. 2 (1987), p. 43.

40 Keith Loveard, *Suharto: Indonesia's Last Sultan* (Singapore: Horizon Books, 1999), p. 111.

41 Radius Prawiro, *Indonesia's Struggle for Economic Development: Pragmatism in Action* (Kuala Lumpur: Oxford University Press, 1998), pp. 230-231.

42 Ibid., p. 264.

43 *The Knapp Commission Report on Police Corruption* (New York: George Braziller, 1972), pp. 67-68.

44 Palmier, *The Control of Bureaucratic Corruption*, pp. 179-181.

45 Syed Hussein Alatas, *Corruption: Its Nature, Causes and Functions* (Kuala Lumpur: S. Abdul Majeed, 1991), p. 121.

46 *Straits Times*, August 1, 1998, p. 14.

47 Hilton Root, "Corruption in China: Has it Become Systemic?" *Asian Survey*, Vol. 36, No. 8 (August 1996), p. 752.

48 *Straits Times*, March 6, 2000, p. 23.

49   *Straits Times*, March 9, 2000, p. 30.

50   *Straits Times*, April 24, 2000, p. 2.

51   Mohammad Mohabbat Khan, *Administrative Reforms in Bangladesh* (New Delhi: South Asian Publishers, 1998), p. 35.

52   Ibid., p. 36.

53   Palmier, *The Control of Bureaucratic Corruption*, p. 279.

54   *Straits Times*, January 27, 1987, p. 11.

55   Palmier, *The Control of Bureaucratic Corruption*, p. 279.

56   For details of China's anti-corruption measures see Chan Kin Man, "Corruption in China: A Principal-Agent Perspective", in H. K. Wong and H.S. Chan (eds.), *Handbook of Public Administration in the Asia-Pacific Basin* (New York: Marcel Dekker, 1999), pp. 300-301.

57   Y. Mansoor Marican, "Combating Corruption: The Malaysian Experience", *Asian Survey*, Vol. 19, No. 6 (June 1979), pp. 601 and 603.

58   Quah, "Bureaucratic Corruption in the ASEAN Countries", p. 170.

59   For more details of this trial see *The Anwar Ibrahim Judgment* (Kuala Lumpur: Malayan Law Journal, 1999).

60   *Building Institutional Capacity in Asia Report 2001: Public Sector Challenges and Government Reforms in South East Asia* (Sydney: Research Institute for Asia and the Pacific, University of Sydney, 2001), p. 131.

61   Quah, "Bureaucratic Corruption in the ASEAN Countries", p. 172.

62   Niels Mulder, *Inside Thai Society: Interpretation of Everyday Life* (Amsterdam: Pepin Press, 1996), pp. 173-174.

63   Catherin E. Dalpino, "Thailand's Search for Accountability", *Journal of Democracy*, Vol. 2, No. 4 (1991), p. 66.

64   Amara Raksasataya, "Bureuacracy vs. Bureaucracy: Anti-corrupt Practice Measures in Thailand", in Ramesh K. Arora (ed.), *Politics and Administration in Changing Societies: Essays in Honour of Professor Fred W. Riggs* (New Delhi: Associated Publishing House, 1992), p. 240.

65   For more details of the NCCC's duties and powers, see *The Office of the National Counter Corruption Commission* (Bangkok: NCCC, n.d.), pp. 9-25.

66   Patrick Glynn, Stephen J. Kobrin and Moises Naim, "The Globalization of Corruption", in Kimberly Ann Elliott (ed.), *Corruption and the Global Economy* (Washington, D.C.: Institute for International Economics, 1997), p. 7.

67   Nathaniel H. Leff, "Economic Development through Bureaucratic Corruption", in Arnold J. Heidenheimer (ed.), *Political Corruption: Readings in Comparative Analysis* (New Brunswick: Transaction Books, 1970), pp. 514-516. This article was originally published in the *American Behavioral Scientist*, Vol. 8, No. 3 (November 1964), pp. 8-14.

68   Ledivina V. Carino, "Tonic or Toxic: The Effects of Graft and Corruption", in Ledivina V. Carino (ed.), *Bureaucratic Corruption in Asia: Causes, Consequences and Control* (Quezon City: JMC Press and College of Public Administration, University of the Philippines, 1986), p. 194.

69   *Human Development in South Asia 1999: The Crisis of Governance* (Karachi: Oxford University Press, 1999), pp. 96 and 105.

CHAPTER 2

Mongolia

INTRODUCTION

Mongolia became the first communist state in Asia in July 1921[1] and was dependent on the former Soviet Union for foreign aid, technical assistance and a large market for her exports for 70 years until the departure of the Soviet advisers in 1991. Corruption existed in Mongolia during its seven decades under communist rule. However, the country's transition from a Soviet-style command economy to a market economy since 1991 has increased the opportunities for corruption and made the environment conducive for corruption for three reasons: the poverty of the population, the low salaries of public officials, and the non-enforcement of the anti-corruption laws.

How serious is the problem of corruption in Mongolia today? What measures have been employed by the Mongolian government to combat corruption? How effective is its anti-corruption strategy? What problems have been encountered in fighting corruption and what are the prospects of minimising corruption in Mongolia? In order to answer these questions, it is necessary to provide a brief description of the Mongolian policy context to enable us to understand the problem of corruption.[2]

POLICY CONTEXT

The policy context refers to the four aspects relevant for analysing the problem of corruption, namely, the geography, economy, demography, and political system of Mongolia.

Geography

Mongolia is the sixth largest country in Asia and the 18th largest in the world with a total area of 1,565,000 sq. km.[3] More importantly, Mongolia is also landlocked by Russia to the north and the People's Republic of China (PRC) to the south, east and west. Indeed, there is a Mongolian saying that "Mongolia exists because Russia and China exist".[4] In fact, Mongolia is the largest land-locked state in Africa and Asia.[5] Since it has a small population of 2,694,432 over a vast area, Mongolia is sparsely populated. Its population density in July 2002 was only 1.7 persons per sq. km.[6]

Mongolia is divided into three zones: the mountains in the north and west; the inter-mountain basins; and the steppe, which includes the Gobi Desert, constitutes 75% of the land. It has a high altitude, with an average elevation of 1,580 metres above sea level. Mongolia has also an extreme climate as there is no sea to moderate its semi-arid continental climate, which has been exacerbated by its high altitude. Indeed, its harsh winters (from October to March) and its vulnerability to earthquakes "add substantial costs to the development of socioeconomic structure".[7] Mongolia's harsh climate and remoteness from sea transport and markets constitute a serious constraint to economic growth. Indeed, Mongolia faces many obstacles to international trade and growth as there is only one railway traversing the country from north to south, without access to ports, and hampered by deteriorating road conditions, and the payment of heavy transit fees through Russia and China.[8] Mongolia's poorly developed infrastructure is reflected in the fact that it has only 1,748 km of railways and 47,600 km of roads even though it measures 2,368 km east to west and 1,260 km north to south. Its telecommunications system is also congested and outdated.[9] The lack of all-weather roads and useful waterways means that 90% of the national freight is carried by the railway system.[10]

Mongolia's geographical context has made the task of fighting corruption much harder for two reasons. First, Mongolia's large size is not advantageous for policy formulation and implementation as there are problems with communication and enforcing the anti-corruption measures, especially in the more remote provinces. Second, Mongolia's proximity to the PRC and Russia, where corruption is rampant, constitutes an obstacle to its government's anti-corruption drive as these countries were role models during the nearly seven decades of communist rule, and the two centuries of Chinese rule.

Economy

As large-scale agriculture is not possible in Mongolia because of its harsh climate and high altitude, its economy is "based primarily upon herding and secondarily upon hunting, both of which were supplemented by trade and raiding".[11] However, the herding economy did not expand because of internecine warfare, the payment of tribute to the Manchu rulers in Peking, and the conversion of the population to Lamaist Buddhism and the consequent growth of the monasteries.[12] In addition to the climate and geography, which do not make the Mongolian steppe suitable for agriculture, "Mongolian nomads have been psychologically conditioned for centuries to feel that toiling in the soil is not a proper way for humans to make a living." Consequently, they prefer "to work on horseback and look after one's animals than to dig in the dirt".[13]

Manufacturing and industry developed very late in Mongolia because of "the non-development of urban life, the far-flung migrations of the Mongolian people, and the recruitment of all able-bodied males for military service" and the "high incidence of warlike activity in Mongol history". Moreover, during the Ch'ing dynasty (1644-1911) the free flow of Chinese goods into the steppe areas and the settling of Chinese artisans in the monasteries hindered the growth of an indigenous class of Mongol artisans. Indeed, manufacturing activity and artisans were only developed in Mongolia in the 1930s and 1940s as a result of the efforts of its nationalist leaders.[14]

With its extensive pasture land and limited arable land, animal husbandry is important in Mongolia as "livestock production using pastoral grazing management strategies has dominated Mongolian agriculture for centuries".[15] Mongolia is a poor country with a weak industrial base and animal husbandry as the major source of livelihood for its nomadic population. While its livestock population has increased from 23.6 million to 26.8 million during 1930 to 1994[16], Mongolia has imported wheat, butter and other dairy products from other countries to feed its livestock and population even though the agricultural sector has grown during the past 30 years.

Mongolia is rich in mineral resources as "600 mineral deposits bearing over 80 minerals have been discovered including coal, iron, tin, copper, molybdenum, gold, silver, tungsten, zinc, lead, phosphates, wolfram, fluorspar, uranium, oil shale, and semiprecious stones (agate, lapis, lazuli, garnet)". The country also has over 170 deposits of construction materials such as marble and granite. Copper is the major mineral as 400,000 tons of it are produced annually at the copper plant in Erdenet.[17] Martha Brill Olcott's description of Kazakhstan as being "blessed with resources but cursed by geography" also applies to Mongolia.[18]

Mongolia's economic history can be divided into five periods: the feudal period; the post-revolutionary period (1921-1948); the development of the command economy (1948-1984); the period of Mongolian *Perestroika* (1984-1989);[19] and the transition to a market economy (1991-1998). What is important for our analysis is the fact that Mongolia was under communist rule and Soviet influence for seven decades, from July 1921 until January 1991, when its Soviet advisers left the country.[20] In fact, Mongolia was the second longest communist-ruled country after the former Soviet Union.[21] This meant the development of a command economy, based on central planning and the Soviet system of economic management, in Mongolia from 1948 until 1984. In 1946, Mongolia signed a Friendship and Mutual Assistance Treaty with the Soviet Union, and it joined the Council for Mutual Economic Assistance (CMEA), the Soviet trade bloc, in 1962.

The former Soviet Union provided Mongolia with foreign aid, technical assistance and "a large market for her exports, a secure supply of required imports and exceptionally favourable terms of trade". Furthermore, Mongolia's trade with CMEA constituted 93% of its total trade in 1988.[22] Until 1990, the Soviet Union had provided Mongolia with US$800 million annually in grants and loans, 40% of its consumer goods, 80% of its supplies for the economy, and 90% of its technical equipment.[23]

Economic reforms were introduced during 1984-1989 within the context of a planned economy. However, in 1991, the Mongolian economy was exposed to three external shocks: "an aid shock, a trade shock and a macroeconomic management shock".[24] First, the reduction of Soviet aid in 1989 and its cessation in 1991 deprived the Mongolian economy of the concessions needed for financing its investment programme. Second, the collapse of the CMEA in 1991 affected Mongolia adversely as its total exports decreased from US$739.1 million to US$348 million during 1988-1991. Finally, the departure of the Soviet technical advisers in 1991 also left Mongolia with few experienced people to run the economy. The combined effect of these three shocks was devastating as "Mongolia suffered the most serious peacetime economic collapse any nation has faced during this century".[25] Indeed, Mongolia's economic collapse "was possibly the greatest of all the (peaceful) formerly socialist countries" as "the decline in domestic absorption equalled approximately 62% of GNP, much more than the decline experienced in Eastern European countries or during wartime destruction".[26] The Mongolian government responded to the economic crisis by rejecting the former Soviet-style command economy and introducing reforms to transform it into a market economy.[27] According to Nixson and Walters, the basic aim of the reform programme was to transform the "centrally planned economy into a free market economy in the shortest possible time".[28]

Official statistics during 1985-1990 revealed that Mongolia's per capita gross domestic product (GDP) was between US$600 to US$2,100. However, the dismantling of the command economy led to the reduction of the per capita GDP from 5,400 togrogs to 3,700 togrogs during 1989 to 1993. Even though Mongolia's per capita GDP rose from US$224 in 1993 to US$260 in 1994,[29] its status as a poor country is confirmed by two surveys on poverty, which found that poverty had increased from 14.5% to 19.2% of the population during

1991 to 1996, and 36% of the population was estimated by the World Bank to be poor in 1995.[30] According to *The Economist*, Mongolia's per capita GDP in 2000 was US$400.[31]

The transition of the Mongolian economy from a centrally planned one to a market economy has two important implications for curbing corruption in the country. First, as the former Soviet Union had exerted tremendous influence on Mongolia for 70 years, it is not surprising that the Soviet forms of corruption were also prevalent in Mongolia during the socialist period. Second, the experiences of other transitional economies have shown that the transition from a command economy to a market economy has also increased the opportunities for corruption.

Demography

Mongolia's small population of 2.3 million people in 1996 consists of 85% Khalkha Mongol, 7% Kazakh, 4.6% Tungusic and 3.4% other groups.[32] The population has an average life expectancy of 64 years and a high literacy rate of 96% among those over 15 years old in 1994.[33] Mongolia's population is young as those under 16 years of age constitute 40% of the total population and 50% of the poor.[34] In terms of religion, 94% of Mongolians are Lamaist Buddhists, while the remaining 6% are Muslim.[35]

What are the values of the Mongolian population which are relevant for curbing corruption in the country? First, the tradition of gift-giving exists and the taboo of returning or presenting "an empty container to a person who has brought a gift" without placing a small token in it[36] encourages reciprocity in human relations and could possibly contribute to extensive bribery of civil servants in the form of "gifts" provided by those citizens wishing to "cut red tape" or to obtain licences improperly. Second, the national currency, the togrog, was established in 1925 by the communist government to pay the civil service and "to benefit the small urban proletariat".[37]

In 1994, the average income for city families was 27,900 togrogs compared to 32,900 togrogs for rural families.[38] However, according to Campi, money was unimportant to the Mongols for two reasons: the limited functions of currency in a nomadic economy; and the low salaries and limited salary range of workers during the communist era as "the most highly rewarded Mongols received only three times the pay of the least skilled workers".[39] Today, the salaries of civil servants are among the lowest in Asia, and constitute an important factor contributing to corruption in Mongolia.

Political System

Mongolia was dominated by the emperors of China for two centuries, but it asserted its autonomy for eight years from 1911 until 1919, when a Chinese army occupied the capital, Urga (known today as Ulaanbaatar). In January 1920, two groups of revolutionaries united to form the Mongolian People's Party (MPP), which was later renamed the Mongolian People's Revolutionary Party (MPRP) in 1922. In February 1921, Mongolia was occupied by an army led by a White Russian, the Baron von Ungern-Sternberg, who provided the Bolsheviks with an excuse to invade and "liberate" it. The Bolsheviks had assisted some Mongols to organise the MPP, a provisional government in exile, and an army. The small Mongolian army and the provisional government appealed to the Soviets for military assistance to liberate their country. The Soviet forces defeated Ungern and a new government was formed in July 1921.[40]

The many Soviet advisers who were placed in important government departments and the MPP became the real rulers of the country from 1921 and they gradually changed Mongolia into "a capsular imitation of the Soviet Union".[41] For example, the MPRP was organised in the manner of its Soviet counterpart, and the supreme organ of government was the Great Khuraldan (now known as the State Great Hural), which resembled the Congress of Soviets, and the Small Khuraldan, which was similar to the Central Executive Committee in the U.S.S.R. According to Hammond, "the chief objective of Soviet economic policy in Mongolia was not the establishment of a socialist system, but rather the exploitation of

Mongolia for the benefit of Russia".[42] Indeed, this policy of exploitation was implemented through the control of Mongolian foreign trade. Consequently, Mongolia's exports to the U.S.S.R. rose from 24.1% to 99.2% during 1925 to 1931.

In 1989, two years after the advent of *perestroika* in the Soviet Union, the Mongolian Democratic Union (MDU) was formed in Ulaanbaatar with the aim of overthrowing the MPRP. However, the MPRP responded to the wave of demonstrations in the capital by launching extensive political reforms. President Batmonh was replaced by Ochirbat, the Central Committee was reorganised, and the government indicated that the Constitution would be amended. The reformed MPRP called for immediate elections to give the urban-based opposition minimal time for organisation.

The first democratic election was held in July 1990 and the MPRP won 62% of the votes and obtained a secure majority of deputies in the new bicameral legislature. In 1991, the MPRP passed a law banning political parties from operating in government organs and required all government officials to drop their party affiliation, thus eroding the relevance of communism. A constitutional drafting committee was formed and the new constitution was passed in 1992.[43]

During the second election in July 1992, the MPRP won 71 out of the 76 parliamentary seats, and secured 56% of the popular vote. The MPRP was the only party that was able to field candidates for every seat and it succeeded in promoting "itself as a reformed party aiming at a more gradual–and socially acceptable–transition towards a market economy".[44] In contrast, the Democratic Coalition was divided and lost its credibility when a banking scandal was revealed implicating central bankers (associated with the opposition), who had squandered the country's entire gold reserves through currency speculation. In October 1992, the four major opposition parties united to form the National Democratic Party (NDP). The Social Democratic Party (SDP) was the second major opposition party and in January 1993, the NDP and SDP agreed to field a single candidate in the presidential election. The MPRP nominated L. Tudev, the editor of the party newspaper, as its presidential candidate and rejected Ochirbat, who accepted the opposition's offer to be their candidate. The opposition won in 14 of the 18 provinces in the first presidential election in June 1993, which resulted in "a new era of divided government between parliament and presidency".[45]

The opposition won a landslide victory in the June 1996 parliamentary election as the Democratic Union coalition captured 50 of the 76 seats in the Hural. The NDP won 34 seats, the SDP won 13 seats, the Conservative party won one seat, and independent candidates won three seats, while the MPRP won 25 seats.[46] The opposition's victory signalled not only the end of more than 70 years of the MPRP's dominance, but also the establishment of a democratic government in Mongolia. However, the second presidential election in May 1997 resulted in the election of the MPRP's candidate , Natsagin Bagabandi, as president. There was a split between the communist-led presidency and the democratic, pro-reform legislature, which was dominated by the ruling Democratic Coalition.[47] Indeed, in mid-October 1998, President Bagabandi rejected Davaadoriin Ganbold, the Democratic Coalition's candidate for prime minister, for the seventh time.[48] However, the Democratic Coalition was ineffective because of political infighting, a corruption scandal, and the MPRP's efforts to obstruct its reform agenda. Consequently, it was not surprising that the MPRP won 72 of the 76 seats in the 2000 parliamentary election and took over power from the Democratic Coalition.

The MPRP consolidated its political power and showed its commitment to keep the market economic reforms on track in 2001.[49] Accordingly, it was not surprising that incumbent President N. Bagabandi won the May 20 presidential election with 58% of the vote. Bagabandi's victory not only "enhanced the MPRP's political dominance" but also demonstrated "the democrats' difficulties in rebuilding public confidence after their four tumultuous years in power".[50]

The transformation of Mongolia's political system from seven decades of communism under the control of the MPRP to a new democracy that has adopted a market economy poses two important challenges for the incumbent government in terms of combating corruption. First, like the former Soviet Union, Mongolia has been afflicted by corruption during its 70 years of communist rule. Second, and more importantly, the task of fighting corruption has been made more difficult as the Mongolian government has to deal with both the legacy of corruption as well as the many opportunities for corruption arising from the democratisation process and the transition to a market economy.

EXTENT OF CORRUPTION

The problem of gathering evidence is particularly difficult in communist or former communist countries. This problem still exists today even though corruption is no longer as sensitive a topic as it was in the 1960s. According to Maria Los, whose study of corruption in Poland was based on reports of corruption in several weekly magazines and daily newspapers, these reports "paint a bleak, deeply disturbing picture of a country plagued by injustice, corruption and exploitation" but she cautioned that such reports "present a rather cautious diagnosis, more likely understated than overstated" because of censorship and other constraints in a totalitarian country.[51] In other words, the reported extent of corruption is incomplete and does not represent the *actual* extent of corruption in a country.[52] This caveat must be noted when analysing the extent of corruption in Mongolia and the other five Asian countries discussed in this book as the analysis below is based on reports of corruption in the press and other publications, and some survey data on corruption.

There is limited information on the extent of corruption in Mongolia during its 70 years of communist rule (1921-1991). One of the earliest observations about the existence of corruption in Mongolia was made by Robert A. Rupen 37 years ago:

> Most members of the Mongolian elite were patriotic, and they differed genuinely in their opinions as to the policies that would be best for their country. *They took bribes, however, and allowed personal concerns to influence their political opinions. In this respect the Church [Buddhist monasteries] also was generally corrupt.*[53]

However, Rupen did not provide any empirical evidence for his generalisation about the practice of bribery among the Mongolian elite and the Buddhist monks.

In 1981, General Secretary Tsedenbal had called for "a clampdown on corruption and promised to root out 'weeds of all kinds' from the party" at the 18th MPRP Congress.[54] In January 1982, Professor B. Shirendev, who was president of the Mongolian Academy of Sciences for 22 years, a member of the MPRP's Central Committee, and a deputy chairperson of Parliament, was accused by the MPRP's Central Committee of embezzling "hundreds of thousands" of dollars, which were used for hosting lavish parties and acquiring luxury items for his personal use.[55]

In her study of communist societies, Maria Hirzowicz found that "under Stalinist rule, the Communist bureaucracies enjoyed many privileges, ranging from better food in their canteens, higher salaries, and special shops, to better flats, chauffeur-driven cars and luxurious holidays in the best health resorts". While corruption among party and state officials was quite common under Stalinist regimes, "there were many disincentives which prevented malpractices from spreading". First, there was "a general feeling of insecurity and fear" among these officials and "constant purges, trials, and witch-hunts" made them cautious. Second, these officials had to work long hours and observe the official "disapproval of 'petty bourgeois' desires for material luxuries". Third, "the range of goods available in the post-war decades was rather limited". Furthermore, overseas trips were restricted to "a narrow circle of functionaries who usually did their best to show their contempt for the decadent West". Fourth, as accommodation and some "consumer durables" could be used but not owned, "flats were nationalised, private cars were rare, chauffeur-driven limousines belonged to state enterprises and offices, and land could not be acquired by private individuals". Fifth, as "officials were subject to tight control by security and party organs both in their official and private lives", they could not spend their money "without attracting the attention of the security apparatus" and "party comrades were alert for any sign of improper conduct in their friends and even in members of their families".[56]

The quality of life of party and state officials was not based on their ownership of material assets but on the various perks associated with their positions. In her study of *blat*, networking and informal exchange in Russia, Alena V. Ledeneva observed that cadres were "the most adept *blat* practitioners" as they "had at their disposal decision-making and resource-allocation powers" which "made them frequent recipients of *blat* overtures".[57] Thus, "the system protected itself against the excessive greed of state functionaries" by providing them with the privileges gained from their official positions and not "with the individual ownership of valuable material assets".[58] As Mongolia was a communist state under the Soviet Union's influence for seven decades, it also exhibited the same pattern of "restrained" corruption during this period.

The most common crimes in Mongolia during the late 1980s were theft and embezzlement of state property, black-marketing, juvenile delinquency, misappropriation of materials (food and drugs), and speculation (such as selling automobiles). The government dealt with these crimes through better enforcement of laws, harsher punishment for criminals, and enhanced public involvement in curbing crime.[59] In 1989, the political leaders were "more concerned with the threats of corruption and of incompetence in law enforcement that allowed for an increase in crime, especially economic crimes".[60]

O. Adiya has observed that corruption was "not an entirely new phenomenon in Mongolian society" as "it existed under the previous regime, in which a few people made decisions and everyone else was held accountable for those decisions". However, "the level of corrupted officials in the former Politburo had far less magnitude and scale than today's wide-ranging, all-encompassing abuses of power. *Today, corruption is everywhere*".[61]

In April 1994, a group which included some opposition MPs, launched a hunger strike in front of the government buildings in Ulaanbaatar to protest against corruption which "was rife among the parliament and government".[62] Colonel L. Sanjaasuren, the former head of counter-intelligence, had "warned that important documentary evidence of bribery and corruption among high-ranking government officials might be destroyed in the reorganisation." A parliamentary commission of inquiry convened to examine the allegations concluded that the allegations were untrue. However, two of the opposition commissioners did not agree with the conclusions of the other four MPRP commissioners and "media reports of the affair suggest that the public was not convinced that their leaders were entirely blameless either".[63] Accordingly, it was not surprising that the opposition MPs, other political parties and organisations, and the general public continued to accuse the prime minister, the chairman and secretary of the State Great Hural and other senior civil servants of corruption and abuse of power.[64] On July 29, 1994, the state procurator refused to file a criminal case against the prime minister, Puntsagiin Jasrai, as he was not guilty of any charges of bribery and corruption.[65]

In August 1994, the press published the results of an opinion poll of 830 persons conducted in eight provinces and two cities by the Academy of Sciences and the Konrad Adenauer Foundation of Germany.[66] The findings showed that the general public was very concerned about bribery and corruption at all levels of administration.[67] First, 68% of the respondents strongly agreed with the "strong social perception that without giving incentives to officials one's matter cannot be processed". Second, regarding the forms of corruption, 75.5% of the respondents gave cash, 55.2% gave gifts, and 43% participated in mutual exchange of services and assistance. Third, 46.6% of the respondents felt that all those who try to process matters will offer bribes to public officials; and 38.6% of them identified businessmen, entrepreneurs and vendors as bribe-givers. Fourth, the most corrupt agencies in Mongolia according to the respondents were: the customs office (55.7%); the banking and financial sector (51.2%); the police and prosecutors (46.5%); the immigration office responsible for foreign and national passports (28.05%); the taxation office (15.3%); and local government (13.4%). Fifth, 54% of the respondents viewed the middle level officials as the most corrupt; 25.5% believed that the senior government officials were the most corrupt; and 18.3% said that the junior officials were the most corrupt. Sixth, Table 2.1 below shows that the banking sector and the customs office were the most corrupt sectors in Ulaanbaatar, the provinces and the counties. Seventh, 44% of the respondents from Ulaanbaatar, 44% of the respondents from the provinces, and 38.4% of the respondents from the counties strongly agreed with the view that corruption was everywhere. Finally, 47.2% of the respondents felt that the government did not take any action to fight corruption, and 37.1% believed that the anti-corruption measures taken were ineffective.

TABLE 2.1 MOST CORRUPT SECTORS IN MONGOLIA BY LOCATION

Corrupt Sector	Ulaanbaatar	Provinces	Counties
1st	Banking Sector	Customs Office	Customs Office
2nd	Customs Office	Banking Sector	Courts
3rd	Immigration Office	Immigration Office	Banking Sector

Source: Tumur-Ochiryn Erdenebileg, "Public Opinion on Corruption in Mongolia" (unpublished paper, 1994), p. 2.

In October 1994, nine senior banking officials were arrested on charges of bribery and corruption.[68] They were accused of misappropriating funds so that they could provide large loans to a businesswoman, D. Tsolmon, who was found guilty of bribery and tax fraud, and sentenced to eight years' imprisonment. Five of the bankers were also found guilty and given various sentences, ranging from one to five years and fines of varying severity.[69] According to the Economist Intelligence Unit (EIU), this case "highlighted the extent of economic crime, which constitutes an obstacle to the success of economic reform and has caused a considerable loss of confidence in the new order among the general public".[70]

In December 1994, the "Gold Dealers" case involving former bankers and senior civil servants who were responsible for the loss of national gold reserves in the 1980s was reopened. However, the chances of resolving this "long-running legal" case were slim as the state prosecutor demanded that the case be dropped in mid-January 1995 and absented himself from court. The judge was forced to postpone the case.[71] This case was finally resolved in November 1996 with the imprisonment of the two defendants, D. Sukh-Erdene, the former head of the Trade and Development Bank, and G. Khuderchuluun, the head of the Bank of Mongolia from 1981-1991. Both were found guilty of embezzling US$82.4 million and were sentenced to six and four years respectively. Sukh-Erdene had obtained loans from the UK government against a guarantee of 4.4 tons of Mongolian gold and lost the money by speculating on international currency markets.[72]

In October 1996, an inspection of a military unit at Nalaikh at the request of the Minister of Defence, Dambiin Dorligjav, revealed a corruption scandal involving senior military officers who sold eight million togrogs (or US$17,500) worth of military hardware for less than its real value and without permission to China through a third party. Among those implicated were the former Minister of Defence, Lieutenant-General Shagalyn Jadambaa, who had died recently, and the former chief-of-staff, R. Davaa.[73] After conducting its investigations, the Ministry of Defence sacked three generals for misappropriating 87 million togrogs (or US$124,000) of assets belonging to military unit 137.[74]

During the same month, another corruption scandal involving the transfer of funds from the Erdenet ore-dressing plant to private business and abroad was uncovered by the State Property Committee, which "revealed corruption, misconduct, neglect of duty and mismanagement of funds by the hierarchy of the State-owned Erdenet Ore Dressing Plant".[75] The plant's commercial director, Sh. Otgonbileg, was accused of misappropriating more than US$23 million and transferring this amount from the joint venture to the privately-owned Erdenet Concern. In late October, the police charged the director, Ch. Zorig, with cheating the state of US$4.6 million as he paid this sum to the Russian Neman company of Novosibirsk in advance for petroleum products which were not delivered.[76] The State Property Committee closed Erdenet Concern at the end of November 1996 after an audit of its finances revealed that it had violated the privatisation law by using its status as a state-owned enterprise to obtain foreign loans. However, President Ochirbat allowed the director, Sh. Otgonbileg, to remain in his position even though the public had called for his dismissal.[77] Otgonbileg's term of office ended on January 1, 1998, but he was allowed to remain as an interim director. He disappeared on August 7, 1998, when he was supposed to hand over his duties to the new director.[78]

Commenting on the above scandals, the EIU observed that "at present it is not easy to judge the extent to which corruption has penetrated Mongolian institutions". However, it noted that there was a great deal of financial mismanagement as:

> Agencies dependent on the state budget for income are often in a desperate situation when trying to meet their obligations. Payment of allocated funds, which are often inadequate, is frequently delayed so the executive tries to find means to fill the gap between income and expenditure. Audits have been conducted in many state and public organisations following the introduction of auditing procedures. These are now being reported and irregularities are being brought to the attention of the public.[79]

In his review of Mongolian society in 1997, Tom Ginsburg observed that "there is also a perception that government corruption is rising as well".[80] Indeed, the director of the General Customs Board, D. Tsend, who was appointed in July 1996, said in early 1997 that the customs service was "riddled with bribery and corruption and suitable candidates for over 100 vacancies were hard to find. Out of 300 recent applicants only ten were deemed suitable".[81] The morale in the education sector was low in recent years and there were several strikes for better wages and working conditions. More importantly, this sector was also not free of corruption as "it was revealed recently that some head teachers and others have been forging secondary-level examination certificates for considerable sums of money".[82] Finally, "a civil service audit in the first half of 1998 has helped to register Tg1.14 billion misappropriated by officials, in some cases by mismanaging foreign aid; and of this, Tg248 million has already been returned to the Treasury".[83]

The above cases indicate clearly that corruption exists in Mongolia today. However, what is more important, is the public perception that they had to bribe officials to get things done. Indeed, this view was expressed by O. Adiya thus:

> The most unfortunate thing with regard to corruption [in Mongolia] is how commonly it is accepted as necessary to ensure the smooth running of one's affairs. We take for granted the giving of a bottle of vodka to a teacher, small presents to a doctor or nurse, incentives to traffic police, hospitality to a tax officer, "sharing" your goods with a customs inspector, bribing an official to get a business license, whether for gold mining or vodka-making. *It is just all around you.* It has to be. "Well, let me see. Who's next on my target list for bribing?"[84]

The major, if not the most important cause for corruption in contemporary Mongolia is the extremely low salaries of its civil servants and politicians. The highest monthly salary of top officers of the Presidency, Parliament, Supreme Court, General Prosecutor and Constitutional Court is 60,113 togrogs or US$71 while the monthly salary for the lowest position is 29,297 togrogs or US$35. Similarly, the monthly salaries of government administrative employees in Mongolia range from 23,377 togrogs or US$28 for the lowest position to 57,836 togrogs or US$68 for the highest position. Finally, the monthly salaries of the Mongolian government special service employees are also low, ranging from 21,556 togrogs or US$25 to 57,836 togrogs or US$68.[85]

The low salaries in the Mongolian civil service relative to the wages in the private sector constitute a source of corruption as "when civil service pay is too low, civil servants may be obliged to use their positions to collect bribes as a way to making ends meet, particularly when the expected cost of being caught is low".[86] Given their low salaries, it is not surprising that teachers have gone on strike for higher wages. For example, on April 17, 1995, teachers went on strike to demand a threefold increase in their salaries. During 1993-1995, 2,000 teachers resigned in Ulaanbaatar. As the average teacher's monthly salary was 12,000-14,000 togrogs (US$28-US$32), this amount was inadequate to support a family. The number of teachers on strike increased to 6,000 by June 1995 as the strikers in the capital were joined by other teachers from five provinces.[87]

According to the State Statistical Board, data on family incomes for August 1995 indicated that some families were spending more than they earn, especially those living in the *aimag* centres, as their average monthly expenditure per family of 40,117.3 togrogs exceeded their average cash income per family of 39,705.6 togrogs. Furthermore, data for September 1995 revealed that the average family in Ulaanbaatar obtained 38% of their monthly cash income from salaries. The percentage increased to 49% for families living in the *aimag* centres, and declined to 9% for rural families.[88]

Judicial salaries during 1995 were comparable to those of civil servants, and ranged from 15,200 togrogs (US$33) to 23,500 togrogs (US$51) per month. However, these salaries are lower than those of lawyers in private practice. The living conditions of judges are difficult, especially in the countryside where "one out of three judges does not have an apartment. Consequently, some judges live in their office, which is clearly not desirable and does not enhance the status of the judiciary". In the view of Stephanie McPhail, such "relatively low salaries and mediocre working conditions are an impediment to attracting highly qualified candidates to the profession".[89]

On February 28, 1997, nearly half of Mongolia's 32,000 doctors and nurses went on strike to demand higher wages. In April 1997, the teachers complained that "they could not survive on the present wage of Tg26,000 (US$33) per month" because of inflation. Public sector salaries were raised on May 1, 1997, but the teachers were not satisfied as not everyone was eligible for the pay increase.[90] When the government did not increase the public sector pay and pensions as promised on April 1, 1998, there were demonstrations outside parliament. On April 15, the government agreed to pay a 10% increase in salaries, and raised the minimum monthly pension from 9,200 togrogs (US$11) to 12,000 togrogs (US$14). Arising from this, the government had to raise an additional seven billion togrogs to cover the increase in wages and pensions.[91]

However, those teachers and health service staff who were not paid for two or three months in 1998 were dissatisfied. On November 2, 1998, between 10,000 to 20,000 people participated in a demonstration in Ulaanbaatar. The Mongolian Association of Trades Unions issued an ultimatum to the government and demanded the implementation of a 20,000 togrogs or US$23 minimum monthly wage, a 10% increase on pensions and salaries, and payment of overdue salaries and benefits.[92]

ANTI-CORRUPTION STRATEGY

Unlike other countries, Mongolia does not have an independent anti-corruption agency to implement the Law on Anti-Corruption (LAC), which was enacted on April 5, 1996. Rather the task of implementing the LAC and other relevant legislation is shared among the police, the General Prosecutor's Office, and the *aimag* courts, the Capital City Court, and the Supreme Court.

Law on Anti-Corruption

The LAC consists of three chapters and 18 articles. It defines bribery as "a process of giving incentives, compensation or advantage by the subject to the subject referred to in Article 4, who abuses his/her position and possibility to do so to receive a bribe, materialistic or other types of incentives or compensation" (Article 2). According to Article 3, the anti-corruption legislation consists not only of the LAC, but also includes the Criminal Code, and the Law on Government Service. Article 4 is very important as it identifies the six categories of civil servants who are subject to the LAC: (1) the political, administrative and special service civil servants identified in the Law on Government Service; (2) the chief and secretary of the province, capital city, soumon, district citizens representatives' hurals; (3) those civil servants in charge of licensing, authorising, distributing and registering of aid; (4) those civil servants in management and administrative positions of the state property; (5) managers and executives of non-governmental organisations; and (6) senior rank civil servants.

Furthermore, all state organisations are required by Article 5 to perform these four duties to prevent corruption: (1) to publicise the procedures of "licensing, authorising, registering, monitoring and selecting in accordance with the function of the specific organisation"; (2) "to define clearly the responsibility distribution"; (3) to define the procedure for a meeting between a civil servant and a citizen; and (4) "to supervise income declaration of civil servants" and "to audit and resolve claims and complaints". All senior officials of state organisations at all levels are expected "to disclose, to stop, to undertake measures to eliminate consequences of corruption".

To prevent corruption, Article 7 prohibits the officials identified in Article 4 from the following nine activities: travelling within the country or abroad at the expense of business firms, citizens, foreign organisations and individuals, except for officially authorised missions; receiving "gifts, money honorarium, compensation from other organisations, economic entities and citizens"; abusing "for non-official purposes the state organisation's assets, facilities, financial and information resources, and official information"; being involved in business activities and serving as a mediator; possession of "securities, assets by credit and an advantageous right abusing the position"; influencing the "activity of other organisations on matters unrelated to his duties"; offering advantage to individuals and legal bodies, and obstructing the legitimate decision-making process; attempting to "illegally influence on the actions of the same rank or supervised officials"; and undertaking activities which involve the possession of illegal income, incentives and advantage abusing the position.

Perhaps the key measure for preventing corruption is the declaration of income and assets of public officials stipulated in Article 8. More specifically, these officials are required to indicate in the "asset, income declaration the sources of income, real estate, securities, bank savings, animals, and other assets, total income, its sources for himself and family members". Furthermore, they are required to submit their income and asset declarations within 30 days of assuming their positions and thereafter to submit their annual declarations during February 1-15 of each year.

Article 14 states that those committing bribery and corruption-related crimes are liable for prosecution according to the relevant provisions of the Criminal Code. Officials who fail to submit their declarations of income and assets can be fined between 5,000 to 25,000 togrogs (US$6 to US$29). Those officials who do not perform their duty of monitoring the declarations are liable to be fined between 20,000 to 30,000 togrogs (US$24 to US$35). Officials who do not declare gifts or their foreign bank accounts are required to pay between 30,000 to 40,000 togrogs (US$35 to US$47) in fines. Finally, officials found guilty of corruption will be discharged or displaced according to the procedure provided in the law.

The Criminal Code

The Criminal Code contains several articles which deal with bribery and related offences. For example, Articles 195-197 focus on bribery. According to Article 195, an official who receives bribes directly or through a mediator can be suspended from his position or sentenced to six years of imprisonment without suspension of power. If an official is a repeat offender or accepts a large bribe, or if bribery is committed by an organised group, or a senior civil servant, the guilty official will be suspended from his position and jailed from 10 to 25 years. Article 196 focuses on the bribe-givers, who can be imprisoned for four years or required to perform public service for 18 months. Recalcitrant bribe-givers can be sentenced for periods ranging from three to ten years' imprisonment. Finally, Article 197 punishes those who mediate in bribe-taking and giving with either a jail sentence of up to four years or 18 months of public service.

Articles 192 and 193 prescribe punishment for those officials who abuse their power or position. The punishment for officials who abuse their power is a three-year jail sentence without suspension or being required to perform public service up to 18 months. Repeat offenders will be suspended and imprisoned for eight years. For excessive abuse of power, the guilty officials will be suspended or jailed for up to four years without suspension, or be compelled to perform 18 months of public service. If officials abuse their power by using violence, weapons, or torturing victims, or are repeat offenders, they will be suspended and imprisoned for up to ten years.

Procedure for dealing with corrupt offences

Reports of crime, including corruption offences, are received by the Criminal Police Department (CPD), which investigates these reports and refers them to the Investigation Department (ID) for the next stage of the investigation, which can last from two to 26 months. The CPD has 10 divisions, but there are two divisions dealing with corruption. The Organised Crime Division (OCD) is concerned with corruption, money-laundering, casino-related crime, environmental crime, crime involving foreigners, terrorism, and trafficking in firearms. The second division is the Economic Crime Division (ECD), which deals with the suppression of financial crime. The Investigation Department has two similar divisions which will continue the work initiated by the OCD and ECD.[93]

The CPD and ID investigate complaints of corruption against public officials and if there is evidence to verify these complaints, the cases will be handed over to the General Prosecutor's Office (GPO), which supervises "inquiries by the police in both criminal and civil cases" and represents "the state in both civil and criminal proceedings".[94] From the GPO, the cases are processed by the *aimag* courts and the Capital City Court (for serious crimes where the amount exceeds 10 million togrogs or US$22,000) and the Supreme Court (for those cases outside the jurisdiction of other courts and appeals from decisions of the *aimag* courts and the Capital City Court).[95]

EVALUATION OF ANTI-CORRUPTION STRATEGY

How effective are the LAC, the Criminal Code, and the above-mentioned agencies in curbing corruption in Mongolia? During

Mongolia's first major corruption trial on October 21, 1999, three Members of Parliament (MPs) from the ruling Democratic Union coalition were jailed from three to five and a half years for receiving bribes amounting to US$210,000 from a casino official in connection with a casino tender in 1998.[96] The fact that only three MPs have been convicted of corruption and that only two cases involving cashiers and accountants have been settled in court[97] even though the LAC has been in existence since April 1996 is a reflection of the LAC's ineffectiveness. The major problem is the difficulty in obtaining evidence for prosecuting those suspected of corruption offences. Indeed, many public officials are not punished for bribery even though the public perception is that they are corrupt as these officials cannot be convicted because of the lack of evidence. Similarly, the public perceives the Mongolian police to be corrupt but it is rare for police officers to be found guilty of bribery in the absence of evidence.

The LAC has two major weaknesses. First, the responsibility for implementing the LAC is not clearly stated as Article 5 indicated that all state organisations are required to perform four common duties to prevent corruption. Furthermore, Article 10 has identified the agencies and officials responsible for registering and storing the declarations of assets and incomes of all public officials. The experiences of the Corrupt Practices Investigation Bureau (CPIB) in Singapore (discussed in Chapter 5) and the Independent Commission Against Corruption (ICAC) in Hong Kong (discussed in Chapter 6) demonstrate the effectiveness of a single anti-corruption agency in implementing respectively the Prevention of Corruption Act (POCA) and the Prevention of Bribery Ordinance (POBO) and the ICAC Ordinance.[98]

The second weakness of the LAC is that the penalties for those public officials who fail to submit and monitor their income and asset declarations specified in Article 15 are not effective deterrents as the fines range from 5,000 togrogs (US$6) to 40,000 togrogs (US$47) and there is no imprisonment. As these fines can easily be paid by those officials who are corrupt, the punishment for corrupt officials should be enhanced by confiscating their properties or cars and dismissing them from the civil service.

The penalties for bribery according to Articles 195-197 of the Criminal Code are different lengths of imprisonment (from three to 25 years) or the performance of public service for 18 months but no fines are imposed. In contrast, as seen in Chapter 5, Article 12 of Singapore's POCA specifies that the punishment for corrupt behaviour is "a fine not exceeding S$100,000 or to imprisonment for a term not exceeding seven years or to both".[99] Similarly, Hong Kong's POBO (discussed in Chapter 6) introduced severe maximum penalties of "a fine of HK$50,000 and three years' imprisonment, or on indictment, a fine of HK$100,000 and seven years' imprisonment. The duration of imprisonment was increased to ten years for offences involving contracts and tenders".[100]

The procedure for dealing with corrupt offences in Mongolia is not effective as it provides opportunities for corruption among the officials concerned as they can interpret the law differently. For example, a case considered as bribery by the police can be viewed as a smuggling offence by the General Prosecutor's Office, and as illegal crossing of borders by the courts.[101] Furthermore, the courts are perceived by the public to be corrupt as individuals can bribe the poorly paid judges to make decisions in their favour. Indeed, Tables 2.2 and 2.3 below show that between 70-71% of respondents in public opinion polls were not confident in Mongolia's judiciary system and 61-62% of them have given it a bad rating.

Finally, as discussed in Chapters 5 and 6, the experiences of Singapore and Hong Kong in controlling corruption demonstrate clearly that the anti-corruption agency must be removed from the police as soon as possible as its location within the police prevents it from functioning effectively, especially when the police are corrupt. Indeed, Singapore took 15 years to set up the CPIB as an independent agency in 1952, outside the purview of the police. However, Hong Kong required 26 years for the creation of the ICAC in 1974.[102]

Since the Mongolian public perceive police officers to be corrupt without providing relevant evidence, few police officers have been convicted for corrupt offences. Under such circumstances, it will be difficult for the CPD and ID to be objective in the investigation of cases of police corruption, especially if their colleagues are involved.

TABLE 2.2 RESPONDENTS' CONFIDENCE IN THE MONGOLIAN JUDICIARY SYSTEM, OCTOBER 1997, MARCH 1998 AND OCTOBER 1998

Confidence Level	October 1997	March 1998	October 1998	Average
Very confident	2.4%	3.5%	5.1%	3.7%
Rather confident	27.7%	25.9%	23.7%	25.8%
Rather not confident	46.8%	45.9%	44.3%	45.7%
Totally not confident	23.1%	24.7%	26.9%	24.9%
Total	100.0%	100.0%	100.0%	100.0%
Sample size	840	795	814	—

Source: Survey data provided by courtesy of Mr. L. Sumati, Director of the Sant Maral Foundation, Ulaanbaatar.

TABLE 2.3 RESPONDENTS' RATING OF THE MONGOLIAN JUDICIARY SYSTEM, JUNE 1996 AND JANUARY 1997

Rating	June 1996	January 1997	Average
Good	9.6%	6.1%	7.9%
Not good or bad	29.2%	32.2%	30.7%
Bad	61.2%	61.7%	61.5%
Total	100.0%	100.0%	100.0%
Sample size	911	951	—

Source: Survey data provided by courtesy of Mr. L. Sumati, Director of the Sant Maral Foundation, Ulaanbaatar.

It can be seen from Chapter 5 that the Anti-Corruption Branch of the Criminal Investigation Department in Singapore was ineffective in curbing corruption because it was understaffed and failed to take measures against corrupt police officers. The discovery by the British colonial government of the involvement of police officers in the opium smuggling racket in October 1951 led to the creation of the CPIB a year later. Similarly, earlier attempts by the Royal Hong Kong Police to curb police corruption were futile until the establishment of the ICAC in 1974.[103]

CONCLUSION

In his critical analysis of Nigeria's problems, Babatunde Oyinade attributed the persistence of these problems to corruption, which has "reached an uncontrollable level" as it has been institutionalised in both the government and private sector. According to Oyinade:

> There is corruption in every society, but the problem of corruption is so pervasive in Nigeria that there is difficulty in knowing precisely how to address the issue. ... in Nigeria the problems exist because of the inability of the government to investigate and bring to justice anyone considered guilty. Most government agencies have become business centres where corruption is so rampant that legitimate work cannot be accomplished without paying off someone. No one is exempt, not the military, the civil servants, the business elites, the politicians, or society at large. *Everyone does it. It is part and parcel of daily life in Nigeria.* Unless Nigerians cease to justify corruption as normal, efforts to eradicate it will fail. Poverty remains the vehicle for corruption.[104]

In October 1998, three MPs and a political analyst urged the public, political parties and non-governmental organisations to fight corruption, which is "growing and endangers to suppress the ongoing process of democracy" in Mongolia. Since MPs declare their incomes on what they earn from their work in parliament, and do not disclose other additional sources of income, H. Hulan, an MP and Chairperson of the Standing Committee on Social Policy, recommended that all MPs should declare all their income sources, including campaign funding. Furthermore, she also proposed that public financial records should be made available for any transaction in tender and project commissions.[105]

Fortunately, the problem of corruption in Mongolia today has still not reached the epidemic proportions of Nigerian or Indonesian corruption yet. Indeed, according to Transparency International's Corruption Perceptions Index (CPI) for 1999, Mongolia was ranked 43rd, Indonesia 96th, and Nigeria 98th in its annual survey of 99 countries.[106] However, whether Mongolia can avoid the same route taken by Nigeria and Indonesia depends mainly on the commitment of its political leaders and population in the fight against corruption. There is still hope if Mongolia's leaders and people are willing to pay the price required for minimising corruption by implementing a comprehensive strategy to reduce both the incentives and opportunities for corruption. However, if such political will is lacking, it will be very difficult to prevent corruption from gradually becoming a way of life in Mongolia in the future. Indeed, a crucial first step in minimising corruption in Mongolia is a concerted national effort by the President, Parliament, the civil service, the academic community, and the business community.

ENDNOTES

1   M.T. Haggard, "Mongolia: The First Communist State in Asia", in Robert A. Scalapino (ed.), *The Communist Revolution in Asia: Tactics, Goals, and Achievements* (Englewood Cliffs: Prentice-Hall, 1965), pp. 82-113.

2   This chapter is based on the research I conducted as a consultant for the United Nations Development Programme's Programme in Accountability and Transparency (PACT) in New York. I visited Ulaanbaatar from September 7-10 and October 19-22, 1998 to interview Members of Parliament and senior civil servants. I am grateful to all of them for sharing their views on corruption in Mongolia with me. I would also like to thank Ms Pauline Tamesis, Programme Coordinator of PACT, and Mr Douglas Gardner, the UNDP Resident Representative in Mongolia for their kind assistance.

3   John Andrews, *Pocket Asia* 7th edition (London: The Economist Newspaper Ltd. and Profile Books Ltd., 2002), p. 14; and *Pocket World in Figures* 2003 edition (London: The Economist Newspaper Ltd. and Profile Books Ltd., 2002), p. 12.

4   Peter Boone, Baavaa Tarvaa, Adiya Tsend, Enkhbold Tsendjav, and Narantsetseg Unenburen, "Mongolia's Transition to a Democratic Market System", in Wing Thye Woo, Stephen Parker, and Jeffery D. Sachs (eds.), *Economies in Transition: Comparing Asia and Eastern Europe* (Cambridge: The MIT Press, 1997), p. 106.

5   Keith McLachlan, "Introduction", in Dick Hodder, Sarah J. Lloyd and Keith McLachlan (eds.), *Land-locked States of Africa and Asia* (London: Frank Cass, 1998), p. 2, Table 1.

6   "Mongolia," *The World Factbook 2002*, see http://www.odci.gov/cia/publications/factbook/geos/mg.html for more details.

7   Elizabeth Milne, John Leimone, Frank Rozwadowski, and Padej Sukachevin, *The Mongolian People's Republic: Toward a Market Economy* (Washington, D.C.: International Monetary Fund, 1991), p. 2.

8   Ole Brun and Ole Odgaard, "A Society and Economy in Transition", in Ole Brun and Ole Odgaard (eds.), *Mongolia in Transition: Old Patterns, New Challenges* (Richmond: Curzon Press, 1996), p. 24.

9   Young C. Kim, "Mongolia", in Pradumna B. Rana and Naved Hamid (eds.), *From Centrally Planned to Market Economics: The Asian Approach*, Vol. 2 *People's Republic of China and Mongolia* (Hong Kong: Oxford University Press, 1996), p. 297.

10   McLachlan, "Introduction," p. 8.

11   Sechin Jachid and Paul Hyer, *Mongolia's Culture and Society* (Boulder: Westview Press, 1979), p. 297.

12   Ibid., pp. 298-299.

13   Ibid., p. 310.

14   Ibid., pp. 316-317.

15   Dennis P. Sheehy, "Sustainable Livestock Use of Pastoral Resources", in Bruun and Odgaard (eds.), *Mongolia in Transition*, p. 42.

16   Ibid., p. 46.

17   Asian Development Bank, *Mongolia: A Centrally Planned Economy in Transition* (Hong Kong: Oxford University Press, 1992), p. 176.

18   Martha Brill Olcott, *Kazakhstan: Unfulfilled Promise* (Washington, D.C.: Carnegie Endowment for International Peace, 2002), p. 10.

19   Michael Kaser, "Mongolia", in Ian Jeffries (ed.), *Industrial Reform in Socialist Countries: From Restructuring to Revolution* (Aldershot: Edward Elgar, 1992), pp. 167-171.

20   Bruun and Odgaard, "A Society and Economy in Transition", p. 23.

21   Boone *et al.*, "Mongolia's Transition to a Democratic Market System", p. 103.

22   Keith Griffin, "Economic Strategy during the Transition", in Keith Griffin (ed.), *Poverty and the Transition to a Market Economy in Mongolia* (Basingstoke: Macmillan Press, 1995), p. 1.

23   Robert A. Scalapino, *The Last Leninists: The Uncertain Future of Asia's Communist States* (Washington, D.C.: The Center for Strategic and International Studies, 1992), pp. 37-38.

24   Griffin, "Economic Strategy during the Transition", p. 3.

25   Bruun and Odgaard, "A Society and Economy in Transition," p. 23.

26   Boone *et al.* "Mongolia's Transition to a Democratic Market System", p. 103.

27   Richard Pomfret, *Asian Economies in Transition: Reforming Centrally Planned Economies* (Cheltenham: Edward Elgar, 1996), pp. 75-90.

28   Frederick I. Nixson and Bernard Walters", Administrative Reform and Economic Development in Mongolia, 1990-1997: A Critical Perspective", in Kuotsai Tom Liou (ed.), *Administrative Reform and National Economic Development* (Aldershot: Ashgate, 2000), p. 217.

29   Ole Odgaard, "Living Standards and Poverty", in Bruun and Odgaard (eds.), *Mongolia in Transition*, pp. 105-107.

30   United Nations Development Programme, *Human Development Report Mongolia 1997* (Ulaanbaatar: UNDP, 1997).

31   Andrews, *Pocket Asia*, p. 121.

32   Mongolian Business Development Agency, *Doing Business in Mongolia: A Guide for European Companies* (Ulaanbaatar: MBDA and European Union Tacis Programme for Mongolia, 1996), p. 11.

33   UNDP, *Human Development Report Mongolia 1997*, p. 2.

34   Ibid., p. 8.

35   MBDA, *Doing Business in Mongolia*, p. 1.

36   Jachid and Hyer, *Mongolia's Culture and Society*, p. 159.

37   Alicia J. Campi, "Nomadic Cultural Values and Their Influence on Modernization", in Bruun and Odgaard, *Mongolia in Transition*, p. 97.

38   Ibid., p. 98.

39   Ibid., pp. 97-98.

40   Thomas T. Hammond, "The History of Communist Takeovers", in Thomas T. Hammond (ed.), *The Anatomy of Communist Takeovers* (New Haven: Yale University Press, 1975), p. 9.

41   Ibid., pp. 9-10.

42   Thomas T. Hammond, "The Communist Takeover of Outer Mongolia: Model for Eastern Europe?" in Hammond (ed.), *The Anatomy of Communist Takeovers*, p. 139.

43   Bruun and Odgaard, "A Society and Economy in Transition", pp. 28-29.

44   Ibid., pp. 29-30.

45   Ibid., pp. 30-31.

46   Ibid., p. 32.

47   Economist Intelligence Unit, *Country Report: China, Mongolia Second Quarter 1997* (London: EIU, 1997), p. 47.

48   Michael Kohn, "Bagabandi keeps tough line against Dem[ocratic] Union", *The Mongol Messenger*, October 21, 1998, p. 1.

49   Christopher M. Finch, "Mongolia in 2001: Political Consolidation and Continued Economic Reform", *Asian Survey*, Vol. 42, No. 1 (January/ February 2002), p. 39.

50   Ibid., p. 40.

51   Maria Los, *Communist Ideology, Law and Crime: A Comparative View of the USSR and Poland* (Basingstoke: Macmillan Press, 1988), p. 150.

52   Jon S.T. Quah, "Police Corruption in Singapore: An Analysis of its Forms, Extent and Causes", *Singapore Police Journal*, Vol. 10, No. 1 (January 1979), p. 17.

53   Robert A. Ruppen, *The Mongolian People's Republic* (Stanford: Hoover Institution Studies, No. 12, Stanford University, 1966), p. 23.

54   Leslie Holmes, *The End of Communist Power: Anti-Corruption Campaigns and Legitimation Crisis* (New York: Oxford University Press, 1993), p. 114.

55   Ibid., pp. 114-115.

56   Maria Hirszowicz, *Coercion and Control in Communist Society: The Visible Hand of Bureaucracy* (Brighton: Wheatsheaf Books Ltd, 1986), pp. 127-128.

57   Alena V. Ledeneva, *Russia's Economy of Favours: Blat, Networking and Informal Exchange* (Cambridge: Cambridge University Press, 1998), p. 127.

58   Hirszowicz, *Coercion and Control in Communist Society*, p. 128.

59   Robert L. Worden and Andrea Matles Savada (eds.), *Mongolia: A Country Study* 2nd ed. (Washington, D.C.: Federal Research Division, Library of Congress, 1991), p. 258.

60   Ibid., p. 259.

61   Oyungerel Adiya, "A Beginner's Guide to Corruption", *UB Post*, September 15, 1998, p. 3, emphasis added.

62   Bruun and Odgaard, "A Society and Economy in Transition", p. 31.

63   EIU, *Country Report: China, Mongolia First Quarter 1994* (London: EIU, 1994), pp. 36-37.

64   EIU, *Country Report: China, Mongolia Second Quarter 1994* (London: EIU, 1994), p. 37.

65   EIU, *Country Report: China, Mongolia Fourth Quarter 1994* (London: EIU, 1994), p. 37.

66   Ibid., p. 37.

67   I am very grateful to Mr Tumur-Ochiryn Erdenebileg, Member of Parliament in Mongolia, for providing me with his paper on "Public Opinion on Corruption in Mongolia" and to Mr Oyungerel Adiya for translating the paper into English.

68   EIU, *Country Report: China, Mongolia Fourth Quarter 1994*, pp. 37-38.

69   EIU, *Country Report: China, Mongolia Fourth Quarter 1995* (London: EIU, 1995), pp. 39-40.

70   Ibid., p. 40.

71   EIU, *Country Report: China, Mongolia First Quarter 1995* (London: EIU, 1995), p. 39.

72   EIU, *Country Report: China, Mongolia First Quarter 1997* (London: EIU, 1997), p. 50.

73   EIU, *Country Report: China, Mongolia Fourth Quarter 1996* (London: EIU, 1996), p. 47.

74   EIU, *Country Report: China, Mongolia First Quarter 1997*, p. 49.

75   "Copper giant caught in corruption web", *The Mongol Messenger*, October 9, 1996, p. 1.

76   EIU, *Country Report: China, Mongolia Fourth Quarter 1996*, p. 51.

77   EIU, *Country Report: China, Mongolia First Quarter 1997*, p. 56.

78   B. Indra, "Otgonbileg gives gov[ernmen]t the slip", *The Mongol Messenger*, August 12, 1998, pp. 1, 3 and 5.

79   EIU, *Country Report: China, Mongolia Fourth Quarter 1996*, p. 47.

80   Tom Ginsburg, "Mongolia in 1997: Deepening Democracy", *Asian Survey*, Vol. 38, No. 1 (January 1998), p. 67.

81   EIU, *Country Report: China, Mongolia First Quarter 1997*, p. 59.

82   EIU, *Country Report: China, Mongolia Third Quarter 1997* (London: EIU, 1997), p. 41.

83   EIU, *Country Report: China, Mongolia Third Quarter 1998* (London: EIU, 1998), p. 43. Tg refers to togrog, the Mongolian currency.

84   Adiya, "A Beginner's Guide to Corruption", p. 3, emphasis added.

85   Information on these monthly salaries were provided by courtesy of the Cabinet Secretariat, Government of Mongolia. The exchange rate was US$1=850 togrogs during September to November 1998.

86   Paolo Mauro, *Why Worry About Corruption?* (Washington, D.C.: International Monetary Fund, 1997), p. 5.

87   EIU, *Country Report: China, Mongolia Third Quarter 1995* (London: EIU, 1995), p. 45.

88   EIU, *Country Report: China, Mongolia Fourth Quarter 1995*, p. 45.

89   Stephanie McPhail, *Developing Mongolia's Legal Framework: A Needs Analysis* (Manila: Asian Development Bank, 1995), p. 45.

90   EIU, *Country Report: China, Mongolia Second Quarter 1997*, p. 51.

91   EIU, *Country Report: China, Mongolia Second Quarter 1998* (London: EIU, 1998), pp. 47-48.

92   EIU, *Country Report: China, Mongolia Fourth Quarter 1998* (London: EIU, 1998), pp. 47-48.

93   United Nations Office for Drug Control and Crime Prevention Centre for International Crime Prevention, *Restructuring the Police in Mongolia* (Vienna: UNODC and CPCICP, 1997), pp.12-14.

94   McPhail, *Developing Mongolia's Legal Framework*, pp.49-50.

95   Ibid., p. 38.

96   "Corrupt Mongolia MPs jailed", *Straits Times* (Singapore), October 22, 1999, p. 23.

97   D. Naruntuya, "Top officials slam door on corruption", *The Mongol Messenger*, October 21, 1998, p. 3.

98   See Jon S.T. Quah, "Controlling Corruption in City-States: A Comparative Study of Hong Kong and Singapore", *Crime, Law and Social Change*, Vol. 22 (1995), pp. 391-414 and Chapters 5 and 6 of this book.

99   Republic of Singapore, *Prevention of Corruption Act (Chapter 241)* Singapore: Government Printer, 1993), p. 8.

100   Quah, "Controlling Corruption in City-States", p. 401.

101   Interview with an officer of the General Council of Courts on October 19, 1998.

102 Quah, "Controlling Corruption in City-States", p. 408, and Chapters 5 and 6.

103 Ibid., pp. 393-394 and 400-402.

104 Babatunde Oyinade, "Ethnicity in the Politics of a Nation: Nigeria and the Problems of Social Transformation", in Valentine Udoh James (ed.), *Capacity Building in Developing Countries: Human and Environmental Dimensions* (Westport: Praeger, 1998), p. 21.

105 D. Naruntuya, "Top officials slam door on corruption", *The Mongol Messenger*, October 21, 1998, p. 3.

106 For details of the 1999 CPI, see Transparency International's website: http://www.transparency.org/documents/index.html.Unfortunately, Mongolia has only been included in the 1999 CPI and not for the other years.

CHAPTER 3

India

INTRODUCTION

Writing in 1968, the Swedish economist Gunnar Myrdal observed that in spite of the anti-corruption efforts of the governments in India, Ceylon (now known as Sri Lanka) and other South Asian countries, corruption was "rampant" and "growing" in these countries, "particularly among higher officials and politicians, including legislators and ministers".[1] In the case of India, he cited a 1963 report that "administrative corruption, in its various forms, is all around us all the time and that it is rising".[2] His assessment was confirmed by John B. Monteiro, who wrote:

> Corruption has spread far beyond the limits of general administration to the police and even the judiciary. ... Rampant corruption in all walks of life has been adequately proved by the various Commissions of inquiry set up from time to time.[3]

Unfortunately today, nearly four decades later, the fight against corruption in India has still not been won, judging from the various studies done.[4] For example, according to S.S. Gill, a former senior civil servant:

> One cannot think of any sphere of public administration which is not infested with corruption. ... As a matter of routine all vendors, hawkers, artisans and traders have to bribe petty police officials for the privilege of being left alone. ... Corruption, unlike a headache, is not confined only to the top; it infects the whole system. Every level devises its own methods of extortion. ... There is also widespread financial corruption in schools and colleges. Teachers take bribes to leak question papers, arrange cheating during examinations, force students to engage them as their tutors, replace answer books, award unmerited high marks—all for a consideration.[5]

Indeed, India's consistently poor ranking on Transparency International's CPI from 1995-2002 and by PERC for the same period reflects the serious extent of the corruption problem and the ineffectiveness of its anti-corruption strategy. Table 1.1 in Chapter 1 shows that, of the 13 Asian countries participating in the CPI, India's average ranking on the CPI from 1995-2002 was 59th among all the participating countries, and 10th among the 13 Asian countries. Similarly, Table 1.2 in Chapter 1 shows that India has an average ranking of joint 10th position with Vietnam among the 12 Asian countries ranked by PERC.

The purpose of this chapter is twofold: to describe the main features of India's anti-corruption strategy; and to evaluate the effectiveness of this strategy. However, before proceeding further, it is necessary to describe the policy context in India first.

POLICY CONTEXT

Geography

India is a huge country with a total land area of 3,287,263 sq. km. It is the seventh largest country in the world and has a land frontier of 15,200 kilometres and a coastline of 7,516 kilometres. India shares its borders with six countries: Pakistan, China, Nepal, Bhutan, Bangladesh, and Myanmar. Given its vast territory, India has a federal system with 28 states and seven Union Territories administered by the central government. Accordingly, there are four layers of administration at the central, state, local and district levels.

Indeed, India's complex administrative structure provides many opportunities for corruption, and its large size and diversity make the enforcement of the anti-corruption laws difficult, especially at the state, local and district levels. N. Vittal and S. Mahalingam have astutely referred to the difficulties posed by India's geography thus:

> In terms of geographical space India may be one country but when it comes to time India is a country which is spread over a few centuries. India is like a snake whose head is in the twentieth

century and the tail is in the seventeenth century. Geographically, India may be in one place but chronologically it occupies different time zones.[6]

Economy

India's economy is the fourth largest in Asia after Japan, China and South Korea as its GDP in 2000 was US$457 billion. However, its GDP per capita in 2000 was US$450, ranking it 24th in Asia.[7] India is rich in such natural resources as rubber, timber, chromium, coal, iron, managanese, copper ore, bauxite, mica salt, limestone, and gypsum. It also has reserves of coal, gas, and oil but India remains a net importer of crude oil as domestic generation cannot meet the demand.[8]

The percentage of arable area is 56% and agriculture contributes about a third of the country's GDP and employs nearly 70% of the workforce. The major crops produced are rice, wheat, pulses, sugar cane, cotton, jute, oilseeds, tea, coffee, and tobacco. India has a diversified manufacturing base and the major manufacturing industries are cotton and jute textiles; iron, steel, and other basic metals; petrochemicals; electrical machinery and appliances; transport equipment; chemicals; cement; fertilisers; medicines and pharmaceuticals; and food products.[9]

In spite of its abundant natural resources, there is a great deal of poverty in India and this is reflected in the following indicators of consumer goods ownership in 2000: there are 29.6 colour television sets per 100 households; 3.4 telephone lines per 100 population; 0.5 mobile telephone subscribers per 100 population; 0.6 computers per 100 population; and 0.1 internet hosts per 1,000 population.[10] According to Michael Todaro, India "epitomises the problem of absolute poverty" as it has "one of the highest poverty rates in the world (52.5% in 1996) and by far the greatest number of people living on less that $1 a day (509 million, compared to China's 274 million)".[11]

India's absolute poverty and its low GDP per capita of US$450 are responsible for the low wages of civil servants and political leaders, which is a major cause for the rampant corruption in the country.

Demography

India's population in 2000 was 1,008.9 million, which is the second largest in the world after China.[12] However, its population density of 307 persons per sq. km makes India the 20th most populated country in the world.[13] The population is heterogeneous in terms of ethnicity and religion. The population consists of 72% Indo-Aryans, 25% Dravidians, and 3% Mongolians. There are three major religious groups: 83% Hindu, 11% Muslim, and 3% Christian.[14] There is also a great deal of linguistic diversity as apart from Hindi, the official language, and English, the language of administration, commerce and higher education, there are 17 other major Indian languages[15] and 1,652 dialects.[16] In addition to its diversity, the literacy rate of the population is 57.2% and the percentage of the urban population is 28.4% in 2000.[17] This means that about 72% of the population live in rural India and "remains traditional and provincial with strict beliefs and practices that have changed very little throughout the centuries".[18]

As 83% of the population is Hindu, it is necessary to discuss the cultural dimension of Hinduism and the implications for fighting corruption. Krishna K. Tummala has astutely identified two aspects of Hinduism which might hinder anti-corruption efforts. First, Hinduism's forgiving nature and the tendency to show leniency towards offenders might undermine the enforcement of the anti-corruption measures. Second, "deviance in personal and material life is accepted and forgiven when the search is for a supposedly higher truth" and "apparently contradictory, but not necessarily conflicting behaviour patterns are manifest and tolerated in India".[19]

Finally, because of the influence of Hinduism, many Indians are fatalistic and believe that there are limits to what an individual can do to change his or her life.[20] This fatalistic attitude of most Indians is not conducive for fighting corruption as they believe that they cannot change the status quo that is, to minimise the problem of corruption.

Political System

India was a British colony for 89 years from September 1, 1858, when the East India Company was dissolved and its powers were transferred to the British Crown, until independence was attained on August 15, 1947. The legacy of British rule was generally positive as it created a centralised administration in the form of the Indian Administrative Service (IAS); introduced meritocracy in recruitment to the IAS; constructed an extensive network of roads, railways, and telecommunications; and promoted the rule of law, respect for personal liberty, and equality.

Richard P. Taub has contended that the British maintained control over India by employing three techniques. First, the British created four levels of administration with the Indian Civil Service, the IAS, and the district and local administration. Second, rules were created to maintain control over decision-making powers of the Indian subordinates. However, these rules cause delay and confusion today and provide ample opportunities for corruption. The third method was the centralisation of decision-making which required junior civil servants to obtain approval from their superiors for their decisions.[21]

Perhaps the most enduring legacy of British colonial rule is the adoption of parliamentary democracy in India, which has a Council of States or *Rajya Sabha* consisting of 245 members elected for six years, and the House of the People or *Lok Sabha* with 543 members elected for five years and two appointed.[22] To accommodate the country's diversity, India adopted a federal system of government and has 28 states and seven Union Territories.[23]

During the first 20 years of independence, the Congress Party was the dominant party in India. In 1967, the Congress Party lost its predominant position at both the national and state levels. The defeat of the Congress Party in the 1977 general election resulted in a split within the party and the emergence of the Congress (I) Party.[24] After the defeat of the Congress (I) Party in the 1989 election, there have been five general elections in 10 years, with eight governments, four of which were minority governments.[25] The growing importance of coalition governments in Indian politics in recent years and the resulting lack of political continuity makes it more difficult for the incumbent governments to combat corruption effectively.

EXTENT OF CORRUPTION

As indicated earlier, corruption has been a serious problem in India for many decades. On September 6, 1974, the *Far Eastern Economic Review* devoted its cover story to a survey of corruption in Asian countries. In his unfavourable assessment of the situation in India, A. Hariharan wrote:

> The prevailing feeling is that corruption in Indian public life is all pervasive. Not only the President and the Prime Minister but lesser dignitaries, businessmen, bureaucrats, contractors, journalists, vice-chancellors, teachers, doctors and nurses all come under suspicion. ... Elections undoubtedly involve corruption, with black money and clandestine expenses for campaigns.[26]

Similarly, in 1975, Chetane Kohli observed that:

> Corruption is the largest single element to be found most in India. All roads, from the maternity hospital to the crematorium, smell of corruption. No individual is free from it, no area can be found where corruption is not a ritual.[27]

In 1997, three separate evaluations confirmed that corruption is a way of life in India. First, Madhav Godbole, a former senior civil servant, described the Indian Civil Service as being "marked by corruption, subservience, venality, misuse of power and position, nepotism and favouritism".[28] The second assessment is by Gurharpal Singh, who contended that political corruption in India is a serious problem as "scams, scandals, charges and counter-charges of corruption have become the daily diet of Indian political life". He referred to a recent poll which found that most of the respondents were "no longer surprised by reports of corruption in politics" and that nearly half of them felt that "one has to be corrupt to survive in politics today".[29]

The third assessment is provided by S. Guhan who argued that corruption in India in the 1980s and 1990s had assumed critical proportions when compared with the situation in the 1950s and 1960s. According to him, it is not "an exaggeration today to talk about corruption in terms of a crisis or a cancer endangering India's society, polity and economy".[30]

Why is corruption a way of life in India? In their analysis of corruption in the public services in India, Samuel Paul and Manubhai Shah identified five contributing factors. First, the government's monopoly in the supply of public goods and services reduced competition and created opportunities for corruption by restricting supply either deliberately or through inefficiency. Second, the discretion of public agencies in decision-making provided opportunities and incentives for those involved to engage in corrupt practices. Third, there is a relative lack of accountability on the part of the service providers to the citizens. Fourth, information barriers contribute to corruption when service providers have information not available to citizens. Finally, as the average citizen is exposed to corruption in the public sector on an episodic and not daily basis, "it is unlikely that he will invest his time and resources in a systemic reform" and this explains "why it is difficult to organise effective collective action against corruption in public services".[31]

However, the above list by Paul and Shah is not exhaustive as they had not included other important causes of corruption in their analysis. In this context, the three major causes of corruption identified by Leslie Palmier are also important in accounting for corruption in India *viz.*, low salaries, ample opportunities, and ineffective policing.

The Third Pay Commission (1970-1973) in India identified the link between low salaries and corruption thus:

> While it is not argued that the payment of high salaries by itself is a guarantee for the honesty and integrity of the public service, it can be confidently stated that the payment of a salary which does not satisfy the minimum reasonable needs of a government servant is a direct invitation to corruption.[32]

In his survey of civil service pay in South Asia, David C.E. Chew found that "despite salary revisions and dearness allowances, starting basic salaries of the five kinds of civil servants in South Asia remained very low in December 1987 by international standards".[33] Table 3.1

below shows that the monthly salary in 1996 for the prime minister, minister and member of Parliament in India is much lower than their counterparts in Singapore, Japan and Thailand.

TABLE 3.1 MONTHLY SALARIES OF PRIME MINISTERS, MINISTERS AND MEMBERS OF PARLIAMENT IN INDIA, JAPAN, SINGAPORE AND THAILAND IN 1996

Country	Monthly salary of Prime Minister	Monthly salary of Minister	Monthly salary of Member of Parliament
Singapore	US$67,738	US$47,873	US$5,431*
Japan	US$32,921	US$24,026	US$19,615
Thailand	US$4,533	US$4,135	US$3,062
India	US$417	US$405	US$381

*   This is an allowance as members of Parliament do not receive a salary as they have their own careers.
Source: Compiled from data provided in *Straits Times* (Singapore), February 24, 1996 and C.P. Srivastava, *Corruption: India's Enemy Within* (New Delhi: Macmillan India Ltd., 2001), pp. 91-93, Tables 9.1 to 9.3.

More specifically, the monthly salary of Singapore's prime minister in 1996 was 162 times more than that of the Indian prime minister. Similarly, a cabinet minister in Singapore earns 118 times as much each month as his Indian counterpart. The Japanese member of Parliament's monthly salary is 51 times higher than that of the Indian member of Parliament. Even the monthly allowance of members of Parliament in Singapore is 14 times more than the monthly salary of their Indian counterparts. Finally, the Thai member of Parliament also earns eight times as much per month as his counterpart in India. In short, "the salaries paid to India's prime minister, ministers and MPs are extremely low compared to the salaries paid to their peers in other developing countries".[34]

As discussed earlier, the British method of creating rules to maintain control over the decision-making powers of the Indian subordinate civil servants had caused delay and confusion and provided many opportunities for corruption. Furthermore, Palmier has argued that delays in investigations, prosecutions, and the courts in India have increased the opportunities for corruption as "delay breeds corruption".[35]

Perhaps, the most important factor responsible for corruption in India is the insufficient policing devoted to corruption.[36] In other words, the probability of detecting and punishing corrupt behaviour is not high in India. In his analysis of corruption in the Indian Civil Service, P. C. Alexander identified as a major cause of corruption, "the ease with which corrupt officials are able to get away without punishments commensurate with their offence". He elaborated thus:

> The constitution has justly given the guarantee to all officials that they cannot be dismissed, removed or reduced in rank except after an enquiry for which they will be given a reasonable opportunity of being heard. However the procedures involved in such enquiries have become so complicated and dilatory that the protection intended for the honest official has also become the loophole for the corrupt to escape ... When punishments are not prompt and deterrent, they cease to be disincentives for the dishonest.[37]

ANTI-CORRUPTION STRATEGY

There are three patterns of corruption control in Asian countries as discussed in Chapter 1. India's anti-corruption strategy exhibits the second pattern of corruption control as the Prevention of Corruption Act (POCA) is implemented by the Central Bureau of Investigation (CBI), the Central Vigilance Commission (CVC), the anti-corruption bureaux and vigilance commissions at the state level. In 1860, the Indian Penal Code defined corruption as "acceptance by public servants of any gratification, other than legal remuneration, in exchange for an official act".[38]

However, the fight against corruption in India began in 1941, when the colonial government created the Delhi Special Police Establishment (DSPE) to "investigate cases of bribery and corruption in transactions" involving the War and Supply Departments. In 1943, the government issued Ordinance no. XXII which empowered the

DSPE's officers to investigate corruption cases involving central government departments in India. This Ordinance lapsed on September 30, 1946 and was replaced by the DSPE Act, 1946, which transferred control of the DSPE to the Home Department (now known as the Ministry of Home Affairs).[39]

In March 1947, the POCA incorporated relevant sections of the Indian Penal Code and became law. In 1949, the government formed a Committee chaired by Baksi Tek Chand to review, *inter alia*, the operation of the POCA and to assess the DSPE's effectiveness in combating corruption. In 1952, the Chand Committee recommended that the DSPE's activities should be expanded. Accordingly, an Enforcement Wing was added to the DSPE in 1953 to handle offences involving violation of import and export regulations at Bombay, Calcutta and Madras. In 1955, an Administrative Vigilance Division (AVD) was formed within the Ministry of Home Affairs (MHA) to coordinate anti-corruption measures within the central government.[40]

In June 1962, a Committee on the Prevention of Corruption was appointed and chaired by K. Santhanam. The Santhanam Committee was appointed "to review the existing instruments for checking corruption in the Central Services" and to provide advice on the "practical steps that should be taken to make anti-corruption measures more effective".[41] The Santhanam Report had far-reaching consequences as it first recommended the formation of a CVC, which has the power to "investigate any complaint or suspicion of improper behaviour" against a civil servant. Secondly, a Chief Vigilance Officer (CVO) was appointed in each ministry or department to supervise its vigilance staff. Finally, the Santhanam Report recommended the amendment of the POCA of 1947 to include the provision that "the possession by a public servant of assets disproportionate to income, and for which a satisfactory explanation could not be made, was itself criminal misconduct".[42]

In April 1963, the government established the CBI by incorporating the DSPE as one of its six divisions *viz.*, the Investigation and Anti-Corruption Division. As the CBI's role is to investigate crimes handled by the DSPE, the DSPE Act of 1946 remains in force and provides the legal sanction and authority for investigations by the CBI, which does not have any statutory basis itself. Thus, the MHA, through its AVD assumed control of the CBI's work and provided for its budget. Arising from the recommendations of the Administrative Reforms Commission of 1966, the CBI and AVD were transferred from the MHA to the new Department of Personnel, Cabinet Secretariat in 1970.[43]

The CBI derives its investigating powers from the DSPE Act of 1946, as its Section 5 states that the central government can empower the CBI to investigate the notified offences in any state, but such empowerment is only possible with the consent of the government of that state. According to the Constitution of India, law and order come under the jurisdiction of the states. In view of this, the CBI, as a police organisation of the central government, cannot operate in the states without the permission of the state concerned because of this constitutional provision.

Narasimhan observed that the CBI did not encounter any difficulty within the states during the post-independent period when the Congress Party was in power in the states and centre. However, the situation changed when different political parties assumed power in the states because some state governments withdrew the consent given by their predecessors "whenever they felt that an investigation taken up by the CBI was politically embarrassing or uncomfortable for them". In short, the CBI's status as an investigating agency in a state depends on that state government's mercy. Narasimhan contends that "this is a serious handicap in planning any nation-wide network of investigating units for anti-corruption inquiries".[44]

The 28 states have their own anti-corruption bureaux (ACBs) for dealing with vigilance and anti-corruption work, but these ACBs derive their powers of investigation from the Police Act as they are regular police units. If there is public pressure for an inquiry into the misconduct of a minister, the central or state government will form a commission to inquire into the specific allegations against the minister. The Commission of Inquiry will present its report on the facts ascertained during the inquiry to the government concerned, which will refer the matter to the

CBI or state ACB for investigation if a person is to be prosecuted. However, the investigation process and the ensuing trial is time-consuming and does not result in quickly awarding a severe punishment to the guilty person. Indeed, no CBI case involving ministers has resulted in a firm court conviction during the last 40 years.[45]

The CVC was formed in February 1964 to perform four functions: (1) investigate any transaction in which a public servant is alleged to act for an improper purpose; (2) examine (a) any complaint that a public servant had exercised his powers for improper or corrupt purposes; and (b) any complaint of corruption, misconduct, lack of integrity or other malpractices by a public servant, including members of the All India Services; (3) request reports from ministries, departments and public enterprises to enable it to check and supervise their vigilance and anti-corruption work; and (4) request the CBI to investigate a case, or to entrust the complaint, information or case for inquiry to the CBI or the ministry, department or public enterprise concerned.[46]

During 1964-1998, the CVC was headed by a Commissioner, who was appointed by the President on the recommendation of the Prime Minister for five years. The enactment of the CVC Ordinance on August 25, 1998, transformed the CVC into a statutory body to supervise the functioning of the CBI. The CVC consists of a Central Vigilance Commissioner appointed for four years, and a Vigilance Commissioner appointed for three years. The CVOs in ministries and departments are appointed in consultation with the Commissioner, who assesses their performance. The CVC submits an annual report on its activities to the MHA. Apart from receiving complaints from individuals, the CVC collects and collates data on corruption and malpractices from such sources as press reports, parliamentary speeches, audit objections, reports of parliamentary committees, and CBI reports.[47] The Commissioner advises the departments on the action to be taken on CBI reports on gazetted officers. He also reviews the preventive work of the CVOs and Vigilance Officers in different departments and provides them with the necessary directions.[48]

EVALUATION OF ANTI-CORRUPTION STRATEGY

How effective is India's anti-corruption strategy? India's 71st ranking among the 102 countries in the 2002 Transparency International's CPI, its average rank of 59th position for the CPI from 1995-2002 (see Table 3.2 below) and its joint 10th ranking among the 12 Asian countries in the PERC survey from 1995-2001, all reflect the ineffectiveness of the various anti-corruption measures employed in India.

TABLE 3.2 INDIA'S RANKING ON THE CPI, 1995-2002

Year	Ranking	Score
1995	35	2.78
1996	46	2.63
1997	45	2.75
1998	66	2.90
1999	72	2.90
2000	69	2.80
2001	71	2.70
2002	71	2.70
Average	59	2.77

Source: Compiled from Transparency International's CPI from 1995-2002. See
http://www.transparency.org

More importantly, the fact that corruption is a way of life in India is clearly an indication of the failure of its anti-corruption strategy. In his book, *The Pathology of Corruption*, S.S. Gill observed that no "sphere of public administration" is "not infested with corruption". Indeed, "corruption, unlike a headache, is not confined only to the top; it infects the whole system".[49] During the first 50 years of India's independence, "corruption has spread like an epidemic to all spheres of public life, and India has the distinction of being rated as one of the most corrupt countries in the world".[50]

In assessing the effectiveness of India's anti-corruption strategy, he wrote: "Looking to the number of agencies created to tackle corruption, it would appear that the government was in dead earnest to eradicate this malady".[51] However, he lamented that "this elaborate and multi-layered apparatus to control administrative corruption has hardly made a dent on the situation". Moreover, the public perceives the CBI to be "a pliable tool of the ruling party, and its investigations tend to become cover-up operations for the misdeeds of the ministers." Indeed, the CBI's ineffectiveness is also reflected in its low conviction rate as only 300 of the 1,349 cases (22.2%) in 1972 and 164 of the 1,231 cases (13.3%) in 1992 resulted in conviction. Gill has also accused the CBI of going "only after the small fry" as only one gazetted officer was dismissed in 1972 and two officers in 1992. Finally, the CBI's record in investigating the various mega scams has been dismal as there has been no conviction.[52]

In his evaluation of India's anti-corruption efforts, Palmier was critical of the "ineffectiveness of the internal controls, consisting of the Vigilance Organisations within departments" as these organisations failed to prevent "departments [from taking] ... advantage of every procedure to delay inquiries, investigations, and prosecutions, ably abetting the similar efforts of suspect officers".[53] A more serious weakness is the lack of commitment from the political leaders as "many politicians are themselves corrupt, and are in no position to cast stones at officials".[54]

Palmier criticised the Indian government's unwillingness to provide adequate resources for its anti-corruption strategy thus:

> The notion is simply ludicrous that one Central Vigilance Commissioner can effectively consider the files of all gazetted officers charged with corruption, or that their cases can be properly investigated by a handful of Commissioners for Departmental Inquiries. True priorities are shown by the allocation of resources more than by any rhetoric; on that score the control of corruption cannot be said to be very high on the list of preferences of the Government of India. The Central Vigilance Commission and the Central Bureau of Investigation appear to have been given just enough powers and resources to permit some activity, but not enough to make them effective.[55]

In his comprehensive analysis of the enforcement of the anti-corruption measures in India, C.V. Narasimhan noted that "the existing scheme of anti-corruption work" was based on these three assumptions:

(1) Functionaries at the topmost level in the Government are sincere and keen on putting down corruption.
(2) Supervisory officials in the administrative system at the middle and top levels will themselves be motivated by the status of their office to check corruption at the lower levels and at the cutting edge of the administration.
(3) Special measures devised for the expeditious conduct of court trials and departmental proceedings against corrupt officials will ensure quick and severe punishment which would deter corruption.[56]

Narasimhan contended that these assumptions were valid during the initial post-independence period but no longer valid in recent decades for three reasons:

> Firstly, political corruption at the level of ministers has grown to monstrous proportions. No one believes that the leaders of any political party are sincere and keen in rooting out corruption. Secondly, when ministers themselves become corrupt, the senior officers in their departments are rendered weak and ineffective to check and put down corruption among the subordinate officers who have political linkage. ... Lastly, court convictions and punishments in departmental disciplinary proceedings in respect of corrupt officials have been relatively few, considering the wide spread of corruption as perceived by the people. ... The slow moving criminal justice system has ceased to have any deterrent effect on the potential bribe-takers.[57]

The final manifestation of the ineffectiveness of India's anti-corruption strategy is the empirical evidence for the high extent of "retail" corruption in five cities which has not spared the poor. In their survey, Samuel Paul And Manubhai Shah found that 33% of the urban poor in Bangalore had to pay a bribe to get a service or solve a problem with a public agency. Table 3.3 below shows that the percentages for the other four cities were: Madras (26%), Ahmedabad (20%), Calcutta (12%) and Pune (6%). Paul and Shah concluded that "corruption is a pervasive phenomenon in India's public services".[58]

TABLE 3.3 THE SPEED MONEY PHENOMENON IN FIVE INDIAN CITIES

City	Percentage of poor who paid bribes	Amount of bribe
Ahmedabad	20%	Rs. 500
Bangalore	33%	Rs. 850
Calcutta	12%	NA
Madras	26%	NA
Pune	6%	Rs. 350

Source: Samuel Paul and Manubhai Shah, "Corruption in Public Service Delivery", in S. Guhan and Samuel Paul (eds.), *Corruption in India: Agenda For Action* (New Delhi: Vision Books, 1997), pp. 151-152.

Similarly, Ramesh Thakur has observed that: "What makes the pervasiveness of corruption in India so distinctive is that graft is necessary to get the lowliest officials to perform their *ordinary* duties for which they are receiving salaries from the public purse".[59] Indeed, "People are forced to pay bribes for securing virtually any service connected with the government, even that which is theirs by right and law".[60]

CONCLUSION

The major reason for India's ineffective anti-corruption strategy is the lack of political will or commitment by its political leaders. Indeed, political will is the critical ingredient for an effective anti-corruption strategy because the political leaders must demonstrate their commitment by providing (1) adequate resources for fighting corruption; (2) comprehensive anti-corruption laws; (3)

an independent anti-corruption agency; and (4) punishment for those found guilty of corruption, regardless of their status or position in society.

The key question is: how can the lack of political will in fighting corruption in India be rectified? As India is the world's largest democracy, the onus lies with the voters to elect responsible and competent persons into office. However, according to Gurharpal Singh, "opinion polls regularly suggest that regardless of caste, ethnicity, gender or region, voters perceive politicians as corrupt". Indeed, an opinion poll showed that most voters preferred "a leader who is corrupt but efficient to one who is honest but inefficient".[61]

Thus, to enhance the political will to curb corruption in India, the citizens must elect to public office honest and non-corrupt political leaders who will strengthen the existing anti-corruption measures and enforce these measures impartially. Since corruption is a way of life in India today, the political leaders must take action to change the population's tolerant attitude towards corruption in the short term by punishing all corrupt officials regardless of their status, and in the long term by informing them of the harmful consequences of corruption to Indian society. In the final analysis, the political will to curb corruption in India ultimately depends on the citizens' willingness to elect honest and competent persons to Parliament. In this connection, the CVC has taken the initiative by publishing the *Citizens' Guide to Fighting Corruption* on its web site (http://www.cvc.nic.in) on August 15, 2001.

If those found guilty of corruption are punished, corruption will be viewed as a high risk, low reward activity. Conversely, if those involved in corrupt practices are unlikely to be caught and severely punished, corruption will be viewed as a low risk, high reward activity. For Indian citizens to perceive corruption as a high risk, low reward activity, the incumbent government must publicise through the mass media the detection of corrupt behaviour among civil servants and politicians and their punishment according to the law if they are found guilty.

Thus, to minimise corruption, the Indian government must first identify those public agencies which are "wet" or vulnerable to corruption. In India, those agencies which provide opportunities for corrupt civil servants to enrich themselves through bribery are described as sensitive agencies. These "wet" or sensitive agencies must review their procedures periodically to reduce opportunities for corruption. The standing order of the CVC that a person's term of office in a sensitive agency should not exceed three years helps to reduce opportunities for corruption.[62] Furthermore, unnecessary regulations and excessive red tape should be reduced and cumbersome administrative procedures streamlined to remove opportunities for corruption.[63]

The CBI personnel must be incorruptible themselves to ensure their credibility and effectiveness. In contrast to Singapore's Corrupt Practices Investigation Bureau (CPIB), which has 84 members, and Hong Kong's Independent Commission Against Commission (ICAC), which has 1,286 members, the CBI has 5,087 members (consisting of 3,856 officers and 1,231 administrative staff). Thus, compared with the CPIB and ICAC, it would be more difficult for the CBI to ensure that all its members are incorrupt, given its large staff.

A more serious problem is that India has still retained the British colonial method of employing the police to curb corruption even though it is ineffective, especially when the police is corrupt. Singapore's experience in combating corruption (discussed in Chapter 5) has shown that from 1937 to 1951, the Anti-Corruption Branch (ACB) within the Criminal Investigation Department of the Police Force was ineffective because of its limited resources and prevalence of police corruption. The discovery by the British colonial government in October 1951 of the involvement of senior police officers in the robbery of S$400,000 worth of opium (known as the "Opium Hijacking" scandal), made it realise the necessity of removing the task of corruption control from the police. Accordingly, the CPIB was established as an independent agency in October 1952.[64]

Even though Hong Kong had learnt from Singapore's experience in fighting corruption from the 1968 study tour conducted by its officials, it took 26 years (1948-1974) to transfer the task of curbing corruption from the Anti-Corruption Branch and the Anti-Corruption Office of the police to the ICAC in February 1974. According to

Jeremiah H.K. Wong, the government had opposed the creation of an independent anti-corruption agency for three reasons: "possible adverse effects on police morale, difficulties for any new organisation to recruit and train an independent team of expert investigators, and the need for co-ordination in any case with other departments in the Police Force related to anti-corruption investigations".[65] However, the escape of a corruption suspect, Chief Superintendent Peter F. Godber, on June 8, 1973, to England angered the public and influenced the Governor, Sir Murray MacLehose, to make the important decision of establishing an ICAC that would be independent of the police.[66]

As the DSPE was created in 1941 and transformed into the CBI in 1963, this means that India has employed the traditional British method of relying on the police to curb corruption for the past 60 years even though this method has been shown to be ineffective. As the CBI is a police agency, it is not only concerned with fighting corruption. The CBI has three main areas of operation: anti-corruption, economic crimes, and special crimes (including organised crime and terrorism). Thus, to enhance the CBI's effectiveness, the following reforms must be introduced: (1) the CBI must be removed from police control; (2) the CBI must be transformed into an independent anti-corruption agency; (3) the powers of the CBI must be increased so that it does not have to obtain permission from a state government to investigate corruption cases in that state; and (4) the CBI should reduce its huge staff of 5,087 members if possible to improve its ability to monitor them.

On March 13, 2001, Tehelka.com released its tapes showing Bangaru Laxman, President of the ruling Bharatiya Janata Party (BJP), receiving money from a Tehelka journalist posing as an arms dealer. This exposé led to the resignation of Laxman and George Fernandes, the Defence Minister. According to Sureshwar D. Sinha, a retired commander in the Indian Navy:

> Corruption and the methods of corruption in the Ministry of Defence and Service Headquarters has been a hush-hush topic of discussion in the officer's mess and service parties. The Tehelka Tapes exposé has revealed what the service officers have been talking about amongst themselves over the past three decades.

The methods, approach, tactics of the defence agents have remained the same, [but] the level of corruption at the highest levels has, on the other hand, gone up.[67]

Joginder Singh, a former CBI director, has expressed his pessimism thus: "The rot is so deep that it can't be solved by one single party. ... The real problem is not the system, the real problem is that the people are corrupt. The malady is too deep, the problem too serious to be solved by speeches".[68]

Is the situation in India hopeless as far as minimising corruption is concerned? Is the above pessimistic assessment by Joginder Singh correct? In my 1982 matrix of anti-corruption strategies, I described the "hopeless" strategy as one with inadequate anti-corruption measures and where the political leaders are not concerned with curbing corruption.[69] Indeed, India's anti-corruption strategy will remain hopeless as long as its political leaders do not demonstrate the political will required to improve its ineffective anti-corruption measures, which appear to have been designed to fail.

In short, to enhance India's anti-corruption strategy, its political leaders must demonstrate political will by increasing the probability of detection and punishment for corrupt offences, reducing the opportunities for corruption in "wet" or sensitive agencies, and removing the CBI from police control.

ENDNOTES

1   Gunnar Myrdal, "Corruption as a Hindrance to Modernisation in South Asia", in Arnold J. Heidenheimer, Michael Johnston, and Victor T. LeVine (eds.), *Political Corruption: A Handbook* (New Brunswick: Transaction Publishers, 1989), p. 407.

2   *The Economic Weekly*, Vol. 15, No. 51, December 21, 1963, p. 2061, quoted in ibid., p. 410.

3   John B. Monteiro, *Corruption: Control of Maladministration* (Bombay: Manaktala and Sons, 1966), pp. 47 and 53.

4   See for examples, Michael L. Hager, "Bureaucratic Corruption in India: Legal Control of Maladministration", *Comparative Political Studies*, Vol. 6, No. 2 (July 1973), pp. 197-219; Suresh Kohli (ed.), *Corruption in India* (New Delhi: Chetana Publications, 1975); Vinod Pavarala, *Interpreting Corruption: Elite Perspectives in India* (New Delhi: Sage Publications, 1996); S. Guhan and Samuel Paul (eds.), *Corruption in India: Agenda For Action* (New Delhi: Vision Books, 1997); S.S. Gill, *The Pathology of Corruption*

(New Delhi: HarperCollins Publishers, 1998); Chandran Mitra, *The Corrupt Society: The Criminalization of India from Independence to the 1990s* (New Delhi: Penguin Books India, 1998); Shiv Visvanathan and Harsh Sethi (eds.), *Foul Play: Chronicles of Corruption 1947-97* (New Delhi: Banyan Books, 1998); N.K. Singh, *The Politics of Crime and Corruption: A Former CBI Officer Speaks* (New Delhi: HarperCollins Publishers, 1999); S.K. Das, *Public Office, Private Interest: Bureaucracy and Corruption in India* (New Delhi: Oxford University Press, 2001); and C.P. Srivastava, *Corruption: India's Enemy Within* (New Delhi: Macmillan India Ltd., 2001).

5   Gill, *The Pathology of Corruption*, pp. 125-127 and 136.

6   N. Vittal and S. Mahalingam, *Fighting Corruption and Restructuring Government* (New Delhi: Manas Publications, 2000), p. 271.

7   John Andrews, *Pocket Asia*, 7th edition (London: The Economist Newspaper Ltd. and Profile Books Ltd., 2002), p. 78.

8   Sanjyot P. Dunung, *Doing Business in Asia*, 2nd edition (San Francisco: Jossey-Bass Publishers, 1998), p. 339.

9   Ibid., p. 339.

10 Andrews, *Pocket Asia*, p. 79.

11 Michael Todaro, *Economic Development*, 7th edition (Reading: Addison-Wesley, 2000), p. 196.

12 *Pocket World in Figures* 2003 edition (London: The Economist Newspaper Ltd. and Profile Books Ltd., 2002), p. 14.

13 Ibid., p. 16.

14 Andrews, *Pocket Asia*, p. 79.

15 Rajiv Desai, *Indian Business Culture* (Oxford: Butterworth-Heinemann, 1999), pp. 93-94.

16 Krishna K. Tummala, "Corruption in India: Control Measures and Consequences", *Asian Journal of Political Science*, Vol. 10, No. 1 (June 2002), pp. 44-45.

17 Andrews, *Pocket Asia*, p. 79.

18 Dunung, *Doing Business in Asia*, p. 341.

19 Tummala, "Corruption in India", pp. 46-47.

20 Dunung, *Doing Business in Asia*, p. 343.

21 Richard P. Taub, *Bureaucrats Under Stress: Administrators and Administration in an Indian State* (Berkeley: University of California Press, 1969), pp. 153-161.

22 Andrews, *Pocket Asia*, p. 79.

23 Ibid., p. 72.

24 For more details of the Congress Party's electoral performance, see Craig Baxter *et al.*, *Government and Politics in South Asia* 4th edition (Boulder: Westview Press, 1998), pp.95-99.

25 Kripa Sridharan, "Indian Politics in the 1990s: Trends and Transformations", *Asian Journal of Political Science*, Vol. 10, No. 1 (June 2002), pp. 55-59.

26   A. Hariharan, "A Common Goal: Get-Rich-Quick", *Far Eastern Economic Review*, Vol. 85, No. 35, September 6, 1974, p. 25.

27   Kohli, "In Cinema", in Kohli (ed.), *Corruption in India*, p. 67.

28   Madhav Godbole, "Corruption, Political Interference and the Civil Service", in Guhan and Paul (eds.), *Corruption in India*, p. 61.

29   Gurharpal Singh, "Understandig Political Corruption in Contemporary Indian Politics", in Paul Heywood, (ed.), *Political Corruption* (Oxford: Blackwell Publishers, 1997), pp. 210-211.

30   S. Guhan, "Introduction", in Guhan and Paul (eds.), *Corruption in India*, pp. 15-16.

31   Samuel Paul and Manubhai Shah, "Corruption in Public Service Delivery", in Guhan and Paul (eds.), *Corruption in India*, pp. 147-149.

32   Quoted in S.K. Das, *Public Office, Private Interest: Bureaucracy and Corruption in India* (New Delhi: Oxford University Press, 2001), p. 105.

33   David C.E. Chew, *Civil Service Pay in South Asia* (Geneva: International Labour Office, 1992), p. 78.

34   Srivastava, *Corruption: India's Enemy Within*, p. 94.

35   Palmier, *The Control of Bureaucratic Corruption*, pp. 83-99.

36   Ibid., p. 280.

37   P. C. Alexander, *The Perils of Democracy* (Bombay: Somaiya Publications, 1995), pp. 79-80.

38   Vijay K. Shunglu, "India's Anti-Corruption Strategy", in *Combating Corruption in Asian and Pacific Economies* (Manila: Asian Development Bank, 2000), p. 13.

39   Palmier, *The Control of Bureaucratic Corruption*, p. 30.

40   Ibid., pp. 13 and 31.

41   Ibid., p. 14.

42   Ibid., p. 14.

43   Ibid., pp. 31-32.

44   C. V. Narasimhan, "Prevention of Corruption: Towards Effective Enforcement", in Guhan and Paul (eds.), *Corruption in India*, pp. 255-256.

45   Ibid., pp. 257-258.

46   Ibid., pp. 264-265.

47   Palmier, *The Control of Bureaucratic Corruption*, p. 52. For a more recent analysis of the CVC's role, see Vittal and Mahalingam, *Fighting Corruption and Restructuring Government*, pp. 231-235 and 248-258.

48   Narasimhan, "Prevention of Corruption", p. 266.

49   Gill, *The Pathology of Corruption*, pp. 125 and 127.

50   Ibid., p. 230.

51   Ibid., p. 237.

52   Ibid., p. 238.

53   Palmier, *The Control of Bureaucratic Corruption*, p. 111.

54   Ibid., p. 112.

55   Ibid., p. 113.

56   Narasimhan, "Prevention of Corruption", p. 253.

57   Ibid., p. 254.

58   Samuel Paul and Manubhai Shah, "Corruption in Public Service Delivery", in Guhan and Shah (eds.), *Corruption in India*, pp. 151-152.

59   Ramesh Thakur, *The Government and Politics of India* (New York: St. Martin's Press, 1995), p. 178.

60   Ibid., p. 179.

61   Gurharpal Singh, "Understanding Political Corruption in Contemporary Indian Politics", in Paul Heywood (ed.), *Political Corruption* (Oxford: Blackwell Publishers, 1997), p. 222.

62   I am grateful to Mr N. Vittal, former Central Vigilance Commissioner, for pointing this out to me.

63   Tan Ah Leak, "The Experience of Singapore in Combating Corruption", in Rick Stapenhurst and Sahr J. Kpundeh (eds.), *Curbing Corruption: Toward a Model for Building National Integrity* (Washington, D.C.: The World Bank, 1999), pp. 61-62.

64   See Chapter 5.

65   Jeremiah K.H. Wong, "The ICAC and Its Anti-Corruption Measures", in Rance P. L. Lee (ed.), *Corruption and Its Control in Hong Kong* (Hong Kong: The Chinese University Press, 1981), p. 45.

66   See Chapter 6.

67   Quoted in tehelka.com, New Delhi, March 17, 2001. For more details, see http://www.tehelka.com/currentaffairs/mar2001/ca031701commander1.htm.

68   See http://www.tehelka.com/currentaffairs/mar2001/ca031401intellectuals1.htm.

69   Jon S.T. Quah, "Bureaucratic Corruption in the ASEAN Countries: A Comparative Analysis of Their Anti-Corruption Strategies", *Journal of Southeast Asian Studiies*, Vol. 13, No. 1 (March 1982), pp. 175-176.

CHAPTER 4

The Philippines

INTRODUCTION

The Philippines attained its independence from the United States on July 4, 1946. John Andrews described the Philippines as "a country which fell from grace" from being "one of Asia's richest countries in the 1950s" to "become one of the poorest" countries in the 1980s.[1] In the same vein, Alasdair Bowie and Danny Unger referred to the Philippines as "the East Asian capitalist laggard" as "its economic performance after the 1950s, and particularly after the early 1980s, was considerably less impressive than that of the other commodity-rich economies of Southeast Asia".[2] There are many reasons for the decline in economic performance in the Philippines.[3]

This chapter focuses on one of the major reasons for the Philippines' economic decline, namely, the rampant corruption in the country. More specifically, it analyses the problem of corruption in the Philippines today by first demonstrating that it is a way of life. The various anti-corruption measures employed by the government are then described and evaluated. This chapter concludes that the anti-corruption measures in the Philippines are ineffective as the "logic of corruption control" has not been observed i.e., these measures have not removed the five major causes of corruption in the country. However, before discussing the extent of corruption, it is necessary describe the nature of the policy context in the Philippines.

POLICY CONTEXT

Geography

The Philippines is an archipelago of 7,107 islands, comprising a total land area of 300,000 sq. km, approximately the same size as

Italy. However, only 1,000 islands are populated and the 11 largest islands constitute 94% of the total land mass.[4] The Philippines is "a highly fragmented country" as its islands are "scattered over some 1,295,000 sq. km of oceanic waters", its beaches are stretched "along its length of 1,851 sq. km and breadth of 1,107 sq. km," and "the boundaries of water and mountain make internal travel and communication difficult".[5]

While its archipelagic nature has resulted in "considerable fragmentation", the relative ease of water transportation in the Philippines has "facilitated inter-island commerce and migration" particularly in the central Visayan region. On the other hand, "the mountainous nature" of the country has made "intra-island interaction more difficult", especially in Mindanao. Indeed, "geography and linguistics overlap to divide the Philippines into three regions", namely, Luzon island, the Visayan islands, and Mindanao island.[6]

While "the boundaries of water and mountain make internal travel and communication difficult" in the Philippines, these boundaries "make more uneconomical and unbalanced the exploitation and utilisation of resources", "hinder governance and administration", and "cultivated parochial loyalties and given rise to internecine conflicts which inhibit nationalism and unified development".[7] A final source of diversity is the tremendous difference between urban and rural life. Almost 54% of the population live in the urban areas, which are "more exposed to Western values". In contrast, the rural Filipinos are "more traditional, more conservative, and less politically active than city dwellers".[8] In short, the archipelagic and fragmented nature of the Philippines has made the task of fighting corruption more arduous, especially in the provinces and rural areas.

Economy

Until the late 1950s, the Philippines' economic growth rate was one of the highest in East Asia. However, under President Ferdinand Marcos' leadership from 1965 to 1986, the Philippines "slipped behind other countries in the region".[9] With its abundance of such natural resources as timber, coconuts, sugar, bananas, rubber and minerals, and its literate and hard-working labour force, the Philippines should have been one of Asia's most prosperous economies today. However, John Andrews observed that the Philippines was "one of the worst-performing economies" among the ASEAN countries for these reasons:

> In the 1950s industrialisation concentrated on import-substitution, but in the 1960s there was no attempt to build export-oriented industries based on the import-substituting factories. By the end of the 1960s the Philippines was the slowest growing economy in non-communist South-East Asia. It compounded its problems by erecting high tariffs to protect its industries (and the profits of their owners) from foreign competition. The consequence was a country living beyond its means.[10]

Thus, it is not surprising that the Philippines' GDP per capita in 2000 was US$990, which is ranked behind Singapore, Hong Kong and South Korea, and higher than that of India and Mongolia. Its GDP is US$74.7 billion and its average annual growth in real GDP from 1990-2000 was 2.9%.[11] However, in 2001, economic growth in the Philippines decreased to 2.9%, which was below the government's forecast of 3.3% for the year.[12]

Since the agricultural area constitutes 41% of the total land area, it is not surprising that "rural life focuses around the production of four main crops: rice, corn, coconut and sugar". Rice and corn are produced for local consumption while coconut and sugar are exported. In spite of the government's Green Revolution of 1969-1971, the production of rice was the lowest in Asia in the early 1970s. According to Wurfel, "low agricultural production is a root cause of rural poverty in the Philippines".[13] In 2001, the poverty level in the Philippines "reached beyond an alarming 40%, with some 35 million Filipinos living below the poverty level".[14] The high level of poverty in the Philippines and the government's inability to raise civil service salaries increase the incentive for corruption and also make it more difficult for the incumbent government to minimise corruption in the country.

In her analysis of the development experience of the Philippines, Helen Cabalu noted that in the early 1960s, the

Philippines "had strong export performance from commodities, a relatively rich and rapidly growing domestic market and a relatively educated and skilled labour force". However, its "subsequent economic history" was "one of unfulfilled promise" as it "quickly became the weakest performer in the region".[15] The reasons for the "persistent macroeconomic imbalances" in the Philippines were the:

> weak macroeconomic policies, a small revenue base and wasteful public investment, an inward-oriented production structure, a repressed financial sector and an overblown bureaucracy associated with a high degree of intervention in the economy designed to offset the distortions created by inappropriate basic policies.[16]

In sum, she concluded that "the Philippine development experience has been an example of what *not* to do" in view of its dismal economic performance.[17]

Cabalu's negative assessment is shared by Clark D. Neher who wrote: "If Thailand has been the favorite case study for capitalist development of agricultural societies in the last several decades, the Philippines became the model for what not to do".[18] In the mid-1970s, Philippines and Thailand had a GDP per capita of just over US$300. In 1997, the Philippines' GDP per capita increased to US$1,265, which is lower than Thailand's GDP per capita of US$2,970. Indeed, during the 1980s, the Philippines was "the only ASEAN state not to share in this period of economic growth" as its growth rates declined.[19]

Demography

The Philippines has a population of 75.7 million persons and a population density of 252 per sq. km. The population's average annual growth rate from 1995-2000 was 2.0%.[20] There are two important aspects of the population which merit attention: its diversity and cultural values which emphasise the importance of the family.

According to anthropologists, the Philippines has 111 different cultural and racial groups, who speak 70 different languages, ranging from the Muslim Malays in the southern Sulu archipelago to the

Episcopalian Igorot aborigines in the mountains of Luzon.[21] In terms of ethnic composition, the Malays constitute the majority with 91.5%, followed by 6% of aborigines and 1.5% of Chinese. However, "the potential divisiveness of these ethnic differences" was mitigated by "a widespread acceptance of mixed marriages in the Philippines".[22] Consequently, both the Spanish and Chinese *mestizos* (those whose blood is mixed) are at the top of the social hierarchy as they receive half the national income.[23] The population is also 92% Christian (83% Roman Catholic and 9% Protestant) and 5% Muslim. As the Catholic Church exerts a pervasive influence in the Philippines, the religious minorities are "tightly-knit and protective of their positions in Philippine society".[24]

The family plays a central role in Philippine society for the following reasons:

> It is the primary vehicle for socialisation of the young; the source of emotional and financial support for its members; and the chief claimant of loyalty. ... The primacy of the family is reinforced by custom, embedded in Catholic teachings, and proclaimed in the 1987 Constitution.[25]

This view is shared by Alfredo and Grace Roces, who contend that "The influence of the family permeates all facets of Philippine society. It is the primary unit of corporate action about which social, economic, and religious activities revolve".[26]

The state has recognised the importance of the family in Philippine society as Article 216 of the Philippine Civil Code states that "The family is a basic social institution which public policy cherishes and protects." Furthermore, Article 2, section 12 of the Philippine Constitution of 1986 stipulates that "The State recognises the sanctity of family life and shall protect and strengthen the family as a basic autonomous social institution".[27]

As the family in the Philippines is viewed as "a mutual assistance community in which the authority of age and birth order is respected",[28] kinship ties extend bilaterally to include the families of both spouses. The Filipino family is further extended through the *"compadre* system, in which a prominent man in the community" is chosen as "the child's godfather and the *compadre* of the parent". The godfather acts as an intermediary in dealings with the government and he receives in return "gifts or free labour services in election campaigns and other political situations". Richard L. Langston has contended that "the *compadre* system reinforces the Filipino tendency to work through an intermediary whenever possible".[29]

During the American colonial period (1898-1913), the bureaucracy was clean for two reasons: the civil servants received higher salaries and corrupt officials were promptly prosecuted. However, the growth of the bureaucracy led to a rise in nepotism as "many Filipinos helped extended family members land government jobs." As Filipinos rely a great deal on their relatives, they are often obligated to employ relatives even though they are not qualified for the job.[30]

According to Gaudioso C. Sosmena Jr., the reverence to the family, which "runs strongly in the Filipino psyche", contributes to the culture of patronage in the Philippines as "whenever one holds a seat of administrative and political power", the members of this person's family and immediate relatives "use the power and influence" of the position "as a bridge in getting preferential government employment".[31] As the corporations in the Philippines are "characteristically family-owned", nepotism is also widespread in the private sector. According to Alfredo and Grace Roces, the prevalence of nepotism in government and business is "a reflection of family cohesiveness".[32]

In short, as Jean Grossholz has astutely observed, the family in the Philippines is "the strongest unit of society, demanding the deepest loyalties of the individual and colouring all social activity with its own set of demands" but its "communal values" are "often in conflict with the impersonal values of the institutions of the larger society".[33]

Finally, mention must be made of the traditional Philippine cultural value of *utang na loob* or "debt of gratitude", because it is an important "operating principle in Philippine interpersonal behaviour".[34] More specifically, *utang na loob* refers to "a feeling of

86

indebtedness which is incurred when one receives a favour, service, or goods, and it carries a deep sense of obligation to reciprocate when the appropriate moment comes". Accordingly, "if one decides to hire an employee, make a purchase, leave an employer, or even cast a vote, *utang na loob* is likely to be a factor".[35] More importantly, *utang na loob* reinforces the strength of the network of strong inter-family groups as it demands that "all favours be returned in like or greater value". Indeed, such favours not only extend across several generations, but also "encourage patronage between superiors and subordinates and perpetuate the domination of elite groups deriving their power from the extensiveness of their networks".[36]

Political System

The Philippines has a presidential system of government, which is a legacy of American colonial rule. To prevent the dictatorship of the Marcos era from occurring again, the Constitution of February 1987 limited the president to a single six-year term. Furthermore, the president cannot overrule a two-thirds vote by Congress or abolish Congress; and he can only impose martial law for a maximum of 60 days. The bicameral legislature consists of a 24-member Senate, directly elected for six years, and a 208-member House of Representatives elected by constituency for a three-year term.[37]

Political power in the Philippines is concentrated in the executive branch through a series of legal provisions. The president has the power to make executive appointments and to control the budget process. Secondly, the political system rewards its incumbents by the use of pluralistic, "winner takes all" voting rules. Accordingly, the two political parties–Nacionalistas and Liberals which have similar policy platforms–have dominated the Philippine political scene. Thirdly, the technocrats were constrained in formulating and implementing macroeconomic policy as they lacked political support. Finally, policy implementation has been hindered by the existence of weak public institutions which have "poor human and financial resources and organisational inadequacies".[38]

EXTENT OF CORRUPTION

Corruption was introduced to the Philippines by the Spanish as the "low salaries and poor working conditions of the bureaucrats and the many opportunities available for corrupt behaviour contributed to the widespread corruption in the colonial bureaucracy".[39] For example, the *gobernadorcillo* or petty governor was paid a miserable salary of two pesos a month which was not commensurate with the extensive duties he had to perform including, among other things, being the village mayor, justice of the peace, and supervisor of tribute and tax-collections.[40] As a public office was viewed as a grant or favour from the king during the Spanish colonial period, "many bureaucrats actually treated the transaction as a business–selling an office at a profit and buying a more lucrative one".[41] According to Corpuz, the most serious weakness of the Spanish colonial bureaucracy was the "internal moral corruption of its members".[42]

During the American colonial period (1898-1913) there were two groups of corrupt bureaucrats: civilians and discharged soldiers appointed without examination by the previous military government; and the justices of the peace who were also appointed without examination and did not receive salaries, but they could collect fees for their judicial services.[43] However, the bureaucracy as a whole was quite clean during this period for two reasons: the bureaucrats received higher salaries and corrupt officials were promptly prosecuted. Thus, the two major causes of corruption responsible for the rampant corruption during the Spanish colonial period–low salaries and ineffective legal measures–were removed in the American colonial bureaucracy and this explains why it was less corrupt than the Spanish colonial bureaucracy.[44]

After World War II, the bureaucracy in the Philippines suffered from "low prestige, incompetence, meager resources, and a large measure of cynical corruption".[45] The colonial bureaucracy's low prestige was the result of its low salaries and the corrupt behaviour of its members. Bureaucratic corruption became a serious problem during the 1950s, especially during the administration of President Elpidio Quirino (1948-53) because corruption "permeated the entire gamut of the Philippine bureaucracy, extending from the lowest level of the civil service to the top, excepting the President himself".[46]

In January 1959, President Carlos Garcia highlighted the problem of graft and corruption in his address to Congress:

> In our essay at making our social and economic objectives a fact accomplished, we are hampered by a cancer gnawing at our national entrails. Graft and corruption ... is ... a national problem. The problem of graft and corruption is not peculiar to our administration in this country. Nor is it a new one. It has plagued all administrations before us. Nevertheless, I do not condone nor minimise the significance of this blight.[47]

In 1969, the Philippine Ethnic Group Attitude Surveys found, among other things, that 66% of the 1,381 Filipinos interviewed believed that graft and corruption were prevalent and constituted a major problem.[48] When the respondents were asked "Which officials are corrupt?" 38% identified politicians as corrupt, 36% viewed government employees as corrupt, and 22% considered local politicians as corrupt.[49] Finally, the respondents from Manila viewed politicians and government employees as corrupt unlike the Ilocano, Muslim, Pampangan and lower-income respondents.[50]

In 1988, Raul P. de Guzman and his associates contended that graft and corruption was a major problem of the bureaucracy in the Philippines.[51] Similarly, David Timberman pointed out that corruption was not only endemic to Philippine politics, but the more serious problem was "the widespread assumption that corruption is unavoidable". Consequently, "few Filipino politicians have left office without having significantly increased their wealth".[52]

Corruption in the Philippines reached its highest level during the 21 years of Marcos' rule (1965-1986). According to Amelia P. Varela:

> Graft and corruption reached its all time high during the martial law regime under Marcos. ... Graft and corruption under Marcos had permeated almost all aspects of bureaucratic life and institutions which saw the start of the systematic plunder of the country.[53]

In the same vein, Joel Rocamora observed that Marcos "perfected ... 'a vacuum cleaner approach' to corruption" as he and his relatives "picked the government clean, siphoned large chunks of the tens of billions of dollar loans which flowed liberally in the 1970s".[54]

The prosecution in the March 1990 trial in New York accused Imelda Marcos of "systematically looting the country." According to one of the prosecution's 95 witnesses, Oscar Carino, the manager of the Philippine National Bank's branch in New York, revealed that "when Imelda was in town, she used the National Bank like her own 'personal piggy bank'. He regularly delivered up to $100,000 in cash to her hotel room as loose change for her shopping sprees. When state investigators examined the books, they found unreimbursed withdrawals totalling over $22 million".[55] During one shopping trip to New York, Copenhagen and Rome, she spent more than 3 million British pounds. There was also a standing order in every hotel she stayed in to furnish her suite with 500 British pounds worth of flowers.[56]

Carmen Navarro Pedrosa estimated that Marcos had amassed "a staggering $15 billion", which was more than half of the country's national debt.[57] Given the massive scale of "official corruption" practised by Marcos, his family and cronies, Belinda A. Aquino accurately described the Philippines under Marcos as the "Politics of Plunder" as "they stole high and low, from both rich and poor" and bled the country of billions of dollars until it became the "basket case of Asia" by the late 1970s.[58] The Marcos regime was "sultanistic" as it was based on personalism and loyalty to Marcos was motivated by a mixture of fear and the promise of rewards to his collaborators.[59]

Yvonne T. Chua's excellent case study of the Philippines' Department of Education, Culture and Sports (DECS) demonstrates graphically "an education bureaucracy so ridden with graft that it is barely able to deliver the most basic educational services to the country's 15 million public school students".[60] She contends that corruption has become systemic at DECS and has permeated all levels of the public educational system. Corruption in the DECS has assumed many forms, from petty or survival corruption to top-level corruption, with procurement and recruitment being the areas most vulnerable to corruption. Furthermore, embezzlement, nepotism, influence peddling, fraud and other types of corruption also flourished at the DECS. According to Chua, corruption has been institutionalised in the DECS that "payoffs have become the lubricant that makes the bureaucracy run smoothly".[61] Finally, Chua observed that "one of the greatest tragedies of corruption in the public school system is when teachers pass on their warped values to students. In some schools, teachers teach young schoolchildren to cheat in tests because it is on the basis of these tests that the school's performance is assessed".[62]

In December 1999, the World Bank estimated that the Philippines government had lost US$47 million annually or a total of US$48 billion to corruption during 1977-97.[63] In short, corruption is a way of life in the Philippines as both grand and petty corruption are rampant at all levels of the government and society.

ANTI-CORRUPTION STRATEGY

The fight against corruption began in May 1950, when President Quirino created the Integrity Board consisting of five members to investigate complaints of graft and corruption against civil servants. However, this first anti-corruption agency was short-lived as the lack of public support led to its dissolution five months later.[64]

After winning the 1953 presidential election, Ramon Magsaysay established the Presidential Complaints and Action Commission (PCAC) to reduce inefficiency and dishonesty in the civil service. He also issued Administrative Order No. 1 to prevent public officials from participating in certain types of official transactions with their real or imaginary relatives. The first anti-corruption law was the Forfeiture Law of 1955, which authorised "the state to forfeit in its favour any property found to have been unlawfully acquired by any public officer or employer".[65] Unfortunately, this law was ineffective as there were no conviction even after four years of the law's implementation.

President Magsaysay's untimely death in an air crash in 1957 led to the emergence of the Garcia administration (1957-62), which abolished the PCAC and replaced it with the Presidential Committee on Administrative Performance Efficiency (PCAPE) and the Presidential Fact-Finding Committee (PFFC) in 1958 to implement the government's anti-graft campaign. In February 1960, President Garcia formed a third agency known as the Presidential Anti-Graft Committee (PAGC).[66] Two months later, the second anti-corruption law, the Republic Act (RA) No. 3019, entitled the Anti-Graft and Corrupt Practices Act, was passed.[67] RA No. 3019 identified 11 types of corrupt acts among public officials and required them to file every two years a detailed and sworn statement of their assets and liabilities.

President Garcia was succeeded by President Diosdado Macapagal, who served from 1962-65. Macapagal created the Presidential Anti-Graft Committee or PAGCOM. In 1965, Ferdinand Marcos replaced Macapagal as President and abolished PAGCOM and formed in its place, the Presidential Agency on Reforms and Government Operations (PARGO) in January 1966. Three other agencies were created to assist PARGO to fight corruption: the Presidential Complaints and Action Office (PCAO), the Complaints and Investigations Office (CIO), and the Special Cabinet Committee in Backsliding.[68] The third anti-corruption law, RA No. 6028, which provided for the formation of the Office of the Citizens' Counsellor, was passed in August 1969, but was not implemented.

President Marcos' declaration of martial law on September 22, 1972 "ended over a quarter century of robust, if often irresponsible and elitist, democratic politics".[69] The remaining anti-corruption laws were the four Presidential Decrees (PD) issued by President Marcos after the establishment of martial law. PD No. 6 identified 29 administrative offences and empowered heads of departments to dismiss guilty officials immediately. This resulted in the sacking of nearly 8,000 public officials. Two months later, PD No. 46 prevented public officials from receiving and private individuals from giving gifts on any occasion including Christmas. Finally, PD No. 677 and PD No. 749 are amendments to RA No. 3019, requiring all government employees to submit statements of their assets and liabilities every year, instead of every other year; and providing immunity from prosecution for those willing to testify against public officials or citizens accused of corruption.[70]

However, these purges were ineffective as "many of those who were fired were already retired or dead, while others were exonerated and the charges were dropped. Ten months later, many implicated officials were still at their posts".[71] Moreover, the criteria for these purges were random and "encouraged fear and indifference rather than excellence". Most importantly, the Marcos regime's efforts in curbing corruption lacked credibility among the public as there was "growing suspicion that the worst offenders were sitting in the president's palace". By 1976, corruption had become rampant as grand corruption by Marcos and his cabinet encouraged the spread of petty corruption.[72]

The Philippines is the Asian country with the most anti-corruption measures as it has relied on seven laws and 13 anti-graft agencies since it began its fight against corruption in the 1950s.[73] The proliferation of anti-graft agencies is the result of the frequent changes in political leadership as these agencies are either created or abolished by the President. From May 1950 to January 1966, five anti-corruption agencies were formed and dissolved as there were five changes in political leadership during that period. Similarly, President Marcos created another five anti-graft agencies during his 21 years in power because the first three agencies were ineffective and lasted between eight months and two years.[74] In July 1979, President Marcos formed the *Sandiganbayan* (Special Anti-Graft Court) and the *Tanodbayan* (Ombudsman) by issuing PD No. 1606 and PD No. 1603 respectively.

When President Aquino assumed office in February 1986, "there was high expectation that the end of the culture of graft and corruption was near".[75] She established the Presidential Commission on Good Government (PCGG) to identify and retrieve the money stolen by the Marcos family and its cronies. Unfortunately, Aquino's "avowed anti-graft and corruption" stance was viewed cynically by the public as two of her Cabinet members and her relatives were accused of corruption. The PCGG was also a target for charges of corruption, favouritism and incompetence.

Indeed, by June 1988, five of its agents faced graft charges and 13 more were being investigated.

In May 1987, Aquino created the Presidential Committee on Public Ethics and Accountability (PCPEA) to respond to increasing public criticism. However, the PCPEA was also ineffective as it lacked personnel and funds. In other words, Aquino's "honesty has not been matched by the political will to punish the corrupt".[76]

In November 1987, Archbishop Cardinal Jaime Sin criticised the "continued graft in government despite the ouster of former president Ferdinand Marcos". He lamented: "Ali Baba is gone, but the 40 thieves [corrupt officials] remain".[77]

Aquino's ineffectiveness in curbing corruption was manifested in the declining proportion of those citizens who were satisfied with the performance of her administration in tackling corruption from 72% in March 1987 to 26% in July 1989. In short, Aquino herself had "shared the people's exasperation and despair that she could not achieve the very thing that she wanted to leave as a legacy: a clean and accountable government".[78] According to Reid and Guerrero, Aquino "left behind a mixed legacy" as the "democratic institutions she struggled to rebuild remained flawed and weak. Corruption prevailed, and Filipinos were increasingly cynical about the state of their nation".[79]

The *Tanodbayan* or Office of the Ombudsman was "reborn" in 1988 during Aquino's term of office and she appointed Conrado Vasquez for the position. However, from 1988 to 1995, the Ombudsman "failed to attract much public scrutiny" as the "limelight" was "hogged by the more high-profile *Sandiganbayan*". Thus, instead of "inspiring confidence in the judicial system", the Ombudsman has elicited "only disappointment–if not contempt–among many of those seeking redress for the wrong done them by public officials" as it has taken a long time to process the complaints received by it.[80]

A more serious weakness was caused by the quota system introduced by Vasquez as it encouraged inefficiency as investigators "finished the easier cases first to fulfill their quota" and left the more complex ones "untouched for months, or even years". Consequently, by December 1994, the Ombudsman had accumulated a backlog of

14,652 cases, or 65% of its total workload. Nearly three years later, in August 1997, the Ombudsman still had pending cases dating back to 1979. The *Sandiganbayan's* record is worse than the Ombudsman as it completed only 13% of its total caseload in 1996.[81]

In May 1992, Fidel Ramos was elected president for a six year term. Even though the major focus of his administration was the recovery of the economy, he established the Presidential Commission Against Graft and Corruption (PCAGC) in 1994 to investigate violations of the anti-graft laws by presidential appointees and appointed Eufemio Domingo as its chairman. After serving for three years, Domingo lamented that "the system is not working" because "we are not making it work" for the following reasons:

> We have all the laws, rules and regulations and especially institutions not only to curb, but to eliminate, corruption. The problem is that these laws, rules and regulations are not being faithfully implemented. ... I am afraid that many people are accepting [corruption] as another part of our way of life. Big-time grafters are lionised in society. They are invited to all sorts of social events, elected and re-elected to government offices. It is considered an honor—in fact a social distinction—to have them as guests in family and community affairs.[82]

Joseph Estrada succeeded Ramos as president and in his State of the Nation Address on July 28, 1998, he identified the struggle against graft and corruption as his major priority. In early 1999, he requested the World Bank to make recommendations to help his government strengthen its fight against corruption in the Philippines. The World Bank submitted its preliminary findings in December 1999 and recommended "a national strategy for fighting corruption" in the Philippines by "reducing opportunities and motivation for corruption" and making "corruption a high-risk, low-reward activity".[83]

The *Financial Times* reported in June 2000 that "perceived corruption in the Philippines reached its highest levels in two decades in 1998 and 1999, the first two years of the Estrada administration".[84] Four months later, on October 5, 2000, the Senate Minority Leader, Teofisto Guingona, accused President Estrada of receiving "large cash payouts from *jueteng*, an illegal numbers game". On October 9, 2000, one of Estrada's cronies, Governor Luis Singson, "claimed that he had given the president 400 million pesos (US$10 million) from *jueteng* collections nationwide".[85] Singson's "revelations triggered a major political earthquake".[86]

Lande contends that "it was Estrada's mismanagement of the economy that most decisively turned the upper and middle classes against him". Moreover, the business community did not accept cronyism and its members were disturbed by the preferential treatment given to Estrada's friends. However, "the last straw was the revelation that he himself was brazenly corrupt".[87] The minority members of the House of Representatives initiated impeachment proceedings against the president. During the impeachment trial, Clarissa Ocampo, senior vice-president of PCI-Equitable Bank, informed the court that Estrada, "under a false identity, was the true owner of several bank accounts holding hundred of millions of pesos".[88]

The impeachment trial was covered live by the mass media from December 6, 2000 to January 16, 2001, and it "broke all audience records" because it was "a telenovela that outclassed all the others simply because it was real". This trial became "the single most important educational event on civics and the rule of law in Philippine political history" as it was "a large classroom where the weaknesses of institutions were exposed and the innermost secrets of political corruption revealed".[89]

On January 16, 2001, two pro-Estrada senators prevented "damning evidence" from being revealed in the trial and their action "provoked a firestorm of public outrage. The House prosecutors walked out in disgust. Senate president Pimentel resigned. Civil society exploded in non-violent anger and, acting where the Senate had failed to act, moved over five days of massive demonstrations to force the president from office".[90]

On January 20, 2001, Gloria Macapagal-Arroyo was sworn in as the president by the chief justice after Estrada agreed to resign when the military withdrew its support. In her inaugural speech, President Arroyo emphasised that one of four core beliefs was to "improve moral standards in government and society, in order to provide a strong foundation for good governance". It is, of course, premature to assess

President Arroyo's commitment to minimising corruption in the Philippines as she has been in office only since January 2001. However, Sheila Coronel, Executive Director of the Philippine Center for Investigative Journalism, astutely observed that Arroyo's government was unlikely to be "reformist" as "I was at her headquarters and I could see the old faces coming out, people who have been accused of corruption in the past".[91]

During the second anniversary of her assumption of office, President Arroyo launched a war against corruption and announced that US$55 million would be allocated for her anti-corruption crusade against "entrenched vested interests" or the "corruption of the powerful". As she would not be standing for re-election in 2004, she claimed that she would be more effective in curbing corruption as "a President without the baggage of re-election can move faster, hit harder and work to greater effect". However, President Arroyo's anti-corruption efforts are not supported by all Filipinos as some opposition politicians had filed an impeachment complaint in Congress against her for alleged graft and other offences.[92]

EVALUATION OF ANTI-CORRUPTION STRATEGY

The fact that corruption is a way of life in the Philippines is a clear manifestation of the ineffectiveness of the various anti-corruption measures employed by the various administrations since the 1950s. The systemic and rampant nature of corruption in the Philippines is further corroborated by its consistently low ranking on Transparency International's CPI from 1995 to 2002. Table 4.1 shows the Philippines' ranking on the CPI declined from 36th position in 1995 to 77th position in 2002. Its average rank from 1995-2002 was 55th position.

Why is corruption such a serious problem in the Philippines? The first factor responsible for corruption in the Philippines is the low salaries of the political leaders and civil servants. For example, employees of the Bureau of Immigration are under-qualified and paid "starvation wages." Consequently they find it "difficult to survive without accepting bribes, one way or the other, because nearly everyone is doing it".[93] The monthly salary of the most junior civil servant (salary grade 1, step 1) in 1976 was 286 pesos (US$36) and the monthly salary of the most senior civil servant (salary grade 28, step 8) was 5,935 pesos (US$747).[94] In 1995, the starting salary of US$200 for civil servants in the Philippines was the lowest compared to those of Thailand, Malaysia, Taiwan, Singapore, Hong Kong and Japan. In a survey of public attitudes towards corruption in the Philippines conducted in September 1998, the problem of low salaries was cited most often as the major cause of the corruption.[95]

TABLE 4.1 RANKING OF THE PHILIPPINES ON TRANSPARENCY INTERNATIONAL'S CORRUPTION PERCEPTIONS INDEX, 1995-2002

Year	Ranking	Score	No. of countries
1995	36	2.77	41
1996	44	2.69	54
1997	40	3.05	52
1998	55	3.30	85
1999	54	3.60	99
2000	69	2.80	90
2001	65	2.90	91
2002	77	2.60	102
Average	55	2.96	—

Source: http://www.transparency.org/documents/index.html

Second, the excessive red tape and inefficiency of the Philippine Civil Service has provided ample opportunities for corruption. Indeed, papers in the government are processed in an unsystematic and time-consuming manner. Furthermore, the cumbersome and complicated procedures also slow down paper processing. The filing systems are disorganised and there is no disposal policy for files accumulated for many years. In other words, "there is much room for simplifying procedures in the bureaucracy".[96] Excessive regulations coupled with increased bureaucratic discretion provide opportunities and incentives for corruption as regulations governing access to goods and services are exploited by civil servants to extract "rents" from groups vying for access to these goods and services.[97] Accordingly, businessmen in the Philippines resort to paying "speed money" (bribes) to expedite the processing of their applications for licences or permits from the relevant government agency.[98]

Third, corruption has flourished in the Philippines because of the low risk of detection of corrupt offences and the low probability of punishment for such offences. Palmier uses the term "policing" to refer to "the probability of detection and punishment".[99] Corruption thrives in a country where the public perceives it to be a "low risk, high reward" activity as corrupt offenders are unlikely to be detected and punished. In his memoirs, Senior Minister Lee Kuan Yew of Singapore attributed the lack of punishment of Marcos, his family and cronies for their corrupt activities to the "soft, forgiving culture" of the Philippines. He observed:

> Only in the Philippines could a leader like Ferdinand Marcos, who pillaged his country for over 20 years, still be considered for a national burial. Insignificant amounts of the loot have been recovered, yet his wife and children were allowed to return and engage in politics. ... General Fabian Ver, Marcos's commander-in-chief had fled the Philippines together with Marcos in 1986. When he died in Bangkok, the Estrada government gave the general military honours at his burial.[100]

Robert P. Beschel Jr. observed that sanctions were imposed inconsistently in the Philippines, "with draconian punishment being meted out for relatively minor infractions and major crimes receiving lenient treatment—particularly when they are committed by the rich, the powerful and the politically well-connected".[101] In his comparative analysis of successful prosecution of corrupt offenders in Hong Kong and the Philippines, Beschel found that a person committing a corrupt offence in Hong Kong was 35 times more likely to be detected and punished than his counterpart in the Philippines.[102]

Fourth, the importance of the family and the cultural value of *utang na loob* among Filipinos have made them more tolerant of corruption. This explains why nepotism is prevalent in the Philippines as public officials readily perform favours for their relatives including the appointment of unqualified persons. In the case of education, many people "unfit for the teaching profession end up teaching in and running public schools" and they "pay P3,000 to P5,000 in 'bribes' to ensure their admission and give up one to three months' pay to recompense their *utang na loob* (debt of gratitude) to their superiors when their initial paychecks arrive".[103]

Finally, the lack of political will is responsible for the rampant corruption in the Philippines. Defining "political will" as "the use of the power one has to effect changes desired by the society", Ledivina V. Carino identified six reasons for the lack of political will in curbing corruption in the Philippines. First, the decentralisation of power was not accompanied by regular monitoring and evaluation of the subordinates' performance. Second, the inability of the political elite and senior civil servants to distinguish between public needs and private interests has resulted in many conflicts of interest. Third, officials were not punished for their failure to perform their duties. Fourth, political will was lacking as there was unequal enforcement of the laws. Fifth, political will did not exist as pronouncements were not followed by action. Sixth, political will was absent as adequate manpower and funds were not provided for the implementation of the anti-corruption measures.[104]

CONCLUSION

Corruption will remain a serious problem in the Philippines as long as the five causes mentioned above are not eliminated. The salaries of the civil servants and political leaders are unlikely to be increased substantially as the government would not be able to afford such an expensive strategy. While the opportunities for corruption can be reduced by reducing red tape and improving the efficiency of the civil service by streamlining the cumbersome and complicated administrative procedures, such opportunities will remain as long as low salaries reinforce the need for civil servants to accept "speed money" for expediting the approval of applications for permits. The population's tolerance for corruption is reinforced by the importance of the family and such particularistic values as *utang na loob* in Philippine society. Finally, without political will, the probability of detection and punishment for corrupt offences cannot be enhanced, and the resources required for a comprehensive anti-corruption strategy will not be allocated by the government.

ENDNOTES

1   John Andrews, *Pocket Asia* 7th ed. (London: The Economist Newspaper Ltd. and Profile Books Ltd., 2002), p. 152.

2   Alasdair Bowie and Danny Unger, *The Politics of Open Economies: Indonesia, Malaysia, the Philippines, and Thailand* (Cambridge: Cambridge University Press, 1997), p. 98.

3   See ibid., pp. 98-128 for a useful analysis.

4   David Joel Steinberg, *The Philippines: A Singular and A Plural Place* (Boulder: Westview Press, 1982), p. 8; and Andrews, *Pocket Asia*, p. 152.

5   Ledivina V. Carino, "The Land and the People", in Raul P. de Guzman and Mila A. Reforma (eds.), *Government and Politics of the Philippines* (Singapore: Oxford University Press, 1988), pp. 4-5.

6   David G. Timberman, *A Changeless Land: Continuity and Change in Philippine Politics* (Singapore: Institute of Southeast Asian Studies, 1991), p. 4.

7   Carino, "The Land and the People," p. 5.

8   Timberman, *A Changeless Land*, p. 6.

9   Bowie and Unger, *The Politics of Open Economies*, p. 99.

10   Andrews, *Pocket Asia*, pp. 158-159.

11   Ibid., p. 160.

12   Mel C. Labrador, "The Philippines in 2001: High Drama, a New President, and Setting the Stage for Recovery", *Asian Survey*, Vol. 42, No. 1 (January/ February 2002), p. 145.

13   David Wurfel, *Filipino Politics: Development and Decay* (Ithaca: Cornell University Press, 1988), p. 53.

14   Labrador, "The Philippines in 2001", *Asian Survey*, Vol. 42, No. 1 (January/ February 2002), p. 145.

15   Helen Cabalu, *The Development Experience of the Philippines: A Case of What Not to Do* (Canberra: Economics Division Working Paper No. 94/2, Research School of Pacific and Asian Studies, Australian National University, 1994), p. 1.

16   Ibid., p. 30.

17   Ibid., p. 1.

18   Clark D. Neher, *Southeast Asia in the New International Era* (Boulder: Westview Press, 2002), p. 98.

19   Ibid., p. 98.

20   Andrews, *Pocket Asia*, p. 161.

21   Ibid., p. 158.

22   Timberman, *A Changeless Land*, p. 5.

23   Andrews, *Pocket Asia*, p. 158.

24   Timberman, *A Changeless Land*, p. 6.

25   Ibid., p. 16.

26   Alfredo and Grace Roces, *Culture Shock Philippines* (Singapore: Times Books International, 1985), p. 41.

27   Quoted in Alfred W. McCoy, "An Anarchy of Families': The Historiography of State and Family in the Philippines", in Alfred W. McCoy (ed.), *An Anarchy of Families: State and Family in the Philippines* (Quezon City: Ateneo De Manila University Press, 1994), p. 7.

28   Carino, "The Land and the People", p. 9.

29   Richard L. Langston, *Bribery and the Bible: Applied to the Philippines* (Singapore: Campus Crusade Asia Limited, 1991), p. 71.

30   Ibid., pp. 71-72.

31   Gaudioso C. Sosmena, Jr., *Breaking the Cocoon: Bureaucracy Reborn* (Manila: Local Government Development Foundation, 1995), p. 13.

32   Alfredo and Grace Roces, *Culture Shock Philippines*, p. 41.

33   Jean Grossholz, *Politics in the Philippines* (Boston: Little Brown and Company, 1964), pp. 86-87.

34   Socorro C. Espiritu *et al.*, *Sociology in the New Philippine Setting* (Quezon City: Alemar-Phoenix Publishing House Inc., 1977), p. 74, quoted in Langston, *Bribery and the Bible*, p. 78.

35   Ibid., pp. 74 and 285, quoted in Langston, *Bribery and the Bible*, pp. 78-79.

36   Homi J. Kharas, "The Philippines: Three Decades of Lost Opportunities", in Danny M. Leipziger (ed.), *Lessons from East Asia* (Ann Arbor: University of Michigan Press, 1997), p. 471.

37   Andrews, *Pocket Asia*, p. 155.

38   Kharas, "The Philippines", pp. 472-473.

39   Jon S.T. Quah, "Bureaucratic Corruption in the ASEAN Countries: A Comparative Analysis of Their Anti-Corruption Strategies", *Journal of Southeast Asian Studies*, Vol. 13, No. 1 (March 1982), p. 158.

40   Onofre D. Corpuz, *The Bureaucracy in the Philippines* (Manila: College of Public Administration, University of the Philippines, 1957), pp. 111-112.

41   Jose N. Endriga, "Historical Notes on Graft and Corruption in the Philippines", *Philippine Journal of Public Administration*, Vol. 23, Nos. 3-4 (July-October 1979), pp. 247-249.

42   Corpuz, *The Bureaucracy in the Philippines*, p. 129.

43   Ibid., p. 169.

44   Endriga, "Historical Notes on Graft and Corruption in the Philippines", p. 254.

45   Corpuz, *The Bureaucracy in the Philippines*, pp. 222-223.

102

46 Ma. Concepcion P. Alfiler, "Administrative Measures against Bureaucratic Corruption: The Philippine Experience", *Philippine Journal of Public Administration*, Vol. 23, Nos. 3-4 (July-October 1979), p. 323.

47 Quoted in Quah, "Bureaucratic Corruption in the ASEAN Countries", p. 160.

48 Harvey A. Averech, John E. Koehler, and Frank H. Denton, *The Matrix of Policy in the Philippines* (Princeton: Princeton University Press, 1971), p. 31, Table 10.

49 Ibid., pp. 31-32.

50 Ibid., p. 33, Table 12.

51 Raul P. de Guzman *et al.*, "The Bureaucracy", in de Guzman and Reforma (eds.), *Government and Politics of the Philippines*, p. 197.

52 Timberman, *A Changeless Land*, pp. 25 and 104.

53 Amelia P. Varela, "Different Faces of Filipino Administrative Culture", in Proserpina Domingo Tapales and Nestor N. Pilar (eds.), *Public Administration by the Year 2000: Looking Back into the Future* (Quezon City: College of Public Administration, University of the Philippines, 1995), pp. 173-174.

54 Joel Rocamora, "Corruption in the Philippines: A Beginner's Guide", in S.S. Coronel (ed.), *Pork and Other Perks: Corruption and Governance in the Philippines* (Quezon City: Philippine Center for Investigative Journalism, 1998), pp. 22-23.

55 Nigel Cawthorne, "Imelda Marcos and the Scandal of the Shoes", in his book, *The World's Greatest Political Scandals* (London: Chancellor Press, 1999), p. 134.

56 Ibid., p. 132.

57 Carmen Navarro Pedrosa, *Imelda Marcos: The Rise and Fall of the World's Most Powerful Woman* (New York: St. Martin's Press, 1987), p. 222.

58 Belinda A. Aquino, *Politics of Plunder: The Philippines under Marcos* (Manila: Great Books Trading and College of Public Administration, University of the Philippines, 1987), pp. 116-117.

59 Mark R. Thompson, "The Marcos Regime in the Philippines", in H.E. Chehabi and Juan J. Linz (eds.), *Sultanistic Regimes* (Baltimore: The John Hopkins University Press, 1998), pp. 206-229.

60 Yvonne T. Chua, *Robbed: An Investigation of Corruption in Philippine Education* (Quezon City: Philippine Center for Investigative Journalism, 1999), p. 1.

61 Ibid., p. 3.

62 Ibid., p. 11.

63 Elena R. Torrijos, "$48B lost to graft in 20 years—WB", *Philippine Daily Inquirer*, December 2, 1999, p. 4; and Nicholas Nugent, "High Cost of Corruption in Philippines", *BBC News*, December 6, 2000. See http://news.bbc.co.uk/hi/english/world/asia-pacific/newsid_1057000/1057716.stm.

64 Quah, "Bureaucratic Corruption in the ASEAN Countries", p. 159.

65 Alfiler, "Administrative Measures against Bureaucratic Corruption", pp. 324-325.

66 Ibid., pp. 331-337.

67 For an account of how this law was passed, see Gabriel U. Iglesias, "The Passage of the Anti-Graft Law", in Raul P. De Guzman (ed.), *Patterns in Decision-Making: Case Studies in Philippine Public Administration* (Manila: College of Public Administration, University of the Philippines, 1963), pp. 17-68.

68 Alfiler, "Administrative Measures against Bureaucratic Corruption", pp. 339-346.

69 Timberman, *A Changeless Land*, p. 75.

70 Alfiler, "Administrative Measures against Bureaucratic Corruption", pp. 326-327.

71 Hilton L. Root, *Small Countries, Big Lessons: Governance and the Rise of East Asia* (Hong Kong: Oxford University Press for the Asian Development Bank, 1996), p. 116.

72 Ibid., p. 116.

73 Jon S.T. Quah, *Comparing Anti-Corruption Measures in Asian Countries* (Singapore: Centre for Advanced Studies, National University of Singapore, CAS Research Paper Series No. 13, 1999), p. 19.

74 Quah, "Bureaucratic Corruption in the ASEAN Countries", pp. 168-169.

75 Varela, "Different Faces of Filipino Administrative Culture", p. 174.

76 Timberman, *A Changeless Land*, p. 235.

77 "Govt files graft charges against Aquino's uncle", *Straits Times*, November 7, 1987, p. 44.

78 Ledivina V. Carino, "Enhancing Accountability in the Philippines: The Continuing Quest", in John P. Burns (ed.), *Asian Civil Service Systems: Improving Efficiency and Productivity* (Singapore: Times Academic Press, 1994), p. 113.

79 Robert H. Reid and Eileen Guerrero, *Corazon Aquino and the Brushfire Revolution* (Baton Rouge: Louisiana State University Press, 1995), p. 2.

80 Cecile C.A. Balgos, "Ombudsman", in Coronel (ed.), *Pork and Other Perks*, pp. 247-248.

81 Ibid., pp. 250-251.

82 Ibid., pp. 267-268.

83 Vinay Bhargava, "Combating Corruption in the Philippines", (Manila: Philippine Country Management Unit, World Bank, 1999), pp. 1 and 5.

84 Carl H. Lande, "The Return of 'People Power' in the Philippines", *Journal of Democracy*, Vol. 12, No. 2 (April 2001), p. 92.

85 Ibid., p. 92.

86 Alexander R. Magno, "Philippines: Trauma of a Failed Presidency", in *Southeast Asian Affairs 2001* (Singapore: Institute of Southeast Asian Studies, 2001), p. 259.

87 Lande, "The Return of 'People Power' in the Philippines", p. 92.

88 Magno, "Philippines: Trauma of a Failed Presidency", p. 251.

89 Ibid., pp. 260 and 262.

90 Lande, "The Return of 'People Power' in the Philippines", p. 94.

91 Deidre Sheehan, "More Power to the Powerful", *Far Eastern Economic Review*, February 1, 2001, p. 17.

92 "Arroyo launches anti-corruption drive on anniversary of popular uprising", *Channel News Asia* (Singapore), February 8, 2003.

93 Yvonne T. Chua and Luz Rimban, "Gatekeeper", in Coronel (ed.), *Pork and Other Perks*, p. 154.

94 Filemon U. Fernandez Jr., "The Civil Service System in the Philippines", in Amara Raksasataya and Heinrich Siedentopf (eds.), *Asian Civil Services* (Kuala Lumpur: Asian Pacific Development Administration Centre, 1980), p. 422.

95 Robert P. Beschel Jr., "Corruption, Transparency and Accountability in the Philippines", (Manila: Unpublished report prepared for the Asian Development Bank, 1999), p. 9.

96 Raul P. de Guzman, Alex B. Brillantes, Jr., and Arturo G. Pacho, "The Bureaucracy", in de Guzman and Reforma (eds.), *Government and Politics of the Philippines*, p. 199.

97 David J. Gould and Jose A. Amaro-Reyes, *The Effects of Corruption on Administrative Performance: Illustrations from Developing Countries* (Washington, D.C.: World Bank Staff Working Papers No. 580, 1983), p. 17.

98 De Guzman *et al.*, "The Bureaucracy", p. 198.

99 Leslie Palmier, *The Control of Bureaucratic Corruption: Case Studies in Asia* (New Delhi: Allied Publishers, 1985), p. 271.

100 Lee Kuan Yew, *From Third World to First, The Singapore Story: 1965-2000* (Singapore: Times Media Private Ltd., 2000), pp. 342-343.

101 Beschel, "Corruption, Transparency and Accountability in the Philippines", p. 8.

102 "In 1997, Hong Kong's Independent Commission Against Commission successfully prosecuted approximately 8.24 cases per 10,000 civil servants. In the Philippines, the comparable figure is less than 0.25 per 10,000". Ibid., p. 8.

103 Chua, *Robbed*, p. 10.

104 Ledivina V. Carino, "Enhancing Accountability in the Philippines: The Continuing Quest", in John P. Burns (ed.), *Asian Civil Service Systems* (Singapore: Times Academic Press, 1995), pp. 115-118.

CHAPTER 5

Singapore

INTRODUCTION

Corruption is a serious problem in many Asian countries but Singapore is the least corrupt country in Asia according to the annual surveys conducted by Transparency International and the PERC from 1995-2002 as shown in Chapter 1. However, the situation was quite different in Singapore during the British colonial period, when corruption was a way of life as it was perceived by the public as a low risk, high reward activity as corrupt officials were seldom caught, and even if they were caught, they were not severely punished.

Singapore's battle against corruption began in 1871, when it was made illegal with the enactment of the Penal Code of the Straits Settlements. As will be discussed below, corruption remained a serious problem throughout the colonial period as the British failed to curb it. The breakthrough came in 1960, when the People's Action Party (PAP) government enacted the Prevention of Corruption Act (POCA), which gave the Corrupt Practices Investigation Bureau (CPIB) more powers to fight corruption.

How did the PAP government minimise corruption in Singapore after assuming power in June 1959? Why is corruption no longer a way of life but a fact of life in contemporary Singapore? To answer these questions, it is necessary to discuss in turn the policy context, the extent and causes of corruption in Singapore during the colonial period, the major features of Singapore's anti-corruption strategy, and the evaluation of this strategy.

POLICY CONTEXT

Geography

Singapore is a city-state consisting of a main island and 63 offshore islands with a total land area of 682.3 sq. km. The majority of the population live on the main island, which is 42 km long and 23 km wide and has a coastline of 150.5 km. The rural sector is negligible as Singapore is highly urbanised and only 9.8 sq. km are farms.[1] This means that Singapore has no natural resources except for its strategic location, deep harbour and resourceful people. Singapore's small land area also implies that there is no large rural hinterland to permit the cultivation of crops or the mining of minerals.

Singapore's compactness and its high degree of urbanisation have assisted the policy-making process in four ways. First, Singapore's small size is advantageous for policy formulation and implementation since communication is seldom a problem and serves to facilitate political control by the leadership. Second, the city-state's compactness enhances administrative coordination and integration and enhances the responsiveness of public officials. Third, unlike Indonesia and Malaysia, Singapore's diminutiveness has contributed to a highly centralised public bureaucracy, which is immune from the problems afflicting a federal bureaucracy in its interaction with the state or provincial bureaucracies. Finally, apart from reinforcing the centralised nature of the public bureaucracy, the absence of a large rural sector means that Singapore is not burdened by problems arising from rural-urban migration, or from rural development programmes as such programmes are not needed.[2] In short, Singapore's small size makes it easy for the CPIB to enforce the POCA.

Economy

Singapore developed rapidly after launching its industrialisation programme and establishing the Economic Development Board (EDB) in August 1961 to promote economic development by attracting foreign investment. Its rapid economic growth during the past four decades has transformed the economy from a purely entrepot economy to an entrepot-manufacturing economy. More specifically, Singapore's per capita GDP has increased from S$1,330 in 1960 to S$33,551 in 2001.[3]

In addition to promoting industrialisation and foreign investment, the PAP government dealt with the absence of natural resources by investing in education to develop the nation's human resources and by developing Singapore into a regional centre for financial, communications, medical and other services. Singapore's heavy investment in education has contributed to a high literacy rate of 92.5%,[4] the best workforce in the world since 1980, and indirectly to political stability as education is an important channel for upward social mobility.[5]

Demography

In June 2001, Singapore had a total population of 4,131,200 persons and a resident population of 3,319,100. It is densely populated with 6,502 persons per sq. km, making Singapore the third most densely populated place in the world after Macau and Hong Kong.[6] The population is heterogeneous in terms of ethnicity, language and religion.

The resident population is multi-racial and consists of 76.7% Chinese, 13.9% Malays, 7.9% Indians, and 1.5% Others. Similarly, it is multi-lingual as apart from the four official languages (English, Mandarin, Malay and Tamil), there are several Chinese dialects (Hokkien, Teochew, Cantonese, Hainanese, Hakka and Foochow) and Telegu, Malayalam, Punjabi, Hindu, and Bengali are spoken by the ethnic Indians. There is also great diversity in religion among the population as Buddhists and Taoists constitute the majority (54%), followed by Muslims (15%), atheists (14%), Christians (13%) and Hindus (4%).

The population's diversity in race, language and religion requires the incumbent government in Singapore to formulate and implement policies for encouraging and promoting racial harmony. A second obligation of the government in a plural society is to ensure that both public and private organisations are fair and impartial in the treatment of their clienteles, regardless of their ethnic origin, language or religion. In other words, there is no room for discrimination of any sort in these organisations. Accordingly, there is a Presidential Council for Minority Rights, which examines bills presented to Parliament to ensure that minority rights are protected. In addition, a Presidential Council for Religious Harmony was created to maintain religious harmony.

Political System

Singapore was a British colony for nearly 140 years and attained self-government peacefully in June 1959. This peaceful transfer of power is significant because it left intact the infrastructure developed by the British and spared the population from the bloodshed and turmoil that would have resulted from a violent transfer of power. The legacy of British colonial legacy is the tradition of meritocracy introduced in January 1951 with the establishment of the Public Service Commission to ensure that candidates are recruited to the Singapore Civil Service on the basis of merit.

The PAP won the May 1959 general election and assumed office in June 1959. Since then, the PAP has been re-elected 10 times, with the most recent general election held on November 3, 2001, where the PAP won 81 of the 83 parliamentary seats. Thus, the most important feature of Singapore's political system is the PAP's predominance which can be attributed to its success in delivering the goods and services to the population and the resulting reservoir of legitimacy accumulated during the past four decades.[7]

In short, the PAP's long term of uninterrupted rule of nearly 44 years has contributed to the effectiveness of the public bureaucracy and to a predictable style of policy-making. This political continuity has enabled the PAP government to enforce impartially the POCA.

EXTENT OF CORRUPTION

In 1879, a Commission of Inquiry was appointed to find out why the Singapore Police Force (SPF) was inefficient. This Commission found, *inter alia*, that corruption existed among both the European inspectors and the Malay and Indian policemen. Similarly, the 1886 Commission appointed to investigate public gambling in the Straits Settlements confirmed that police corruption was rampant.[8] As cases of police corruption were reported in the local press, an analysis of the *Straits Times* from 1845 to 1921 showed that 172 cases were reported during this period. Bribery was the most common form of police corruption (109 cases or 63.4%) followed by 42 cases (24.4%) of involvement in such direct criminal activities as theft and robbery.[9]

Corruption was also widespread during the Japanese occupation (1942-1945) as the rampant inflation made it difficult for civil servants to live on their fixed salaries. The situation deteriorated during the post-war period as "corruption had also become a way of life for many people" to enable them to cope with their low salaries and rising inflation.[10] Indeed, the British Military Administration (BMA), which took over after the Japanese surrender in August 1945, was also referred to derisively as the "Black Market Administration". Finally, in his 1950 Annual Report, the Commissioner of Police indicated that graft was rife in government departments in Singapore.[11]

What were the causes of corruption in colonial Singapore? Following Palmier's analysis, which was discussed in Chapter 1, low salaries, ample opportunities and weak policing were responsible for the rampant corruption in colonial Singapore.

Low salaries

The most important factor responsible for police corruption in colonial Singapore was the low salaries of the policemen, especially those in the lower ranks. Table 5.1 shows the range of salaries for both the European and local members of the SPF in 1887. This table clearly demonstrates the lower salaries of the native contingent, as the monthly salaries of the ranks of Sergeant and Constable for the European contingent were more than three times those of their local counterparts. Given the poor salaries of the policemen, it was not surprising that the *Straits Times* made this comment: "It is at once evident that the native constables and the European police of the Inspector class are so underpaid that scandals are unavoidable".[12]

TABLE 5.1 MONTHLY SALARY IN THE SINGAPORE POLICE FORCE BY RANK, 1887

Rank in SPF	Monthly Salary
European Contingent	
Inspector 1st Class	S$100 (no rations)
Inspector 2nd Class	S$80 (S$5 rations)
Inspector 3rd Class	S$60 (S$10 rations)
Sergeant	S$50 (S$10 rations)
Constable	S$40 (S$10 rations)
Native Contingent	
Sergeant	S$15
Corporal	S$12
Constable 1st Class	S$10
Constable 2nd Class	S$9
Constable 3rd Class	S$8
Peon 1st Class	S$5
Peon 2nd Class	S$4

Source: *Straits Times*, October 4, 1887.

Ample opportunities for corruption

In addition to low salaries, a second reason for police corruption in Singapore during the colonial period was the inadequate controls over policemen in those areas most vulnerable to temptation. Indeed, the many cases of police involvement in illegal gambling were symptomatic of the lack of controls over those inspectors and constables who took bribes from the gambling house owners.

In April 1846, an European constable, Charles Cashin, was convicted of receiving bribes from illicit gambling dens and sentenced

111

to 18 months' imprisonment. Cashin reported that for the past three years all the constables in the SPF had received S$20 each monthly, and that the constable who had brought the charge against him had also received bribes himself.[13] The Deputy Superintendent of Police, Thomas Dunman, admitted in court that the police were in the regular pay of gambling promoters and that it was difficult to rectify the situation.[14] In June 1849, the *Straits Times* observed that the police did not take action to suppress gambling activities conducted within 50 yards of a police station in town because the policemen were paid for their silence.[15] Finally, it is surprising that even though the 1886 Commission of Inquiry confirmed the existence of widespread police corruption in gambling activities, nothing was done to prevent the policemen from being involved in illegal gambling activities.

Another reason why members of the SPF had many opportunities for corruption during the colonial period was the fact that many local policemen had other jobs too even though they were not allowed to do so. Indeed, as many of them owned buffalo carts and food stalls they were unable to perform their official duties impartially and were exposed to more opportunities for misbehaviour.[16]

Apart from the police, other government agencies like the customs, immigration and internal revenue departments provided more opportunities for corruption than those public agencies that had limited contact with members of the public, did not issue licences or permits, or collected fees or taxes. Indeed, corruption in colonial Singapore was not confined to the SPF only, but was widespread throughout the entire public bureaucracy. Conditions deteriorated during the post-war period as their low salaries and inflation increased the civil servants' need to be corrupt on the one hand, while their poor supervision by their superior officers provided them with many opportunities for corrupt behaviour with minimal risk of being caught, on the other hand.[17]

Low risk of detection and punishment

What accounted for the low risk of detecting and punishing corrupt offences in colonial Singapore? The British colonial government's efforts to curb corruption failed because the Prevention of Corruption Ordinance (POCO) and the Anti-Corruption Branch (ACB) were ineffective.

Although corruption was made illegal in 1871 in Singapore, nothing was done for the next 66 years until December 1937, when the first anti-corruption law was introduced with the enactment of the POCO. The POCO's rationale was "the prevention of bribery and secret commissions in public and private business". The POCO was a short document consisting of 12 sections. Section 3 identified three instances of corrupt behaviour and specified the penalty for those found guilty of corruption as a prison term of two years and/or a fine of S$10,000. As corrupt offences were not seizable offences given the short prison term of two years, this limited the powers of arrest, search and investigation of the police as warrants were required before arrests could be made. It took another nine years before the POCO was amended in 1946 to increase the penalty to a prison term of three years, thus making corrupt offences seizable ones and automatically gave police officers "much wider powers of arrest, search and investigation".[18]

The ACB of the Criminal Investigation Department (CID), which was responsible for combating corruption in colonial Singapore, was ineffective for three reasons. First, the ACB was a small police unit consisting of 17 men who were given a difficult task to perform i.e., the eradication of corruption in the SPF and other government departments. Second, the ACB had to compete with the other sections of the CID for limited manpower and other resources. Indeed, the Assistant Commissioner of the CID was responsible for 16 duties, including checking corrupt behaviour, secret societies, gambling promoters, fraud (commercial crime), anti-vice (traffickers), pawnshops, second-hand dealers, narcotics (traffickers), criminal records, banishment, naturalisation, missing persons, fingerprints, photography, police gazette, house-to-house and street collections.[19]

The third and most important reason for the ACB's ineffectiveness was the prevalence of police corruption in colonial Singapore. In October 1951, a consignment of 1,800 pounds of opium worth S$400,000 was stolen by a gang of robbers, which included three police detectives.[20] A special team appointed by the British colonial government and headed by a senior Malayan Civil Service officer was formed to investigate the robbery. The team found that there was widespread police corruption especially among those policemen involved in protection rackets. Unfortunately, not all the senior police officers were prosecuted as some of them were not convicted because of insufficient evidence. When the investigation was completed, only an Assistant Superintendent of Police was dismissed and another officer retired.[21]

This opium hijacking scandal made the British colonial government realise the importance and value of creating an independent anti-corruption agency that would be separate from the police. Accordingly, it replaced the ACB with the special team as an independent agency to curb corruption in Singapore. Thus, the ACB's failure to curb corruption in colonial Singapore led to its demise and the formation of the CPIB in October 1952.

ANTI-CORRUPTION STRATEGY

As corruption was rife during the colonial period, the newly-elected PAP government realised in June 1959 that it had to curb the problem of corruption in order to ensure that the Singapore Civil Service (SCS) attained the country's development goals. Indeed, its commitment to the elimination of corruption in Singapore was a major reason for its victory in the May 1959 general election.

After winning the December 1957 City Council election on its platform of curbing corruption, the PAP launched its electoral campaign by revealing that the Labour Front's Minister for Education, Chew Swee Kee, had corruptly accepted political funds from the United States government to defeat the PAP in the 1959 general election. The Chief Minister, Lim Yew Hock, appointed a commission of inquiry to investigate this scandal. During the investigation, Chew admitted that he had received, with his party's knowledge, a total of S$700,000 (or US$233,000) on two occasions

114

from the United States government. Chew's confession of his corrupt dealings sealed his party's fate and enabled the PAP to win the May 1959 general election.[22]

In his memoirs, former Prime Minister Lee Kuan Yew, explained his government's commitment to curbing corruption thus:

> When the PAP government took office in 1959, we set out to have a clean administration. We were sickened by the greed, corruption and decadence of many Asian leaders. … We had a deep sense of mission to establish a clean and effective government. When we took the oath of office at the ceremony in the city council chamber in June 1959, we all wore white shirts and white slacks to symbolise purity and honesty in our personal behaviour and our public life. … We made sure from the day we took office in June 1959 that every dollar in revenue would be properly accounted for and would reach the beneficiaries at the grass roots as one dollar, without being siphoned off along the way.[23]

The PAP leaders also realised that they could not minimise corruption if they had continued with the British colonial government's incremental anti-corruption strategy. Accordingly, their immediate tasks were twofold: to minimise corruption and to change the public perception of corruption from a low risk, high reward activity to a high risk, low reward activity. The PAP leaders initiated a comprehensive anti-corruption strategy in 1960 by enacting the POCA and strengthening the CPIB. Since corruption is caused by both the incentives and opportunities to be corrupt, the PAP government's comprehensive strategy is based on the "logic of corruption control" as "attempts to eradicate corruption must be designed to minimise or remove the conditions of both the incentives and opportunities that make individual corrupt behaviour irresistible".[24]

Prevention of Corruption Act

In 1960, Singapore was a poor country as its GDP per capita was S$1,330 or US$443.[25] As the PAP government could not afford to

115

raise the salaries of the civil servants, it focused on strengthening the existing legislation to reduce the opportunities for corruption and to increase the penalty for corrupt behaviour.

The POCA, which was enacted on June 17, 1960, had five important features to eliminate the POCO's deficiencies and to empower the CPIB in performing its duties. First, the POCA's scope was increased as it had 32 sections in contrast to the POCO's 12 sections.[26] Second, corruption was explicitly defined in terms of the various forms of "gratification" in section 2, which also identified for the first time the CPIB and its Director. Third, to enhance the POCA's deterrent effect, the penalty for corruption was increased to imprisonment for five years and/or a fine of S$10,000 (section 5).[27] Fourth, a person found guilty of accepting an illegal gratification had to pay the amount he had taken as a bribe in addition to any other punishment imposed by a court (section 13). The fifth and most significant feature of the POCA was that it gave the CPIB more powers and a new lease of life. For example, section 15 provided CPIB officers with powers of arrest and search of arrested persons. Section 17 empowered the Public Prosecutor to authorise the CPIB's Director and his senior staff to investigate "any bank account, share account or purchase account" of any one suspected of having committed an offence against the POCA. Section 18 enabled the CPIB officers to inspect a civil servant's banker's book and those of his wife, child or agent, if necessary.

To ensure the POCA's effectiveness, the PAP government amended it whenever necessary or when it needed to introduce new legislation to deal with unanticipated problems. In 1963, the POCA was amended to empower CPIB officers to require the attendance of witnesses and to question them. The aim of this amendment was to enable CPIB officers to obtain the co-operation of witnesses to help them in their investigations. Two important amendments were introduced in 1966 to further strengthen the POCA. The first amendment (section 28) stated that a person could be found guilty of corruption even though he did not actually receive the bribe, as the intention on his part to commit the offence constituted sufficient grounds for his conviction. The second amendment (section 35) was directed at those Singaporeans working for their government in embassies and other government agencies abroad as Singapore citizens would be prosecuted for corrupt offences committed outside Singapore and would be dealt with as if such offences had occurred in Singapore.[28]

In 1981, the POCA was amended for the third time to increase its deterrent effect by requiring those convicted of corruption to repay all the money received besides facing the usual court sentence. Those who were unable to make full restitution would be given heavier court sentences.[29] On December 14, 1986, the then Minister for National Development, Teh Cheang Wan, committed suicide 12 days after he was interrogated for 16 hours by two senior CPIB officers regarding two allegations of corruption against him by a building contractor. Teh was accused of accepting two bribes amounting to S$1 million in 1981 and 1982 from two developers to enable one of them to retain his land which had been acquired by the government, and to assist the other developer in purchasing State land for private development.[30] An important consequence of the Commission of Inquiry that followed was the enactment on March 3, 1989 of the Corruption (Confiscation of Benefits) Act 1989, which was concerned with the confiscation of benefits derived from corruption. If a defendant is deceased, the court would issue a confiscation order against his estate.

Corrupt Practices Investigation Bureau

The CPIB is the anti-corruption agency responsible for enforcing the POCA's provisions. It has grown by nearly 17 times from five officers in 1952 to its present establishment of 84 officers, comprising investigators and clerical and support staff. Table 5.2 shows the growth of the CPIB's personnel from 1952 to 2001. Even though the CPIB has increased its manpower during the last five decades, it is a small agency on two counts: first, in terms of the current size of the Singapore Civil Service (SCS) (62,739), the CPIB's personnel constitute only 0.13%; and second, compared to the Independent

117

Commission Against Corruption (ICAC) in Hong Kong, the ICAC
has 15 times more staff than the CPIB.[31] Thus, unlike Hong Kong's
ICAC, the CPIB is much smaller in size and does not need a large
staff even though it has a heavy workload, as its location within the
Prime Minister's Office and its legal powers enable the CPIB to obtain
the required co-operation from both public and private organisations.

TABLE 5.2 GROWTH OF CPIB'S PERSONNEL, 1952-2001

Year	No. of Personnel
1952	5
1959	8
1962	9
1963	33
1968	40
1970/71	50
1976/77	61
1980/81	69
1985/86	65
1990/91	62
1995/96	67
1998/99	79
2000/01	84
2001/02	84

Source: Compiled from Jon S.T. Quah, *Administrative and Legal Measures for
Combatting Bureaucratic Corruption in Singapore* (Singapore: Department of Political
Science, University of Singapore, Occasional Paper No. 34, 1978), p. 17, Table 2 and
Republic of Singapore, *The Budget for the Financial Years 1980/81 to 2001/02*
(Singapore: Budget Division, Ministry of Finance, 1981-2002), various pages.

The CPIB performs three functions: (1) to receive and investigate
complaints concerning corruption in the public and private sectors;
(2) to investigate malpractices and misconduct by public officers; and
(3) to examine the practices and procedures in the public service to
minimise opportunities for corrupt practices.[32]

The CPIB's organisational structure is divided into three
branches. The largest branch is the Investigation Branch which has

four units, each headed by a Senior Assistant Director or an Assistant Director who is responsible for directing and supervising the investigations undertaken by his subordinate officers. Investigation papers prepared by the investigators are submitted to the Director, who reviews the evidence and makes appropriate recommendations to the Public Prosecutor, whose consent is required for prosecution under the POCA. When there is insufficient evidence to prosecute civil servants in court, these officials are referred to their head of department for disciplinary action.[33]

The Data Management and Support Branch manages the CPIB's Computer Information System which enables the CPIB to formulate its corruption prevention strategies and to screen candidates for public appointments, promotions, scholarships and training courses, applicants for citizenship, and contractors competing for government contracts. It consists of two support units: the Research Unit and the Intelligence Unit. The Research Unit reviews the work procedures of corruption-prone departments to reduce the opportunities for corruption and examines completed cases to identify the *modus operandi* of corrupt civil servants. The Intelligence Unit provides the intelligence required for meeting the Investigation Branch's operational needs.[34]

The Administration Branch provides secretarial support to the other two branches and is responsible for the financial and personnel administration of the CPIB.[35] Unlike the ICAC, the CPIB does not have a Community Relations Department to publicise its activities or educate the public on the negative consequences of corruption. In 1986, S. Chandra Mohan contended that "the CPIB plainly does not see the need to give publicity to its existence in order to encourage the public to come forward with information to the Bureau or even to create public awareness of Singapore's anti-corruption laws" as the CPIB "has already won both public recognition and confidence with an impressive record for law enforcement" during 1952-1986.[36] He further justified the CPIB's neglect of public relations by arguing that "because of existing public support for the Bureau's work, it might be considered offensive to maintain a campaign to publicise the Bureau's existence or to exhort the public not to offer bribes to the extent as is done in Hong Kong, in posters and advertisements, or even to educate the citizens on Singapore's anti-corruption laws".[37]

Improving Civil Service Salaries

The PAP government was only able to implement the second prong of its comprehensive anti-corruption strategy–the reduction of incentives for corruption by means of improving salaries and working conditions in the SCS–in the 1980s long after it had achieved economic growth. The improvement in wages began in March 1972, when all civil servants were given a 13th-month non-pensionable allowance comparable to the bonus in the private sector.[38] The rationale for this allowance was not to curb corruption but to prevent the brain drain of talented civil servants to the private sector by enhancing working conditions in the SCS *vis-à-vis* the private sector.

In March 1985, the then Prime Minister Lee Kuan Yew justified his government's approach to combating corruption by reducing or removing the incentives for corruption through the improvement of the salaries of political leaders and senior civil servants when he explained why the wages of the cabinet ministers had to be raised. He contended that political leaders should be paid the top salaries that they deserved in order to ensure a clean and honest government. If they were underpaid, they would succumb to temptation and indulge in corruption. Lee contended that Singapore needed a corruption-free administration and an honest political leadership to preserve its most precious assets. He concluded that the best way of dealing with corruption was "moving with the market," which is "an honest, open, defensible and workable system" instead of hypocrisy, which results in duplicity and corruption.[39]

In addition to reducing the incentives for corruption, the PAP government had to improve the salaries and working conditions in the SCS to stem the brain drain of competent senior civil servants to the private sector by offering competitive salaries and fringe benefits to reduce the gap between the public and private sectors. Accordingly, the salaries of civil servants in Singapore were increased in 1973, 1979, 1982, 1989 and 1994 to reduce the brain drain to the private sector and the gap between salaries in the two sectors.

In October 1994, a *White Paper on Competitive Salaries for Competent and Honest Government* was presented to Parliament to justify the pegging of the salaries of ministers and senior civil servants to the average salaries of the top four earners in six private sector professions: accounting, banking, engineering, law, local manufacturing companies and multinational corporations. The White Paper recommended the introduction of formal salary benchmarks for ministers and senior bureaucrats, additional salary grades for political appointments and annual salary reviews for the SCS. The adoption of the long-term formula suggested in the White Paper will eliminate the justification of the salaries of ministers and senior bureaucrats "from scratch with each salary revision" as well as ensure the building of "an efficient public service and a competent and honest political leadership, which have been vital for Singapore's prosperity and success".[40]

The 1989 and 1994 salary revisions have increased the salaries of senior civil servants in Singapore to such a high level that they are earning perhaps the highest salaries in the world compared to their counterparts in other countries. Table 5.3 shows the monthly salary for Superscale Officers in the Singapore Administrative Service in 1994. For example, the monthly salary for a permanent secretary in Staff Grade V is S$51,155 (or US$30,091), which is more than four times that of the top monthly salary of GS-18 (the highest salary scale for the United States Federal Service) of US$7,224 (S$12,280).[41]

In 1996, the salaries of ministers and senior civil servants were increased as both benchmarks went up. However, the Asian financial crisis in 1997 and the subsequent slowing down of the Singapore economy resulted in a 2% decrease in Superscale G and a 7% decrease in Staff Grade I salaries because of the reduction of the employers' contribution to the Central Provident Fund from 20% to 10% for all employees, including ministers and senior civil servants.[42]

TABLE 5.3 MONTHLY SALARY OF SUPERSCALE OFFICERS IN THE SINGAPORE ADMINISTRATIVE SERVICE IN 1994

Grade	Monthly Salary (US$)*
Permanent Secretary	
Staff Grade V	S$51,155 (US$30,091)
Staff Grade IV	S$43,865 (US$25,802)
Staff Grade III	S$36,570 (US$21,511)
Staff Grade II	S$31,710 (US$18,652)
Staff Grade I	S$26,845 (US$15,791)
Superscale A	S$22,935 (US$13,491)
Superscale B	S$19,340 (US$11,376)
Superscale C	S$16,065 (US$9,450)
Deputy Secretary	
Superscale D1	S$13,635 (US$8,020)
Superscale D	S$12,365 (US$7,273)
Superscale E1	S$11,465 (US$6,744)
Superscale E	S$10,570 (US$6217)
Superscale F	S$9,720 (US$5,717)
Superscale G	S$8,875 (US$5,220)

*   The exchange rate in 1994 was S$1.70=US$1.
Source: Public Service Commission, *Careers That Count* (Singapore: PSC, 1994).

The recovery of the economy in 1999 led to reduced unemployment and improved wages in the private sector. In June 2000, Deputy Prime Minister Lee Hsien Loong informed Parliament that attracting and retaining talent in the SCS was "quickly becoming a real problem" as eight administrative officers had already resigned during the first six months of 2000. Accordingly, he recommended that the government had to respond quickly by improving both the salaries and terms of service for those in leadership positions in the SCS.[43] To reinforce the link between pay and individual performance, Lee suggested that a performance-related component be included in the total wage package of every civil servant. The benchmark was also expanded from the top four earners in six professions to the top eight earners in six professions. Table 5.4 provides details of the salaries of selected ministers and senior civil servants in Singapore arising from the June 2000 salary revision.

TABLE 5.4 SALARIES OF SELECTED MINISTERS AND SENIOR CIVIL SERVANTS IN SINGAPORE, JUNE 2000

Grade	Monthly Salary	Annual Salary	Revised Monthly Salary	Revised Annual Salary
Prime Minister	S$85,000	S$1.69 million	S$85,300	S$1.94 million
Minister Staff Grade II	S$48,900	S$1.13 million	S$55,700 S$49,900 S$44,600	S$1.42 million S$1.27 million S$1.13 million
Minister Staff Grade I	S$37,800	S$861,000	S$47,400 S$37,900	S$1.21 million S$968,000
Permanent Secretary Superscale B	S$28,000	S$638,000	S$39,800 S$28,800	S$1.01 million S$736,000
Deputy Secretary Superscale G	S$13,400	S$242,000	S$18,800 S$17,500	S$390,000 S$363,000

Source: *Straits Times*, June 30, 2000, p. 53.

In short, Singapore's comprehensive anti-corruption strategy since 1960 consists of (1) the combined use of the POCA and CPIB to reduce the opportunities for corruption; and (2) the periodic increase in salaries of the political leaders and senior civil servants to reduce the incentive for corruption.

EVALUATION OF ANTI-CORRUPTION STRATEGY

In 1996, the Hong Kong based PERC ranked Singapore as the third least corrupt country in the world, after Switzerland and Australia, and the least corrupt of the 12 Asian countries[44] in the study. According to PERC:

> All countries have laws aimed at fighting corruption, but very few governments apply such laws as strictly and consistently as Singapore ... Corrupt officials, particularly high-ranking ones, are dealt with in Singapore with a severity rarely seen elsewhere.[45]

Indeed, the following political leaders and civil servants in Singapore have been investigated and prosecuted by the CPIB:

1. Wee Toon Boon, a minister of state, was investigated in 1975 for accepting bribes from a property developer. He was sentenced to four years and six months' imprisonment, which on appeal was reduced to one year and six months.
2. Phey Yew Kok, a member of Parliament and a prominent trade union leader, was investigated in 1979 and charged in court for criminal breach of trust and other offences. He jumped bail and is now a fugitive.
3. Teh Cheang Wan, a minister was investigated in 1986 for accepting bribes from two property developers. He committed suicide before he could be charged in court.
4. Glen Jeyasingam Knight, a senior state counsel, and the director of the Commercial Affairs Department, was investigated in 1991 and charged in court for corruption and cheating. He was jailed and fined.
5. Yeo Seng Teck, the chief executive officer of the Trade Development Board, Singapore, was investigated in 1993 and charged in court for corruption, cheating and forgery. He was sentenced to four years' imprisonment.
6. Choy Hon Tim, the deputy chief executive of the Public Utilities Board (PUB), was investigated in 1995 and charged for accepting bribes from PUB contractors. He was sentenced to 14 years' imprisonment.[46]

During 1996, Singapore's seventh ranking on Transparency International's CPI made it the least corrupt of the 13 Asian countries in the 54-nation study, with Pakistan (ranked 53rd) as the most corrupt Asian country.[47] Even though Singapore's ranking on the 1997 CPI dropped to ninth position, it was still the least corrupt of the 13 Asian countries in the 52-nation survey, with Pakistan (ranked 48th) retaining its position as the most corrupt Asian country.[48] In the 1998 and 1999 CPI, Singapore's seventh ranking confirmed its status as the least corrupt Asian country. Singapore's ranking on the CPI improved to 6th position in 2000, 4th position in 2001, and 5th position in 2002. Singapore has been consistently ranked as the least corrupt Asian country by the PERC in Hong Kong from 1995-2002. Table 5.5 provides details of Singapore's ranking on the CPI and PERC from 1995-2002.

TABLE 5.5 SINGAPORE'S RANKING ON THE CPI AND PERC, 1995-2002

Year	Corruption Perceptions Index	Political and Economic Risk Consultancy
1995	3rd (41)	1st (11)
1996	7th (54)	1st (12)
1997	9th (52)	1st (12)
1998	7th (85)	1st (11)
1999	7th (99)	1st (12)
2000	6th (90)	1st (12)
2001	4th (91)	1st (12)
2002	5th (102)	1st (12)
Average	6th	1st

Source: Compiled from Transparency International's CPI, 1995-2002; and PERC's Ranking on Corruption in Asian Countries, 1995-2002.

CONCLUSION

In short, Singapore's success in minimising corruption can be attributed to its dual strategy of reducing *both* the opportunities and incentives for corruption. Former Prime Minister, Lee Kuan Yew, identified the five factors responsible for Singapore's effective anti-corruption strategy in his statement to Parliament in January 1987 during the Teh Cheang Wan Commission of Inquiry.

> The effectiveness of our system to check and punish corruption rests, first, on the law against corruption contained in the Prevention of Corruption Act; second, on a vigilant public ready to give information on all suspected corruption; and third, on a CPIB which is scrupulous, thorough, and fearless in its investigations. For this to be so, the CPIB has to receive the full backing of the Prime Minister, under whose portfolio it comes. But the strongest deterrent is in a public opinion which censures and condemns corrupt persons; in other words, in attitudes which make corruption so unacceptable that the stigma of corruption cannot be washed away by serving a prison sentence.[49]

Indeed, Singapore's experience in curbing corruption demonstrates that it is possible to minimise corruption if there is a strong political will. Needless to say, the situation becomes hopeless if such political will is lacking as political leaders and senior civil servants pay only lip service to implementing anti-corruption strategies in their countries.

ENDNOTES

1 Republic of Singapore, *Singapore Facts and Pictures 2002* (Singapore: Ministry of Information, Communication and the Arts, 2002), p. 2.

2 Jon S.T. Quah, "The Public Policy-Making Process in Singapore", *Asian Journal of Public Administration*, Vol. 6, No. 2 (December 1994), pp. 9-10.

3 Republic of Singapore, *Singapore Facts and Pictures 2002*, p. 61.

4 Ibid., p. 8.

5 Jon S.T. Quah, "Singapore's Model of Development: Is It Transferable?" in Henry S. Rowen (ed.), *Behind East Asian Growth: The Political and Social Foundations of Prosperity* (London: Routledge, 1998), p. 110.

6 John Andrews, *Pocket Asia* 7th edition (London: The Economist Newspaper Ltd. and Profile Books Ltd., 2002), p. 15.

7 For more details of Singapore's political system, see Jon S.T. Quah, "Singapore: Meritocratic City-State", in John Funston (ed.), *Government and Politics in Southeast Asia* (Singapore: Institute of Southeast Asian Studies, 2001), pp. 296-308.

8 Jon S.T. Quah, "Police Corruption in Singapore: An Analysis of its Forms, Extent and Causes", *Singapore Police Journal*, Vol. 10, No. 1 (January 1979), pp 24-27.

9   Ibid., pp. 18-24.

10   Yoong Siew-Wah, "Some Aspects of Corruption", *National Youth Leadership Training Institute Journal* (January 1973), pp. 55-56.

11   Jon S.T. Quah, *Administrative and Legal Measures for Combating Bureaucratic Corruption in Singapore* (Singapore: Department of Political Science, University of Singapore, Occasional Paper No. 34, 1978), p. 14.

12   *Straits Times*, October 4, 1887, quoted in Quah, "Police Corruption in Singapore", p. 29.

13   Charles Burton Buckley, *An Anecdotal History of Old Times in Singapore* (Kuala Lumpur: University of Malaya Press, 1965), pp. 446-447.

14   Ibid., p. 447.

15   *Straits Times*, June 13, 1849.

16   Quah, "Police Corruption in Singapore", pp. 29-31.

17   Jon S.T. Quah, "Bureaucratic Corruption in the ASEAN Countries: A Comparative Analysis of Their Anti-Corruption Strategies", *Journal of Southeast Asian Studies*, Vol. 13, No. 1 (March 1983), pp. 161-162.

18   Colony of Singapore, *Twentieth Meeting of the Advisory Council* Public Session, September 5, 1946-February 20, 1947 (Singapore: Government Printing Office, 1947), p. 4.

19   Colony of Singapore, *Distribution of Work 1st May, 1952* (Singapore: Government Printing Office, 1952), p. 31.

20   Tan Ah Leak, "The Experience of Singapore in Combating Corruption", in Rick Stapenhurst and Sahr J. Kpundeh (eds.), *Curbing Corruption: Toward a Model for Building National Integrity* (Washington D.C.: The World Bank, 1999), p. 59.

21   Ibid., p. 59.

22   Jon S.T. Quah, "Controlling Corruption in City-States: A Comparative Study of Hong Kong", *Crime, Law and Social Change*, Vol. 22 (1995), p. 394.

23   Lee Kuan Yew, *From Third World to First: The Singapore Story: 1965-2000* (Singapore: Times Media Private Ltd., 2000), pp. 182-184.

24   Jon S.T. Quah, "Singapore's Experience in Curbing Corruption", in Arnold J. Heidenheimer, Michael Johnston and Victor T. LeVine (eds.), *Political Corruption: A Handbook* (New Brunswick: Transaction Publishers, 1989), p. 842.

25   Republic of Singapore, *Economic Survey of Singapore 1985* (Singapore: Ministry of Trade and Industry, 1986), p. ix.

26   The POCA has now 37 sections as a result of subsequent amendments. See "Prevention of Corruption Act (Chapter 241)", revised edition 1993 (Singapore: Singapore National Printers, 1993).

27   The amount of the fine was increased to S$100,000 in 1989. See ibid., p. 4.

28   Quah, *Administrative and Legal Measures for Combatting Bureaucratic Corruption in Singapore*, p. 13.

29   *Straits Times*, October 26, 1981.

30   *Report of the Commission of Inquiry on Investigations concerning the late Mr Teh Cheang Wan* (Singapore: Singapore National Printers, 1987), pp. 1 and 36.

31 Data on the size of the SCS are provided by the Public Service Division and the size of the ICAC is taken from *2001 Annual Report by the Commissioner of the Independent Commission Against Corruption Hong Kong Special Administrative Region* (Hong Kong: ICAC, 2001), p. 24.

32 *The Corrupt Practices Investigation Bureau* (Singapore: CPIB, 1990), p. 2.

33 Ibid., pp. 3-4.

34 Ibid., p. 4.

35 Ibid., p. 3.

36 S. Chandra Mohan, "The Control of Corruption in Singapore", Volume 2 (Ph.D. thesis, Faculty of Law, School of Oriental and African Studies, University of London, December 1987), p. 600.

37 Ibid., p. 600.

38 Jon S.T. Quah, "The Public Bureaucracy in Singapore, 1959-1984", in You Poh Seng and Lim Chong Yah (eds.), *Singapore: Twenty-Five Years of Development* (Singapore: Nan Yang Xing Zhou Lianhe Zaobao, 1984), p. 296.

39 *Straits Times*, March 23, 1985, pp. 14-16.

40 *White Paper on Competitive Salaries for Competent and Honest Government: Benchmarks for Ministers and Senior Public Officers* (Singapore: Presented to Parliament by the President on 21 October 1994) Command 13 of 1994, pp. 7-14.

41 John W. Wright and Edmund J. Dwyer, *The American Almanac of Jobs and Salaries* (New York: Avon Books, 1990), p. 6.

42 Jon S.T. Quah, "Paying for the 'Best and Brightest': Rewards for High Public Office in Singapore", in Christopher Hood and B. Guy Peters with Grace O.M. Lee (eds.), *Rewards for High Public Office: Asian and Pacific Rim Cases* (London: Routledge, 2003), p. 154.

43 Ibid., p. 154.

44 *Straits Times*, April 9, 1996, p. 3.

45 Ibid., p. 3.

46 Tan, "The Experience of Singapore in Combating Corruption", pp. 64-65.

47 *The Fight Against Corruption: Is the Tide Now Turning? Transparency International Report 1997* (Berlin: Transparency International, 1997), p. 65.

48 *Combating Corruption: Are Lasting Solutions Emerging? Transparency International Report 1998* (Berlin: Transparency International, 1998), p. 195.

49 Quoted in *Report of the Commission of Inquiry on Investigations Concerning the Late Mr Teh Cheang Wan*, p. 2.

CHAPTER 6

Hong Kong

INTRODUCTION

Hong Kong was a British colony for 156 years as it was ceded to Britain in 1841. On July 1, 1997, it was handed over to the People's Republic of China. Corruption was a serious problem in Hong Kong before the advent of the Independent Commission Against Corruption (ICAC) in February 1974. However, as a result of the ICAC's efforts, corruption is no longer a way of life in Hong Kong, which is perceived to be the second least corrupt country in Asia after Singapore.

How did the ICAC minimise corruption in Hong Kong? What are the main features of Hong Kong's anti-corruption strategy? Why has Hong Kong succeeded in curbing corruption? This chapter addresses these questions after describing the policy context and analysing the extent of corruption in Hong Kong.

POLICY CONTEXT

Geography

Hong Kong has a total land area of 1,100 sq. km and consists of three parts: Hong Kong Island, Kowloon peninsula, and the New Territories.[1] Hong Kong is highly urbanised as its arable area constitutes only 6% of the total land area.[2] Like Singapore, Hong Kong has no natural resources except a deep harbour and a strategic location at the southern tip of China. Its proximity to China provides a gateway to the mainland and, until June 1997, was a source of refugees and illegal immigrants.

Unlike other small underdeveloped states, Hong Kong has not encountered the communications problems which hinder implementation because of its "heavy reliance on the values of classical bureaucracy matched by congruent Chinese values" and its allocation of more human resources to line rather than staff positions. There is effective top-down implementation because of the "strong emphasis on hierarchy, discipline, and neutrality", the clear lines of authority and communication, and the efficient implementation of orders by the junior civil servants. In short, top-down implementation is the rule and not the exception in Hong Kong.[3] This strength of the Hong Kong bureaucracy has assisted the ICAC in implementing the anti-corruption laws effectively.

Economy

Like Singapore, Hong Kong has no natural resources except for its harbour and strategic location. Indeed, Hong Kong's small size, rugged terrain, and lack of natural resources not only make it dependent on other countries for food, supplies and raw materials but also require it to provide services to these countries.[4] Hong Kong's status as a free port, its open economy, and political stability have enabled it to attract foreign investment and encouraged the establishment of multinational corporations.[5] In fact, Hong Kong's economy has been successful because of these "precious assets": "a low tax environment [15% flat rate], free and fair market competition, a sound legal and financial framework, a fully convertible and secure currency, a highly efficient network of transport and communication", and "a competent workforce working along with a pool of enterprising entrepreneurs".[6]

Its GDP in 2000 was US$163 billion and its GDP per capita was US$23,930. Its average annual growth in real GDP from 1990-2000 was 4.3%. Hong Kong's affluence is demonstrated by its consumer goods ownership in 2000: there are 99.2 colour television sets per 100 households; 58.1 telephone lines per 100 population; 84.4 mobile phone subscribers per 100 population; and 38.5 computers per 100 population. Furthermore, government spending on education is 2.9% of the GDP and 5% of the latter has been allocated to health.[7]

Hong Kong's economic wealth is advantageous for fighting corruption as the incumbent government can afford to pay its civil servants competitive salaries and also devote the human and financial resources required by the ICAC to curb corruption effectively.

Demography

Hong Kong's population of 6.9 million persons is homogeneous as it consists of 95% Chinese. Its population density of 6,564 persons per sq. km makes it the second most densely populated place in the world after Macau.[8] Unlike Singapore's multi-racial population, Hong Kong's homogeneous Chinese population and its high literacy rate of 93.6% have proved advantageous for the ICAC's emphasis on community relations to educate Hong Kongers on the adverse effects of corruption.[9]

On the other hand, the fact that Hong Kong's population is mainly Chinese has made the task of curbing corruption a challenging one for the ICAC when it was created in February 1974 for four reasons. First, as most of the population were immigrants from China, where corruption was rampant, they also expected public officials in Hong Kong to behave in the same manner as their counterparts in mainland China, who had demanded gifts in return for the performance of services. Without a sense of belonging or national identity, most Hong Kongers "regarded bribes as a small price to pay for being able to get on with their lives with minimum interference from alien officialdom".[10]

Second, it should be noted that in China the terms "government" and "citizen" were unknown until the end of the T'sing Dynasty. There were no civil servants, as the Emperor appointed all the officials. "Every act done by an official was regarded as a favour; and any omission a dispensation. Payment for such favour or dispensation was ... taken as a *quid pro quo*".[11] Given this historical background, it is not surprising that "a Chinese in Hong Kong is more ready to pay a bribe ... without thinking of any moral issue. ... [as] they do not see anything wrong in buying their way out ...".[12] Indeed, the use of *guanxi* (connections) to get things done and for bureaucrats to accept bribes for their personal gain were accepted by the population.

Third, many middle-aged and elderly residents came to Hong Kong as refugees from China with the overthrow of the Kuomintang (KMT) government by the communists in 1949. As the KMT government was corrupt, these refugees believed that civil servants in Hong Kong were also corrupt. "This belief in itself breeds corruption because it leads to voluntary bribery by people who consider it normal practice in dealing with government".[13]

Finally, the ICAC's task of fighting corruption was made more difficult by the Chinese custom of paying "tea money" to workers as a tip in the commercial sector. For example, housewives give tips to mechanics or repairmen to ensure good service. Junior civil servants like postmen are usually given "red packets" containing money during the Chinese Lunar New Year in appreciation for their services during the past year. Those Hong Kongers who pay tea money do not consider this practice as something wrong. Moreover, as junior civil servants are paid low salaries, many Hong Kongers are tolerant of petty corruption and sympathetic towards these officials making some extra money.[14]

Political System

Hong Kong was a British colony for 156 years as it was ceded to Britain in 1841 and returned to the People's Republic of China (PRC) on July 1, 1997 as a Special Administrative Region (SAR). As a British colony, power in Hong Kong was concentrated in a colonial governor appointed by the British government. Administration was conducted by career civil servants with no elected ministers to control their activities. After July 1, 1997, the Chief Executive replaced the Governor as the Head of Government, and he is assisted in policy-making by the Executive Council of 12 members, who are appointed by the Chief Executive from among the principal officials of the executive authorities, members of the Legislative Council, and public figures.[15] The second term of the Legislative Council (2000-2004) consists of 60 members, 24 of whom are directly elected by geographical constituencies, 30 members elected by different functional constituencies, and six members appointed by an Election Committee of 800 elected representatives of the community.[16]

The legacy of British colonial rule in Hong Kong has been positive in three respects. First, the British introduced meritocracy in the civil service with the establishment of the Public Service Commission. Second, the British left Hong Kong with an efficient civil service and a well-developed infrastructure. Finally, the most important legacy of British colonial rule is the commitment to clean government, which the SAR government has inherited and maintained.

EXTENT OF CORRUPTION

In his address to the Legislative Council on 26 February 1969, Governor Sir David Trench said: "Much has been said over the years about corruption in Hong Kong. That it exists here, as everywhere else, I do not doubt; but its extent is a matter of conjecture. However, that it exists at all is intolerable, and everything possible must be done to stamp it out".[17]

Other scholars disagree with Trench's view that the extent of corruption in Hong Kong cannot be ascertained. For example, Leslie Palmier contended that corruption was already a way of life in Hong Kong when the British acquired it in 1841 because:

> The Chinese who formed its population had long been accustomed to a system where most of an official's income depended on what he was able to extort from the public. Not surprisingly, during the first decades of the colony's history corruption prospered at all levels of government.[18]

Similarly, H.J. Lethbridge observed that "syndicated corruption, the satisfied customer variant, paying for convenience, protection rackets, extortion, squeeze, kickbacks, and commissions" had existed "in a primal state" in pre-war Hong Kong. Indeed, corruption "infected" all government departments that "provided any opportunity for its occurrence" and was considered "an unofficial tax levied on all those who laboured or who lived exiguously on the fringes of private enterprise–factory workers, artisans, craftsmen, shop assistants and small shopkeepers, clerks and others".[19] However, "in pre-1941 Hong Kong corruption was not in any sense a serious social problem" as it "did not give rise to great public concern, prolonged debate, uninterrupted administrative action, and the spending of large sums of public money on its control".[20] As the scale and incidence of corruption had increased after 1945, corruption began to emerge as a social problem "primarily because it is regarded as a moral problem or issue, related to the concept of social justice".[21] A 1971 survey of 1,065 household heads in the Kwun Tong District found that 29.2% of the respondents viewed corruption as a serious social problem and "the older or the less educated tended to be less likely to regard corruption as a social problem".[22]

In his *Report of a Commission of Enquiry* in 1973, Sir Alastair Blair-Kerr used the popular bus metaphor to describe corruption in Hong Kong:

1. 'Get on the bus' i.e., if you wish to accept corruption, join us;
2. 'Run alongside the bus' i.e., if you do not wish to accept corruption, it matters not, but do not interfere;
3. 'Never stand in front of the bus' i.e., if you try to report corruption, the 'bus' will knock you down and you will be injured or even killed or your business will be ruined. We will get you somehow.[23]

In short, when the ICAC was established in February 1974, corruption had become rampant. According to Bertrand de Speville, a former ICAC commissioner, "corruption was deeply rooted, widespread, generally tolerated and, in some sectors, highly organised. Every part of the public service was infected, especially the disciplined services, namely the police, the customs and excise service, the immigration department, the fire and ambulance services and the prison service. Certain other government departments shared the notoriety of the disciplined services: housing, public works, education and health".[24]

Why was corruption a way of life in Hong Kong when the ICAC was created in 1974? Bertrand de Speville has argued that Hong Kong provided "a fertile soil for corruption to flourish" for four reasons. First, the increase in population from 600,000 in 1945 to 4.3 million in 1974 severely strained the social services, government resources and manpower. Consequently, "everything was in short supply: food, housing, water, schools, health care, services of every kind".[25] Under such conditions of scarcity, it was not surprising that "doing business by bribing public servants and paying secret commissions to agents and employers was accepted in business circles as the way to get things done, even though such methods were deplored by senior administrators".[26]

The second reason for the prevalence of corruption in Hong Kong was the immigrant nature of the population. As the majority of the Hong Kongers came from China, where corruption was endemic, they expected civil servants in Hong Kong to behave as their counterparts in China did and to require a gift to perform any service for them. Indeed, they were encouraged to pay bribes to the police and other civil servants to avoid being harassed by them.[27]

The third cause of corruption in Hong Kong was the government's control and regulation of such activities as "construction, import and export, health, hygiene, safety, prostitution, gambling, drugs, markets and stalls, immigration and emigration".[28] The government's monopoly and regulation of these activities and the discretion given to those civil servants in charge provided many opportunities for corruption.

The final factor identified by de Speville was the widespread police corruption, which prevented the police from resolving the problem of corruption. Palmier had identified the police as the "most corrupt government body" in Hong Kong.[29] Police corruption was a serious problem as "daily extensive contact with the public provided ample opportunity".[30] In spite of its ineffectiveness in curbing corruption, the Royal Hong Kong Police refused to relinquish its responsibility for investigating corruption.

In short, corruption was a serious problem in Hong Kong in 1974 as it was perceived as a "low risk, high reward" activity where corrupt offenders were unlikely to be detected and punished, especially if they were police officers.

ANTI-CORRUPTION STRATEGY

Hong Kong's anti-corruption strategy can be divided into two phases: the incremental strategy (1898-1973) and the comprehensive strategy (1974-present).

Incremental Strategy (1898-1973)

During 1842-1897, the bribery of civil servants in Hong Kong was a misdemeanour under the Common Law. The June 1897 gambling house scandal, which involved the police, "soiled the reputation of the Civil Service as a whole and it moved the legislature to enact the first local law against corruption: the Misdemeanours Punishment Ordinance [MPO]" in 1898.[31] Section 2 of the MPO defined a bribe as "any fee, perquisite, reward or gratification, whether pecuniary or otherwise, not payable or receivable by law".[32] Sections 3 and 4 made bribery an offence for both the person offering a bribe and the civil servant accepting it.[33] The MPO increased the maximum penalty to two years' imprisonment with or without hard labour or a fine not exceeding HK$500, or both. However, the MPO was ineffective because it was applicable only to civil servants and its definition was restricted to bribery only.[34]

To cope with the increase in corruption after the Second World War, the British colonial government enacted the Prevention of Corruption Ordinance (POCO) in 1948. The POCO was wider in scope than the MPO as it was also applicable to legislators, and employees of both public and private organisations. Moreover, the POCO identified two major types of corruption: corruption in office

136

and corrupt transactions with agents, which included civil servants and private sector employees.[35] More importantly, the POCO authorised the Attorney General to investigate a suspect's bank account, share account or purchase account (section 10 (1)).[36] Another important provision was concerned with the unexplained enrichment of those persons who possessed or disposed of pecuniary resources or property *disproportionate* to their known sources of income.[37] Finally, the POCO raised the maximum penalty for corruption to five years' imprisonment, a fine of HK$10,000 and a "possible forfeiture of the bribe to be paid to the public body or to the agent's principal".[38]

An Anti-Corruption Branch (ACB) was also established in 1948 as a special unit within the Criminal Investigation Department (CID) of the Royal Hong Kong Police Force (RHKPF) to handle the investigation and prosecution of corruption cases.[39] The ACB was separated from the CID in 1952 but it still remained within the RHKPF. The ACB had limited success as its prosecution of corruption offences resulted in between two to 20 court convictions per year.[40] However, the government was criticised by the Advisory Committee for retaining the ACB within the RHKPF.[41]

Accordingly, the ACB initiated a review of the POCO in 1968 and it recommended a scrutiny of the anti-corruption legislation of Singapore and Ceylon (now known as Sri Lanka). During the same year, a study team visited these two countries to examine how their laws worked in practice. The study team was impressed with the independence of their anti-corruption agencies and attributed Singapore's success in curbing corruption to the CPIB's independence from the police.[42] The knowledge gained from the study tour contributed to the formulation of the Prevention of Bribery Bill on October 16, 1970, and its enactment as an ordinance on May 15, 1971.[43]

The Prevention of Bribery Ordinance (POBO) had three important features. First, it enabled the government to prosecute a civil servant for corruption if he could not provide a satisfactory explanation for maintaining a standard of living or controlling excessive pecuniary resources that were not commensurate with

his or her present or past official salaries.[44] Second, the POBO
provided extensive powers of investigation as the Attorney-General
could authorise the inspection of bank accounts, safe-deposit boxes,
books, documents or articles. He could also require the suspect or
any other person to submit information, and authorise the entry
into and search of any premises.[45] Third, the POBO introduced
severe maximum penalties: the general maximum penalty was a
fine of HK$50,000 and three years' imprisonment, or on
indictment, a fine of HK$100,000 and seven years' imprisonment.
The duration of imprisonment was increased to 10 years for
offences involving contracts and tenders.[46]

The POBO's enactment in May 1971 led to the upgrading of
the ACB into an Anti-Corruption Office (ACO), which was headed
by an Assistant Commissioner of Police as its Director. The ACO's
location within the RHKPF resulted from a compromise between
the Attorney-General's view that the ACB should remain within the
RHKPF and the four Unofficial Members of the Legislative Council
who believed that the ACB should be an independent body. The
consequence was that the ACO was given a grace period of three
years to demonstrate its worth.[47] The ACO was given more
manpower and it worked hard and brought 152 cases to court in
less than two years.[48]

However, the escape of a corruption suspect, Chief
Superintendent Peter F. Godber, on June 8, 1973, to the United
Kingdom angered the public and undermined the ACO's credibility.
The government reacted by appointing a Commission of Inquiry
chaired by Sir Alastair Blair-Kerr to investigate the circumstances
which enabled Godber to leave Hong Kong, and to evaluate the
effectiveness of the POBO.[49]

The immediate consequence of Godber's escape was the
amendment of the POBO to remove the safeguards in the interests
of the suspect, and to require a suspect to surrender all his or her
travel documents.[50]

In his second report, Sir Alastair dealt with the question of
whether the anti-corruption agency should be independent of the
RHKPF by stating that "the arguments for retaining the Anti-

Corruption Office in the Police Force are largely organisational and the arguments for removing it are largely political and psychological". He also advised the Governor to consider the "widespread loss of confidence in the police on the part of the public" in making his decision on the fate of the ACO.[51]

The Governor, Sir Murray MacLehose, accepted Sir Alastair's advice of considering public opinion and made the important decision for political and psychological reasons to establish a new anti-corruption agency that was independent of the RHKPF. According to Lethbridge, the Governor's decision to create an independent body was influenced mainly by the exposure of Godber's corrupt activities in the RHKPF. He wrote:

> Godber's activities had thus awakened and illuminated the Governor as to the seriousness of the problem [of corruption]. Godber had fortified his resolve to create an anti-corruption organisation that would be independent of the police, a force which had sheltered Godber comfortably for so many years.[52]

In short, the revelation of Godber's corrupt activities and the unfavourable publicity concerning his escape to the United Kingdom was the catalyst that made the Governor accept the risk of breaking the RHKPF's control over the investigation of corruption. Indeed, Governor MacLehose's decision was a ground-breaking one as

> Governor after governor, committee after committee, had deferred to the police for a variety of reasons but principally because they feared a collapse of police morale if the control of corruption was handed over to an independent body.[53]

On October 17, 1973, Governor MacLehose informed the Legislative Council that an independent anti-corruption agency was needed for two reasons: the RHKPF should not be responsible for combating corruption but should leave this function to an independent and full-time anti-corruption body; and the public would have more confidence in an independent anti-corruption agency that was separate from the police.[54] Four months later, the ICAC was formed.

Comprehensive Anti-Corruption Strategy (1974-present)

On February 15, 1974, the ICAC was established with the enactment of the ICAC Ordinance and was entrusted with two tasks: "to root out corruption and to restore public confidence in the Government".[55] The ICAC inherited 181 police officers and 44 civilian employees from the ACO and recruited 144 new staff members, making a combined total of 369 employees, or 54% of its establishment of 682 positions in 1974.[56] Since then, the ICAC has succeeded in recruiting more staff and has grown by three and a half times during its first 27 years as its actual strength in December 2001 was 1,286 employees or 97% of its establishment of 1,326 positions.[57]

The ICAC is independent in terms of structure, personnel, finance and power. Before the 1997 handover, it was directly responsible to the Governor, and its Commissioner reported directly to the Governor and had easy access to him. Section 12 of the ICAC Ordinance described the Commissioner's duties as the investigation and prevention of corruption including the "education of the public against the evils of corruption and the enlisting and fostering of public support in combatting it".[58] However, after July 1997, the ICAC is directly responsible to the Chief Executive, and its Commissioner reports directly to and has easy access to him. In short, the ICAC has adopted the three-pronged approach of investigation, education and prevention to combat corruption in Hong Kong.

In terms of structure, the ICAC is divided into three unequal departments and the Administration Branch. The Operations Department is the investigative arm of the ICAC and is the largest department as it has 943 employees or 73% of the ICAC's actual strength. The Head of the Operations Department is also the Deputy Commissioner, who is assisted by two Directors of Investigation, one responsible for the government sector and the other for the private sector. There are four investigation branches, each of which has four investigation groups. For example, the Director of Investigation (government sector) is responsible for Investigation Branch 1 (covering Groups A, B, C and Y) and Investigation Branch 3 (covering Groups G, H, R and X).[59]

The Community Relations Department is headed by a Director and has two divisions, which deal respectively with the mass media and the public. It is the second largest department and has 202 employees or 16% of the ICAC's total staff.[60] According to section 12 (g) and (h) of the ICAC Ordinance, this department is responsible for "educating the public against the evils of corruption and harnessing support for the ICAC".[61] It has conducted an intensive education programme for the schools, the commercial and industrial sectors, and the public sector. It has also maintained close contacts with the mass media and district organisations to enhance the public's confidence and to mobilise their support in fighting corruption.[62]

The smallest department is the Corruption Prevention Department (CPD), which has 57 employees or 4% of the ICAC's total staff. It is headed by a Director and two Assistant Directors, and consists of five Assignment Groups (responsible for government departments), the Advisory Services Group (deals with requests from the private sector), and the Management Group (which provides administrative support). More specifically, the department's role is to examine the "practices and procedures of government departments and public bodies, identifies corruption loopholes and makes recommendations to reform work methods for reducing the potential for graft".[63]

The CPD undertakes assignments from government departments to streamline their work procedures, monitors completed assignments, and provides corruption prevention advice through its consulting activities. It also provides training for civil servants in corruption prevention-related subjects. Its final function is the provision of a confidential and free internal audit service on request to private companies to prevent corruption and fraud.[64]

Finally, the Administration Branch is responsible for managing human and financial resources, supplies, accommodation and general matters, the administration of the ICAC's training, staff relations and welfare activities, and the coordination of information technology services affecting the ICAC. It is headed by an Assistant Director and consists of 84 employees or 7% of the ICAC's total staff.[65] Table 6.1 provides details of the number of staff members in the ICAC's three departments and the Administration Branch.

TABLE 6.1 ICAC'S STAFF BY DEPARTMENT, 2001

Department	No. of Staff	Percentage
Operations Department	943	73.0
Community Relations Department	202	16.0
Administration Branch	84	7.0
Corruption Prevention Department	57	4.0
Total	1,286	100.0

Source: *2001 Annual Report by the Commissioner of the Independent Commission Against Corruption Hong Kong Special Administrative Region* (Hong Kong: ICAC, 2002), p. 24.

To ensure the ICAC's integrity, its activities are scrutinised by several independent committees made up of citizens from different sectors of the community and appointed by the Governor before July 1997, and the Chief Executive after July 1997. The Advisory Committee on Corruption reviews the overall policy of the ICAC and the work of the three departments and the Administration Branch. The work of each department is also examined by an advisory committee. Accordingly, the Operations Review Committee focuses on the Operations Department, the Corruption Prevention Advisory Committee deals with the CPD, and the Citizens Advisory Committee on Community Relations advises the Community Relations Department on its activities.[66]

The ICAC Commissioner is appointed by the Chief Executive and the ICAC staff are recruited separately from the civil service and are outside the purview of the Public Service Commission. This means that the ICAC staff cannot be transferred to other government departments and an ICAC officer cannot be "posted later under a more senior civil servant whom he may have investigated".[67] Finally, the ICAC has its own independent staff recruitment practices and it processes the advertisements, examinations, screening, interviewing, appointment and training of its officers.[68]

The ICAC receives its resources from the government and its expenditure is charged to the general revenue. Its budget has increased by 81 times from HK$8.5 million for the 1974/1975 financial year to HK$686.7 million for the 2001/2002 financial year.[69] As the Operations Department is the largest department in the ICAC with 943 members, it receives HK$517.3 million or 75% of the 2001/2002 budget.[70] The tremendous increase in the ICAC's budget during its first 28 years is a clear indication of the government's political will and support for the ICAC's activities.

The ICAC's powers are specified in the ICAC Ordinance of 1974 and the POBO of 1971. The ICAC Ordinance enables the Director of the Operations Department to authorise his officers to restrict the movement of a suspect, to examine bank accounts and safe-deposit boxes, to restrict disposal of a suspect's property and to require a suspect to provide full details of his financial situation. ICAC officers can also arrest without warrant for the offences indicated in the two ordinances and they can search premises and seize and detain any evidence for such offences.[71]

EVALUATION OF ANTI-CORRUPTION STRATEGY

According to Transparency International's CPI from 1995-2002, Hong Kong is perceived to be the second least corrupt country in Asia after Singapore. Table 6.2 shows that Hong Kong's ranking on the CPI improved from 17th position in 1995 to 14th position in 2002, and its average ranking from 1995-2002 is 16th position. A second indicator of the ICAC's effectiveness is its success in transforming the population's attitude towards corruption. In its 1994 report, the ICAC Review Committee indicated that:

> [The ICAC] has also brought about a change in public attitudes from widespread tolerance to outright rejection of corruption. Before the advent of the ICAC, corruption was not regarded as the social evil it is seen to be today. Many members of the community are now prepared to play their part in the constant battle against corruption as shown by the continuing increase in the numbers of identifiable and pursuable complaints made to the ICAC.[72]

TABLE 6.2 HONG KONG'S RANKING ON THE CPI, 1995-2002

Year	Ranking	Score
1995	17th	7.12
1996	18th	7.01
1997	18th	7.28
1998	16th	7.80
1999	15th	7.70
2000	15th	7.70
2001	14th	7.90
2002	14th	8.20
Average	16th	7.58

Source: Compiled from Transparency International's CPI from 1995-2002. See http://www.transparency.org

The third indicator of the ICAC's success is its output in terms of the number of corruption cases investigated and the number of persons prosecuted for corruption. During its first 20 years, the ICAC investigated a total of 22,828 cases and prosecuted 6,261 persons. These cases involved 1,355 civil servants, 218 public corporations, with the rest from the private sector.[73] In 2001, the Operations Department received a total of 4,476 corruption reports, or 2% more than those received in 2000. The number of corruption reports in the private sector rose by 6% from 2,402 in 2000 to 2,542 in 2001. The number of corruption reports concerning members of public bodies increased by 36% from 256 to 347 during 2000-2001. In contrast, the number of corruption reports on police officers decreased by 15% from 602 to 513 during the same period. Similarly, the number of corruption reports involving other civil servants also declined by 5% from 1,130 in 2000 to 1,074 in 2001.[74] During 2001, the Operations Department completed 3,093 investigations, prosecuted 535 persons, and formally cautioned 85 persons.[75]

The above analysis has shown that the ICAC is responsible for minimising corruption in Hong Kong. Why has the ICAC succeeded in making corruption a fact of life in Hong Kong? Betrand de Speville, a former ICAC Commissioner has identified five factors for the ICAC's success. The most important factor is the recognition by the government of the seriousness of the problem of corruption and the provision of adequate resources to deal with it. Second, to gain public confidence, the ICAC must be unimpeachable and its staff "must have unblemished integrity" and be "dedicated and effective graft fighters".[76] The third factor responsible for the ICAC's success is its formulation and implementation of a carefully designed long-term three-pronged strategy, which focuses on investigation, prevention and education. Fourth, the ICAC succeeded in gaining public confidence by ensuring that all reports of corruption, no matter how small, are investigated. Finally, the ICAC succeeded because it ensured confidentiality to those reporting corruption offences. In short, the ICAC succeeded because of "a combination of factors that collectively produced an advantageous environment in which to counter corruption".[77]

The critical factor for the ICAC's success is the political will of the incumbent government before and after July 1997 to recognise corruption as a problem and its commitment to solve it. According to de Speville, "The decision at the highest executive level of government to tackle the problem of corruption is the *sine qua non* of effective action. That decision must be accompanied by the willingness to provide adequate funding, realising that overcoming corruption will be expensive".[78] This also implies that the government ensures that there is comprehensive anti-corruption legislation, which is impartially enforced by a professional, independent and adequately funded ICAC. The ICAC has gained the confidence of the population in Hong Kong by investigating all reports of corruption and protecting the confidentiality of those reporting such offences. Indeed, the proportion of complainants who identified themselves in corruption reports increased from one-third of all reports during the ICAC's early years to nearly two-thirds of all reports in the late 1990s.[79]

In May 1997, the Joint Standing Committee on Foreign Affairs, Defence and Trade of the Australian Parliament indicated its concern about corruption in Hong Kong after the handover in July 1997 when it stated that "... the corruption, rampant in China, if extended to Hong Kong, could prove disastrous for the territory".[80] This concern

145

was not original as it had been expressed earlier by Emily Lau in 1988, and by Michael Yahuda in 1996 when he referred to the "pervasive fear" of the "seepage of corruption" from mainland China to Hong Kong after July 1997.[81]

In 2001, the then ICAC Commissioner, Alan N. Lai, referred to the "considerable trepidation in the community concerning Hong Kong's ability to preserve its essentially corruption-free culture" and posed these questions: "Would the SAR Government have the will and determination to fight graft? Now that the territory had reintegrated with mainland China, would the irregular practices so common across the border spill over to Hong Kong?"[82] His answers to these two questions were "Yes" and "No" respectively:

> Four years have passed since the 1997 sovereignty change and today, Hong Kong can say with pride that her credentials as a champion in fighting graft have remained as strong as ever. The ICAC continues to tackle the corrupt without fear or favour, and our track record of catching not only small flies, but also big tigers remains unblemished. Since July 1997, ICAC activities have regularly hit the headlines. ... Once known to the ICAC, no one can escape our scrutiny.[83]

CONCLUSION

Jack Lo concluded his evaluation of the ICAC by indicating that its "real challenge" was its ability "to preserve and maintain its institutional health and organisational integrity" and "to adapt to the environment without losing public support".[84] Similarly, Alan Lai ended his analysis by emphasising that "building up and upholding an anti-corruption culture is never an easy task" as it requires "determination, perseverance and expertise at the government level". As new situations arise, the ICAC must remain responsive to ensure that Hong Kong "stays a leader in the world's anti-corruption efforts".[85] In short, even though Hong Kong has succeeded in curbing corruption through the implementation of the ICAC's three-pronged strategy, it must remain vigilant as "keeping corruption at bay requires constant effort".[86]

ENDNOTES

1. *Hong Kong 2001* (Hong Kong: Information Services Department, 2002), p. 284.
2. John Andrews, *Pocket Asia*, 7th edition (London: The Economist Newspaper Ltd. and Profile Books Ltd., 2002), p. 68.
3. Ian Scott, "Administration in a Small Capitalist State: The Hong Kong Experience", in Randall Baker (ed.), *Public Administration in Small and Island States* (West Hartford: Kumarian Press, 1992), p. 111.
4. C.P. Lo, *Hong Kong* (London: Bedhaven Press, 1992), p. 49.
5. Ibid., p. 63.
6. Bob Howlett (ed.), *Hong Kong 1997: A Review of 1996* (Hong Kong: Information Services Department, 1997), p. 47.
7. Andrews, *Pocket Asia*, pp. 68-69.
8. *Hong Kong 2001*, p. 432 and Andrews, *Pocket Asia*, pp. 15 and 69.
9. Andrews, *Pocket Asia*, p. 69.
10. Bertrand de Speville, *Hong Kong: Policy Initiatives Against Corruption* (Paris: Development Centre of the Organisation for Economic Co-operation and Development, 1997), p. 13.
11. Ibid., pp. 13-14.
12. Ibid., p. 14.
13. Ibid., p. 15.
14. Ibid., p. 17.
15. *Hong Kong 2001*, pp. 4 -5.
16. Ibid., pp. 6 and 12.
17. Quoted in Steve Tsang (ed.), *Government and Politics: A Documentary History of Hong Kong* (Hong Kong: Hong Kong University Press, 1995), p. 186.
18. Leslie Palmier, *The Control of Bureaucratic Corruption: Case Studies in Asia* (Delhi: Allied Publishers, 1985), p. 123.
19. H.J. Lethbridge, *Hard Graft in Hong Kong* (Hong Kong: Oxford University Press, 1985), pp. 51-52.
20. Henry Lethbridge, "The Emergence of Bureaucratic Corruption as a Social Problem in Hong Kong", in his *Hong Kong: Stability and Change* (Hong Kong: Oxford University Press, 1978), pp. 229-230.
21. Ibid., pp. 231 and 233.
22. Rance P.L. Lee, "Incongruence of Legal Codes and Folk Norms", in Rance P.L. Lee (ed.), *Corruption and Its Control in Hong Kong: Situations Up to the Late Seventies* (Hong Kong: The Chinese University Press, 1981), p. 77.
23. Sir Alastair Blair-Kerr, *Report of a Commission of Enquiry* (Hong Kong: September 1973), p. 24.
24. de Speville, *Hong Kong*, p. 11.
25. Ibid., p. 13.
26. Ibid., p. 13.
27. Ibid., p. 13.
28. Ibid., p. 14.

29   Palmier, *The Control of Bureaucratic Corruption*, p. 123.

30   de Speville, *Hong Kong*, p. 14.

31   Hsin-Chi Kuan, "Anti-Corruption Legislation in Hong Kong–A History", in Lee (ed.), *Corruption and Its Control in Hong Kong*, pp. 16-17.

32   Ibid., p. 18.

33   Ibid., p. 17.

34   Ibid., pp. 18-20.

35   Ibid., p. 20.

36   Ibid., p. 23.

37   Ibid., pp. 23-24.

38   Ibid., p. 23.

39   Ibid., p. 24.

40   Jeremiah K.H. Wong, "The ICAC and Its Anti-Corruption Measures", in Lee (ed.), *Corruption and Its Control in Hong Kong*, p. 45.

41   Ibid., p. 46.

42   Ibid., p. 47.

43   Kuan, "Anti-Corruption Legislation in Hong Kong", p. 29.

44   Ibid., p. 32.

45   Ibid., p. 38.

46   Ibid., pp. 38-39.

47   Lethbridge, *Hard Graft in Hong Kong*, p. 98; and Wong, "The ICAC and Its Anti-Corruption Measures", p. 48.

48   Wong, "The ICAC and Its Anti-Corruption Measures", p. 49.

49   Kuan, "Anti-Corruption Legislation in Hong Kong", p. 39.

50   Ibid., p. 39.

51   Ibid., pp. 40-41.

52   Lethbridge, *Hard Graft in Hong Kong*, p. 98.

53   Ibid., pp. 101-102.

54   Ibid., p. 101.

55   Wong, "The ICAC and Its Anti-Corruption Measures", p. 45.

56   Lethbridge, *Hard Graft in Hong Kong*, p. 107.

57   *2001 Annual Report by the Commissioner of the Independent Commission Against Corruption Hong Kong Special Administrative Region* (Hong Kong: ICAC, 2002), p. 24.

58   Quoted in Lethbridge, *Hard Graft in Hong Kong*, p. 104.

59   *Operations Department Review 2001* (Hong Kong: ICAC, 2002), p. 18.

60   *2001 Annual Report by the Commissioner of the Independent Commission Against Corruption*, p. 24.

61   Ibid., p. 57.

62   *Annual Report on the Activities of the Independent Commission Against Corruption for 1991* (Hong Kong: Government Printer, 1992), pp. 24-25.

63   *2001 Annual Report by the Commissioner of the Independent Commission Against Corruption*, p. 42.

64   *Annual Report by the Commissioner of the Independent Commission Against Corruption for 1991*, pp. 119-21.

65   *2001 Annual Report by the Commissioner of the Independent Commission Against Corruption*, p. 24.

66   For details of the composition of these advisory committees and the report on their activities in 2001, see *Reports of ICAC Advisory Committees* (Hong Kong: ICAC, 2002).

67   Wong, "The ICAC and Its Anti-Corruption Measures", p. 53.

68   Ibid., p. 54.

69   *2001 Annual Report by the Commissioner of the Independent Commission Against Corruption*, p. 77.

70   Ibid., p. 77.

71   Quoted in Kuan, "Anti-Corruption Legislation in Hong Kong", p. 40.

72   Quoted in de Speville, *Hong Kong*, p. 61.

73   Jack M.K. Lo, "Controlling Corruption in Hong Kong: From Colony to Special Administrative Region", *Journal of Contingencies and Crisis Management*, Vol. 9, No. 1 (March 2001), p. 27.

74   *2001 Annual Report by the Commissioner of the Independent Commission Against Corruption*, p. 30.

75   Ibid., pp. 32-33.

76   Bertrand E. D. de Speville, "The Experience of Hong Kong, China, in Combating Corruption", in Rick Stapenhurst and Sahr J. Kpundeh (eds.), *Curbing Corruption: Toward A Model for Building National Integrity* (Washington, D.C.: The World Bank, 1999), p. 53.

77   Ibid., pp. 55-56.

78   de Speville, *Hong Kong*, p. 71.

79   Ibid., p. 61.

80   Joint Standing Committee on Foreign Affairs, Defence and Trade, *Hong Kong: The Transfer of Sovereignty* (Canberra: Parliament of the Commonwealth of Australia, May 1997), p. 98, paragraph 5.79.

81   See Emily Lau, "Graft-busters and 1997: Concern arises over anti-corruption commission's future", *Far Eastern Economic Review*, December 8, 1988, p. 29; and Michael Yahuda, *Hong Kong: China's Challenge* (London: Routledge, 1996), pp. 128-129.

82   Alan N. Lai, "Keeping Hong Kong Clean: Experiences of Fighting Corruption Post 1997", *Harvard Asia Pacific Review*, Vol. 5, No. 2 (Fall 2001), p. 51.

83   Ibid., pp. 51-52.

84   Lo, "Controlling Corruption in Hong Kong", p. 28.

85   Lai, "Keeping Hong Kong Clean", p. 54.

86   de Speville, *Hong Kong*, p. 63.

CHAPTER 7

South Korea

INTRODUCTION

Corruption has been a serious problem in South Korea since the 16th century, when the participation of the King's family in politics led to "increasing nepotism and corruption in administration".[1] As a result of the spate of corruption scandals in South Korea in recent years, Young Jong Kim, a leading Korean scholar of corruption studies, contends that his country has been described as "a ROTC" or Republic of Total Corruption by the people and mass media".[2]

Why is corruption such a serious problem in South Korea? When did the fight against corruption begin? What are the various measures employed to combat corruption in South Korea? How effective have such measures been? This chapter will attempt to answer all these questions. However, before assessing the extent of corruption in South Korea, it is necessary to describe the salient features of its policy context because of their impact on the formulation and implementation of the anti-corruption measures.

POLICY CONTEXT

Geography

South Korea has a total area of 99,274 sq. km and is the 26th largest country in Asia.[3] It is a mountainous country as rugged mountains constitute between 70% and 80% of the land area.[4] According to Donald Stone Macdonald, "the Koreans themselves speak of their 'three thousand *ri* [about 0.5 kilometres] of beautiful rivers and mountains' in song and often go to the mountains for meditation or enjoyment".[5] With its "restricted valleys and lack of major river systems" there was no need to mobilise labour and develop administrative mechanisms for flood control and management of irrigation in South Korea.[6]

While the Korean peninsula is moderately endowed with natural resources, South Korea has been less endowed than North Korea with only tungsten, graphite, and limestone. However, it has 19% of arable area and is the "traditional rice bowl of Korea, with somewhat greater rainfall, [and] warmer climate".[7] Thus, like Hong Kong and Singapore, South Korea is also resource-poor, but South Korea is better endowed with mineral resources and has a higher proportion of arable land than the two city-states. Indeed, South Korea's ample reserves of limestone for producing cement has enabled it to expand its construction industry domestically and to the Middle East in the 1970s.[8]

On the other hand, regional cleavages have developed in response to "wide regional economic disparities, the continued political dominance of one region (Kyongsang) over others until recently, and political manipulation and amplification of regional conflicts by political elites".[9] Indeed, regional cleavages affect many aspects of South Korean society, namely, "choice of marriage partner, recruitment and promotion of employees in firms, support for specific political leaders and political parties, formation and fragmentation of the political parties, and much more".[10] Regionalism was suppressed during the Japanese colonial period, the U.S. military administration, and the pre-1987 era of authoritarian rule.[11] However, with the transition to democracy in 1987, regional ties "fully surfaced and became the pre-eminent line of cleavage in party politics".[12] Political parties became more regionally focused in the 1990s and the origins of their leaders determined the location of their strength. For example, Kim Dae Jung's stronghold was in the Cholla provinces and Seoul; Kim Young Sam's strength was in Pusan and South Kyongsang Province; and Kim Jong Pil came from the Chungchong provinces.[13]

Regionalism is an important factor affecting South Korea's anti-corruption strategy as regional cleavages can undermine the incumbent government's commitment to fighting corruption as "reliance on regionalism undercuts effective national debate on national public policy issues essential to democratic governance".[14]

Economy

In 2000, South Korea's GDP was US$457.2 billion and its GDP per capita was US$9,670. Its average annual growth in GDP during 1990-2000 was 6.4%. Given its lack of natural resources, it is not surprising that South Korea has allocated 4.1% of its GDP to education, and 5.4% of its GDP to health. The relatively high standard of living in South Korea is reflected in the high consumer goods ownership per 100 households of the population. More specifically, there are 92.5 colour television sets per 100 households, 47.6 telephone lines per 100 population, 60.8 mobile telephone subscribers per 100 population, 25.1 computers per 100 population, and 9.4 internet hosts per 100 population.[15]

The growth of South Korea's economy since independence has been remarkable as its GDP per capita has grown by 68 times from US$50 in 1948 to US$3,396 in 1990.[16] During 1990-2000, its GDP per capita had more than doubled to US$9,670. Steinberg has attributed South Korea's success in economic development to these factors: "political will, sound economic policies, effective implementation, mass mobilisation, a skilled but often exploited labour force, a vigorous private sector under the guidance and control of an interventionist centralising government, a strong subsidisation programme to induce exports and rural growth and to open new sectors for expansion, and an international scene conducive to Korean exports".[17]

South Korea's economy is the third largest in Asia after Japan and China. Its GDP per capita is ranked ninth after Japan, Hong Kong, Singapore, Australia, Brunei, Macau, Taiwan, and New Zealand.[18] In short, South Korea is rich enough to devote sufficient resources for fighting corruption and for President Kim Dae Jung's government to raise the salaries of civil servants.

Demography

South Korea has a population of 46.7 million persons in 2000 and a population density of 472 persons per sq. km. Unlike the other countries discussed in this book, the population in South Korea is homogeneous with 99% being Korean and 50,000 Chinese as the only minority group. In terms of religion, 47% of the population are Buddhist and 49% are Christian. The adult literacy rate of South Koreans is 97.8%.[19] With a homogeneous population, common language, and the tremendous importance given to education, the incumbent government in South Korea will be able to spread anti-corruption messages easily throughout the country. Indeed, Steinberg has argued that "the cultural, ethnic, and linguistic homogeneity of the Korean people" gave South Korea "a developmental edge" as it provided "an easier milieu in which a powerful regime could mobilise for developmental (or political) purposes".[20]

On the other hand, Sung Chul Yang has argued that some aspects of Korean culture or "traditional mores" have contributed to the spread of corruption in South Korea:

> A reciprocal giving and receiving common in a traditional setting, for example, may lose its original virtue and become the root cause of corrupt practices in urban and industrial life. Corruption, which permeates contemporary Korean society, may also have originated from some transplantation of rural and traditional values and behaviour to urban and industrial living. Like cancer, it has spread through the entire community—schools and academe, business, commercial and labour establishments, civil services, mass media and political parties. Few individuals or organisations are, in fact, free of, or immune from, such a nexus of corruption and bribery. Two scandals of the Roh administration, the Suso real estate development project irregularities and the Ministry of Defence land scam ... are only conspicuous symptoms of a much deeper socio-political disease rooted in agrarian belief systems and traditional behaviour transplanted into a rapidly urbanising milieu.[21]

In his analysis of Korean political culture, Woon-Tai Kim identified four distinctive features: communitarian identity, authoritarian values, factionalism, and formalism.[22] More specifically, he argued that the negative effects of factionalism outweighed the positive aspects as "rent-seeking, corruption, irrational pattern of recruitment, and the politics of exclusion, all of which are closely associated with factionalism, have undermined political development and economic efficiency".[23]

Political System

Korea's history can be traced to Tangun, who was made the first king in 2333BC. However, political unity was only attained in 668AD, with the establishment of the Silla dynasty. Korea was colonised twice, first by the Mongols, and later, by the Japanese. The Mongols ruled Korea for 113 years from 1259 until 1392, when Yi Song-gye, a former Koryo general, created the Yi or Chosun dynasty. In contrast, the Japanese colonised Korea for 40 years from 1905-1945. While "Japanese colonialism improved Korea's agriculture and gave it the infrastructure for its subsequent economic success," such improvements however, only benefited Japan's own settlers at the expense of the Koreans, who lost their land.[24]

On May 10, 1948, Korea was divided into two at the 38th parallel: the Republic of Korea under Syngman Rhee in the south, and the Democratic People's Republic of Korea under Kim Il Sung in the north. On June 25, 1950, the North attacked the South and this led to the Korean War, which claimed four million lives and ended on July 27, 1953, and confirming the division of the Korean peninsula along the 38th parallel.[25] Since then, Korea has remained divided and the United States has maintained 40,000 troops in South Korea to protect it from invasion by North Korea.

South Korea became independent on August 15, 1948. After 26 years of authoritarian rule under President Park Chung Hee (1961-1979) and President Chun Doo Hwan (1980-1988), South Korea became democratic when President Roh Tae Woo assumed power in 1988.[26] South Korea is a parliamentary democracy with a National Assembly consisting of 299 members who are elected for four years. The president is elected for a five-year term. Kim Young Sam became the first civilian president in February 1993. He was succeeded by Kim Dae Jung, who became president in February 1998. The transformation of South Korea's political system from authoritarianism to democracy has certainly assisted the governments of Kim Young Sam and Kim Dae Jung in curbing corruption.

EXTENT OF CORRUPTION

Corruption is a way of life in South Korea. Its origins can be traced to the Yi Dynasty (1392-1910) which had introduced various anti-corruption measures. The most important measure was the King's Secret Mission or *Amhaing-osa*, whose duty was to investigate the corruption of government officials and to report their investigations secretly to the King. There were also other criminal, personnel and financial regulations which were designed to prevent the abuse of power by the officials and to protect the population from their corrupt behaviour. The various anti-corruption measures were effective until the beginning of the 16th century.[27]

However, corruption became a serious problem from the 16th century onwards for three reasons. First, the participation of the King's relatives in politics and governmental affairs and their acquisition of farm land from independent farmers contributed to nepotism and bureaucratic corruption. Second, the officials abandoned their rectitude and thrifty behaviour for a luxurious lifestyle, which was supported by their involvement in corrupt activities. Finally, the many anti-corruption measures were no longer effective and their ineffectiveness aggravated the problem of corruption.[28]

From January 1894 to March 1897, Isabella L. Bird, a British travel writer made four visits to Korea and recorded her impressions in her book, *Korea and Her Neighbours*, which was published in two volumes in 1898. In her last chapter on "Last Words on Korea" in Volume 2 of her book, Bird referred to the problem of corruption by observing that there were two classes in Korea: "the Robbers and the Robbed–the official class recruited from the *yang-bans*, the licensed vampires of the country, and the *Ha-in*, literally 'low men', a residuum of fully four-fifths of the population, whose *raison d'etre* is to supply the blood for the vampires to suck".[29] The Treasury Department was "in a more chaotic and corrupt condition, and the ramifications of its corruption were spread all through the Provinces" as earlier attempts to reform it were thwarted by "the rapacity of the King's male and female favourites, and the measureless cunning and craft of corrupt officials". However, after one year of "firm and capable foreign supervision", the Treasury Department was "cleansed" as the accounts were "kept on a uniform system, and with the utmost exactitude". Consequently, Korea closed the financial year in April 1897, "with every account paid and a million and a half in the Treasury, out of which she has repaid one million of the Japanese loan of three millions".[30]

Bureaucratic corruption increased during the post-independence period and the government introduced the criminal code and administrative restrictions to curb it. According to Myoung-Soo Kim:

> Corruption has been recognised since the early days of the first Republic, which began in 1948, as one of the most social ills facing Korea and, therefore, is a problem to be tackled by all the means at the country's disposal. ... After the early 1960s, all new administrations in Korea waged anti-corruption drives because it was recognised that corruption was widespread in the public, as well as in the private, sectors and was one of the major concerns of the time ... Corruption has survived and outlived administrations that campaign against it and has proven to be indestructible.[31]

The anti-corruption measures introduced in the 1950s and 1960s were formal and ineffective. During the 1960s and 1970s, the United States Army in South Korea "could not procure local goods and services without encountering collusion and corruption".[32] Even though "bribery and corruption were not applauded in Korean culture" on the one hand, "collusion and kickbacks were also facilitated by certain 'cultural traits'" such as the custom of gift-giving on the other hand.[33] The Korean suppliers subverted the U.S. army's policy of competitive bidding by colluding to over-charging the army by 30% or more above competitive prices. They also gave gifts (including money) to the Korean accountants and contract specialists working for the army to induce them to provide higher cost estimates, as their low salaries made them vulnerable to corruption. If the gifts did not work, the Korean accountants would be threatened by the suppliers.[34] Furthermore, no other legal or administrative anti-corruption measures were initiated until 1974 when major corruption scandals involving civil servants were exposed and there was increasing public dissatisfaction with bureaucratic corruption.[35]

Corruption was also manifested in the 1987 presidential election and the April 1988 legislative election. As the ruling Democratic Justice Party (DJP) had a great deal of money to spend, many observers believed that it spent between US$300 million to US$1 billion in the 1987 presidential election.[36] Vote-buying was rampant as both the DJP and opposition parties were corrupt in handling their campaigns. However, as the DJP had more resources than the opposition parties, it gave US$30 to US$60 to junior civil servants and rice to low-income families. The DJP threatened to dismiss the civil servants if either of the two opposition candidates won the election.[37]

Unlike previous legislative elections where corruption, vote-buying, and mobilisation of civil servants to campaign for the ruling party were conducted discreetly, the DJP performed these activities openly in the April 1988 legislative election, which was considered by many observers to be "the most corrupt in the nation's history" as "money, violence, corruption, mudslinging, fraud, and every other conceivable means were permitted to determine" its outcome.[38] As the average DJP candidate spent about US$1.5 million (the cost of 50,000 votes) to get elected, each vote costs between US$25 to US$30. However, some candidates spent nearly US$3.5 million and "several spent over US$7 million to gain a legislative seat".[39]

A 1990 survey conducted by Seoul National University's Social Science Research Centre found that 40.7% of the respondents identified the corruption of politicians as the most important obstacle to South Korea's democratisation.[40] More importantly, as shown in Table 7.1 below, politicians were considered by 70.1% of the same respondents to be the most corrupt in South Korea, followed by businessmen (10.9%), government officials (9.3%), journalists (3.3%), military (2.5%), and educators (2.1%).[41]

TABLE 7.1 CORRUPTION IN SOUTH KOREA
BY GROUP OR PROFESSION, 1990

Group or Profession	Number of Responses	Percentage of Responses
Politicians	1071	70.1
Businessmen	167	10.9
Government officials	141	9.3
Journalists	50	3.3
Military	38	2.5
Educators	31	2.1
Others	20	1.3
No answer	85	5.6
Total	1526	100.0

Source: Adapted from *A Survey Report of the Korean People's Belief System in Reference to the Coming 21ˢᵗ Century* (Seoul: Seoul National University Social Science Research Centre, 1990), p. 73, quoted in Sung Chul Yang, "An Analysis of South Korea's Political Process and Party Politics", in James Cotton, *Politics and Policy in the New Korean State: From Roh Tae-Woo and Kim Young-Sam* (Melbourne: Longman Australia Pty Ltd, 1995), p. 29, Table 2.6.

Similarly, the Korea Survey (Gallup) Polls conducted a public opinion survey on the government's anti-corruption activities since 1993 in August-September 1993 and found that the respondents believed that "South Korean society seriously suffers from corruption of politicians (85.3%), public employees (52.9%), lawyers (34.3%), and the military (30.2%), and that the two most contributing factors to current corruption are selfishness and mammonism of each individual member of society".[42] Another important finding was that 78.5% of the respondents wanted more punishment and a stricter control system for those found guilty of corrupt practices.[43]

An analysis of the 237 reported cases of corruption by public employees in *HanKuk-Ilbo*, a major newspaper in South Korea, in 1993-1994 by KeeChul Hwang found that bribery (53.6%) was the most common form of corruption, followed by fraud (21.1%), forgery of official documents (8%), embezzlement of public money (7.2%), misappropriation of public money (4.6%), and others (5.5%).[44] Another important finding was that the amount of the average bribe exceeded two million Won (or US$2,000) or more than a month's salary for a lower-level civil servant. Furthermore, Hwang found that 22.4% of the 237 cases involved the police, 19.4% dealt with licensing, 15.6% involved registration, 13.9% concerned taxation, and 7.2% focused on health. Hwang attributed the higher proportion of cases of police corruption to the 36 years of Japanese colonial rule when the police was employed as the primary tool of control over the Korean population.[45] In his 1995 survey of 957 public employees and 925 members of the public, Hwang found that while 81.3% of the public viewed public employees as corrupt, only 47.3% of public employees considered themselves to be corrupt.[46]

Finally, in their analysis of Korean public administration, Jong S. Jun and Myung S. Park argued that "deeply rooted corruption" was a major reason for the incapability of Korean public administrators and the recent financial crisis. They wrote:

> Corruption is the cancer of Korean society, and it is found at every level of Korean society, from top officials down to minor civil servants. ... Corruption at high-level is widespread, but scandals involving bureaucrats, particularly those who collect taxes and enforce customs regulations, are often reported in newspapers as well.[47]

They substantiated their argument by referring to three scandals: the scandal involving the development of the *Soosuh Area* suburb in Seoul; the Hanbo scandal; and the procurement of fighter planes by the Ministry of Defence. They concluded that "corruption will not go away until high-level government officials and politicians live morally and ethically and become models of honesty".[48]

What are the major causes of corruption in South Korea? In addition to the historical reasons for the emergence of corruption in South Korea in the 16th century, the low salaries of civil servants is an important reason for the pervasive corruption in contemporary South Korea. During the First Republic (1948-1960), corruption was rampant because the salaries of civil servants were inadequate for them to support their families. In 1994, Young Jong Kim argued that as the salaries of civil servants are about 70-80% of the salaries of their counterparts in the private sector, the "low salary structure of public officials forces them not only [to] tolerate corruption, but also initiate corruption".[49] The problem of corruption was aggravated during the 1997 financial crisis as civil service salaries were further reduced by 30%. Apart from being lower than private-sector salaries, the current wage level of South Korean civil servants is lower than the salaries of their counterparts in Japan, Singapore and Hong Kong.[50]

Second, according to John Kie-Chiang Oh, there is "a culture of corruption in Korea". The Koreans have a long tradition of gift-giving which causes corruption because "when the gift was an expensive item presented to a powerful individual with the expectation of receiving a favour it was akin to a bribe".[51] Indeed, gift-giving is an honoured tradition in all Asian countries, but in "Korea the tradition has [been] transformed into what can only be called bribery".[52]

Third, the plethora of government regulations in South Korea has given rise to ample opportunities for corruption. For example, to obtain a permit for building a factory, a company must prepare an average of 44.2 documents. These complex procedures requiring many documents resulted in delays, which increased the costs in time and money for the clients, private persons, or business firms. Thus, the latter are "tempted into collusion with the bureaucrats who have control over the matter to seek other, easier ways to get what they need, even by illegitimate means".[53]

Finally, the collusion between the politicians, civil servants and businessmen also contributed to corruption in South Korea. Wan-Ki Paik contended that "the administration-led economic growth policy, by necessity, brought about a connivance between the public administration and enterprises" which resulted in "structural corruption and irregularities".[54] For example, the fire in an illegal beer hall in Inchon in November 1999 was caused by negligence by the police, who ignored repeated complaints about the bar's illegal drinking sales and the fire safety inspectors, who overlooked inadequate safety standards in return for bribes.[55]

ANTI-CORRUPTION STRATEGY

Anti-Corruption Campaigns of Presidents Park, Chun and Roh, 1963-1992

In 1509 during the Chosun Dynasty, secret royal inspectors were appointed by the king from those who passed the state-administered examination to investigate administrative practices and "any possible corruption within local governments".[56] However, the fight against corruption in South Korea began with President Park Chung Hee, who assumed office in May 1961 after ousting the government of Chang Myon because of its involvement in corruption, its inability to defend the country from communism, and its incompetence in initiating economic and social change.[57] Park formed the Board of Audit and Inspection (BAI) in 1963 by merging the Board of Audit and the Commission of Inspection, which were established in 1948, to act as a direct check on the economic bureaucracy.[58] The BAI was thus the first *de facto* anti-corruption agency in South Korea. In March 1975, Park introduced the *Seojungshaeshin* (General Administration Reform) Movement to curb corruption in the civil service[59]. As punishment was stressed by the *Seojungshaeshin* Movement, the number of civil servants prosecuted rose from 21,919 in 1975 to 51,468 in 1976.[60]

Park's assassination in October 1979 led to the assumption of power a year later by his successor, Chun Doo Hwan, who re-affirmed his government's anti-corruption stance by purging corrupt public officials and introducing ethics laws to reward honest officials and to enhance the structures for civil service reforms.[61] However,

Chun's government lacked legitimacy because of opposition by rival political parties, student leaders, intellectuals, and progressive Christians.[62] Chun's unpopularity led to his retirement in February 1988, at the end of his seven-year term. Caiden and Kim have criticised the anti-corruption campaigns of Park and Chun for being sporadic, periodic, episodic, incidental and improvisatory, too cosmetic and lip-serving, and for being implemented quickly and without careful preparation.[63]

The peaceful transfer of power to President Roh Tae Woo enabled him to investigate the abuses and corruption during his predecessor's regime. During the parliamentary hearings in November and December 1988, Chun, his two brothers, and his wife's family were accused of massive corruption. On November 23, 1988, Chun and his wife apologised for their misbehaviour and returned 13.9 billion Won (US$20 million) to the government. In his statement of apology to the country, Chun said:

> When I was inaugurated as president, most relatives of mine, including close relatives were not so well-off. They were proud and surprised at first, but then they started to be disturbed by the temptations around them. They began to cause various problems. I asked them many times to be prudent and sometimes I controlled them. I really am sorry that many relatives of mine have been involved in irregularities and made you very angry. I sincerely apologise and beg your pardon.[64]

In July 1989, Chun's brothers were convicted for corruption and sentenced to between four and seven years' imprisonment. Mark L. Clifford has commented on the consequences of the corruption of Chun and his family thus:

> What became apparent after Chun left office was the depth of corruption and the degree to which it had been quietly tolerated, even expected. The pervasive corruption is another of the ugly legacies bequeathed by the Fifth Republic. Corruption had long been part of the Korean system, but *Chun did the country a tremendous disservice by allowing his relatives to prosper.* For all his faults, Park had never allowed his family to profit personally from his position.

> Unfortunately, the Chun and Lee families set an example of egregiously corrupt behaviour that still undermines the Korean social contract.[65]

While President Roh remained committed to the establishment of democracy during his term of office, he was nevertheless plagued by the long-festering problem of political corruption, as six legislators were found guilty of extorting funds from the business community. The Hanbo scandal of 1992 shocked the country when Chung Tae Soo, chairman of Hanbo Construction Company, was accused of contributing substantial funds to the ruling and opposition political parties for favours involving land development.[66] However, Roh himself was not immune as it was discovered in October 1995 that the major business conglomerates and numerous individuals had contributed almost US$600 million to his private political fund, which he had used to reward supporters and kept for himself and his family.[67]

President Kim Young Sam's Anti-Corruption Campaign

When Kim Young Sam became the first civilian president in February 1993, he launched an intensive anti-corruption campaign to curb the Korean disease, namely, corruption. He began with the voluntary disclosure of his personal assets and those of his extended family amounting to 1.77 billion Won (US$2 million).[68] President Kim encouraged his cabinet colleagues and ruling party members to follow suit. In June 1993, the Public Officials' Ethics Law was revised to institutionalise the disclosure of public officials' assets, and all senior officials were required to periodically register and disclose their assets.[69] He gave up golf, which had become a symbol of corporate-government cronyism and the exchange of corrupt gifts.[70] In August 1993, President Kim issued an emergency presidential decree to establish the Real-Name Financial Transaction System, which prohibited the use of anonymous financial accounts and required individuals to use their own names for operating bank accounts, as the anonymous or false-name account had been the backbone of the black economy and massive fraud, corruption and tax evasion schemes.[71] The use of fake or borrowed accounts enabled individuals to avoid paying tax and conceal the trail of recipients of illicit incomes.[72]

In March 1994, the Election for Public Office and Election Malpractice Prevention Act was introduced to reduce corruption in politics by ensuring transparency in campaign financing, limiting campaign expenditures, preventing electoral irregularities, and imposing heavy penalties for offenders.[73] However, the most important reforms introduced by President Kim were the strengthening of the BAI, and the creation of the Commission for the Prevention of Corruption (CPC), which is an advisory body of private citizens formed to assist the BAI's chairman in the task of fighting corruption.

The BAI performs three functions: to confirm the closing accounts of the state's revenues and expenditures; to audit the accounts of the central government agencies, provincial governments and other local autonomous bodies, and government-invested organisations to ensure proper and fair accounting; and to inspect the work done by government agencies and the duties of public officials to improve the operation and quality of government services.[74]

The BAI's chairman was appointed by the president for four years with the consent of the National Assembly. The BAI's commissioner was also appointed by the president for four years on the recommendation of the chairman.[75] In March 1993, the government formed a team of 100 special inspectors within the BAI to implement President Kim's anti-corruption campaign by focusing on officials handling taxes, government contracts, procurement, military conscription and licences, who were suspected of being corrupt.[76] In August 1993, the BAI had 776 officials involved in audit and administrative inspection. The number of BAI staff increased to 849 officials by July 1998.[77] Article 24 of the BAI Act enabled the BAI to conduct anti-corruption activities by scrutinising the behaviour of civil servants.[78]

Kim Dae Jung's Comprehensive Anti-Corruption Campaign

Kim Dae Jung won the December 1997 presidential election and was inaugurated as president on February 25, 1998. He demonstrated his concern in combating corruption through the implementation of a comprehensive anti-corruption strategy with the objectives of ensuring clean and upright public office, transparent and reliable government, and a just and fair society in order to become a transparent state and to improve its ranking on Transparency International's CPI from 43rd position in 1998 to 20th position by 2003.[79]

President Kim's comprehensive anti-corruption strategy has six major components in response to the various causes of corruption in South Korea.[80] The first component is the improvement of the existing system of corruption control through the implementation of these measures: the creation of an Anti-Corruption Committee for the co-ordination of anti-corruption programmes and activities; and the formulation of the Anti-Corruption Law to provide protection for whistle-blowers, to strengthen citizen watch and participation in anti-corruption movements, and to reinforce detection and punishment for corrupt practices.

The second component of President Kim's anti-corruption campaign involves the reform of the attitudes and consciousness of civil servants by enforcing codes of conduct and education, and revising the salaries of medium to low level bureaucrats to match their counterparts in the private sector within five years. Third, public awareness of corruption is promoted by means of education in school and other social and cultural education centres, the use of mass media to publicise anti-corruption materials, a national movement against corruption, and strengthening of international co-operation in fighting corruption.

The fourth aspect concerns the creation of a social and cultural environment against corruption through the scrutiny and strict control of former government officials, enhancing the transparency of private industries, and eroding the collusion between politicians, government officials, and businessmen. Fifth, detection and punishment for corruption is reinforced by improving the reward/protection system for informers, activating citizen watch and report against corruption, creating a special inspection office to focus on the corruption of senior government officials, and increasing the financial penalty for corrupt officials by retrieving personal gains and government losses, and confiscating the bribes.

Finally, administrative reforms have been introduced in six corruption-prone areas of tax administration, construction, housing, food and entertainment, environmental management, and police work. In 1998, President Kim formed the Regulatory Reform Committee (RRC) to make the country more business friendly by eliminating unnecessary or irrational economic and social regulations that hindered business activities or interfered in people's lives. For example, to obtain a permit to build a factory, a company has to prepare an average of 44 documents and wait for several months for approval. These excessive regulations encourage corruption as businessmen are prepared to bribe the relevant officials to bypass the cumbersome and tedious procedures for obtaining a factory permit.[81] In April 1999, the Seoul Metropolitan Government launched an "Online Procedure Enhancement for Civil Applications (OPEN)" system to improve civil applications covering 54 common procedures, which could be filed through the Internet.[82]

EVALUATION OF ANTI-CORRUPTION STRATEGY

President Kim Young Sam's anti-corruption campaign confirmed that corruption is a way of life in South Korea and exposed its pervasiveness in the country. As he turned the spotlight on corrupt practices, "it exposed more dirt than the Korean people had ever imagined or are comfortable with".[83] Young Jong Kim has lamented the lack of political will in South Korea's efforts to curb corruption, especially under the regimes of Presidents Rhee, Park and Chun.[84] Although Kim's anti-corruption drive was hindered by the May 17, 1997 arrest of his son for bribery and tax evasion in the Hanbo loan scandal and his sentencing to three years' imprisonment five months later, President Kim has clearly demonstrated his commitment to eliminating corruption by not obstructing the legal arrest and sentencing of his son to three years' imprisonment.[85] Nevertheless, the Hanbo scandal and his son's arrest and imprisonment had seriously undermined Kim's legitimacy and jeopardised the continued success of his anti-corruption campaign. Moreover, despite all these efforts made against corruption, there is no evidence that corruption has been contained during President Kim Young Sam's administration.[86]

How effective was President Kim Young Sam's anti-corruption strategy in curbing the endemic corruption in South Korea which has been fuelled by 30 years of authoritarian rule? How effective was his moral crusade against illicit and unethical behaviour in transforming the primordial and particularistic standards of behaviour among the Korean people?[87] The 1996 Korean Democratisation Survey found that 71% of the respondents experienced some degree of decrease in political corruption and only 4% reported having experienced an increase in corruption. However, the 1997 Korean Democratisation Survey reported that 49% and 36% of the respondents perceived the level of corruption of Kim Young Sam's government to be high and very high respectively.[88] Doh C. Shin contends that this finding illustrates the fact that for all the important steps President Kim Young Sam took during 1993-1997, the age-old custom of corruption was not dying at all in the South Korean political marketplace; instead the informal norms were still overpowering the formal rules of the newly-implanted democratic political game.[89] Myoung-Soo Kim contended that corruption was a serious problem in South Korea because of the lack of effective anti-corruption measures, the lack of independence of anti-corruption agencies, and the lack of consistent and fair enforcement of the anti-corruption laws.[90]

A similar negative assessment has been provided by Jon Moran, who has argued that President Kim Young Sam's anti-corruption reforms were initially successful but floundered later because of three problems. First, these reforms were viewed as part of Kim's strategy of removing past opponents to secure his position. Second, the economic crisis and the need for economic growth compelled Kim to abandon by 1995 his attempts to reform chaebol structures in production and finance. Finally, Kim's anti-corruption reforms rebounded on himself as the real name system flushed into the open massive secret accounts held by Chun and Roh and exposed the full extent of informal network politics and the links between the state elite, the chaebol and the politicised financial system.[91] On the other hand, Kim's anti-corruption reforms were successful because they inaugurated important legislative initiatives, laid the groundwork for future reforms and provided a further legitimation for the oppositional activities of civil society activities.[92]

Indeed, the adoption of the real name system in August 1993 was Kim's "most potent antidote to the 'Korean disease'" of corruption as it "dealt a major blow to the prevalent practice of amassing unearned income, and soliciting bribes or political funds through fake or borrowed accounts". Credit should be given to Kim for implementing a policy that was deferred in 1982 and 1987 because of "fears of its negative impact on growth". The implementation of the real name system "proved reform seekers correct" as "billions stashed in fake and borrowed accounts had to be transferred to real-name accounts".[93]

In contrast, President Kim Dae Jung's comprehensive anti-corruption strategy was much more effective for three reasons. First, after its first year of operations, the Regulatory Reform Committee formed by President Kim abolished 5,226 or 48% of 11,125 administrative regulations.[94] Furthermore, the OPEN system has also enhanced the transparency of civil procedures and reduced the opportunities for corruption. By May 2000, the OPEN system had handled 28,000 cases of civil applications and over 648,000 visitors had visited its website. Thus, the OPEN system has improved "customer-oriented delivery of public services" and "transparency of city administration" as those officials responsible for permit or approval procedures (usually perceived to be corruption-prone) are "required to upload their work reports and documents to the Internet" to enable citizens to monitor the progress of their applications.[95]

Second, even though the implementation of President Kim's comprehensive anti-corruption strategy met with stiff resistance, the Anti-Corruption Act was passed on July 24, 2001, more than two years after its proposal.[96] Six months later, in January 2002, the Korean Independent Commission Against Corruption (KICAC) was formed as the country's *de jure* anti-corruption agency. Finally, and most importantly, the recent arrests of President Kim Dae Jung's two sons for corruption show the effectiveness of the newly-formed KICAC and his commitment to curbing corruption as he did not prevent the arrests. President Kim admitted that the arrests of his two sons were "heartbreaking" but he said that he would not interfere and would let the court decide on their fate.[97]

CONCLUSION

This chapter has shown that corruption is a serious problem in South Korea in spite of the attempts by various governments to curb it. The anti-corruption strategies of President Kim Young Sam and President Kim Dae Jung appear to have borne some fruit. First, the number of officials reprimanded for corruption increased by 10.8% from 17,674 during 1995-1997 to 19,597 during 1998-2000.[98] Second, the number of corruption cases reported by the "Anti-Corruption Citizens' Coalition", consisting of 30 citizen groups, increased from 59,000 in 1998 to 123,000 in 2000.[99] Third, the number of officials punished for corruption has decreased from 7,420 in 1998 to 5,091 in 2000, and the proportion of citizens recognising the seriousness of corruption also declined from 91% in November 1999 to 75.6% in September 2000, according to surveys conducted by Hyundai Research.[100]

TABLE 7.2 RANKING OF SOUTH KOREA BY TRANSPARENCY INTERNATIONAL AND POLITICAL ECONOMIC RISK CONSULTANCY, 1995-2002

Year	Transparency International	Political Economic Risk Consultancy
1995	27	4
1996	27	5
1997	34	8
1998	43	7
1999	50	8
2000	48	7
2001	42	6
2002	40	NA
Average ranking	39	6

Source: Compiled from Transparency International's CPI, 1995-2002; and PERC annual corruption surveys, 1995-2001.

Table 7.2 above shows that South Korea's ranking on Transparency International's CPI from 1995-2002 had declined from 27th position in 1995 to 50th position in 1999. However, from 2000 onwards, South Korea's rank on the CPI had improved from 48th position in 2000 to 42nd position in 2001 and to 40th position in 2002. Its average rank during 1995-2002 is 39th position. Thus, the objective of President Kim Dae Jung's comprehensive anti-corruption strategy of improving South Korea's CPI ranking to 20th position by 2003 is unlikely to be attained. In contrast, South Korea's ranking on the PERC annual corruption surveys declined from 4th position in 1995 to 8th position in 1997 and 1999. Its ranking on PERC improved from 7th position in 2000 to 6th position in 2001. South Korea's average ranking by PERC from 1995-2001 is 6th position.

South Korea has shifted from Pattern 1 to Pattern 3 with the implementation of Kim Dae Jung's comprehensive anti-corruption strategy which resulted in the enactment of the Anti-Corruption Act on July 24, 2001, and the establishment of the KICAC to implement the Anti-Corruption Act in January 2002. As Roh Moo Hyun succeeded Kim Dae Jung as President on February 25, 2003, it remains to be seen whether President Roh will demonstrate the same sense of commitment towards the elimination of the "Korean disease" as his two predecessors.

ENDNOTES

1   A.T.R. Rahman, "Legal and Administrative Measures against Bureaucratic Corruption in Asia", in Ledivina V. Carino (ed.), *Bureaucratic Corruption in Asia: Causes, Consequences and Control* (Quezon City: JMC Press and College of Public Administration, University of the Philippines, 1986), p. 118.

2   Young Jong Kim, *Bureaucratic Corruption: The Case of Korea* 4th ed. (Seoul: Chomyung Press, 1994), p. 215.

3   John Andrews, *Pocket Asia* 7th edition (London: The Economist Newspaper Ltd. and Profile Books Ltd., 2002), pp. 14 and 172.

4   Richard Saccone, *The Business of Korean Culture* (Seoul: Hollym Corporation Publishers, 1994), p. 4.

5   Donald Stone Macdonald, *The Koreans: Contemporary Politics and Society* 3rd edition, edited and revised by Donald N. Clark (Boulder: Westview Press, 1996), p. 6.

6   David I. Steinberg, *The Republic of Korea: Economic Transformation and Social Change* (Boulder: Westview Press, 1989), p. 12.

7   Macdonald, *The Koreans*, pp. 8-9; and Andrews, *Pocket Asia*, p. 180.

8   Byung-Nak Song, *The Rise of the Korean Economy* 2nd edition (Hong Kong: Oxford University Press [China], 1997), p. 13.

9   Kyoung-Ryung Seong, "Civil Society and Democratic Consolidation in South Korea: Great Achievements and Remaining Problems", in Larry Diamond and Byung-Kook Kim (eds.), *Consolidatiing Democracy in South Korea* (Boulder: Lynne Rienner Publishers, 2000), p. 98.

10   Ibid., pp. 98-99.

11   David I. Steinberg, "Continuing Democratic Reform: The Unfinished Symphony", in Diamond and Kim (eds.), *Consolidating Democracy in South Korea*, p. 225.

12   Byung-Kook Kim, "Party Politics in South Korea's Democracy: The Crisis of Success", in Diamond and Kim (eds.), *Consolidating Democracy in South Korea*, p. 79.

13   Steinberg, "Continuing Democratic Reform", pp. 225-226.

14   Ibid., p. 226.

15   Andrews, *Pocket Asia*, pp. 180-181.

16   Steinberg, *The Republic of Korea*, p. 123.

17   Ibid., p. 157.

18   Andrews, *Pocket Asia.*, pp. 18-19.

19   Ibid., p. 181.

20 Steinberg, *The Republic of Korea*, p. 188.

21 Sung Chul Yang, "An Analysis of South Korea's Political Process and Party Politics", in James Cotton (ed.), *Politics and Policy in the New Korean State: From Roh Tae-Woo to Kim Young-Sam* (Melbourne: Longman Australia Pty Ltd, 1995), pp. 11-12.

22 Woon-Tai Kim, "Korean Politics: Setting and Political Culture", in Soong Hoom Kil and Chung-In Moon (eds.), *Understanding Korean Politics: An Introduction* (Albany: State University of New York Press, 2001), pp. 25-29.

23 Ibid., p. 28.

24 Andrews, *Pocket Asia*, p. 172.

25 Ibid., p. 173.

26 For more details of South Korea's political development under these three presidents, see Steinberg, *The Republic of Korea*, pp. 55-68.

27 Rahman, "Legal and Administrative Measures Against Bureaucratic Corruption in Asia", pp. 117-118.

28 Ibid., pp. 118-119.

29 Isabella L. Bird, *Korea and Her Neighbours: A Narrative of Travel, with an Account of the Recent Vicissitudes and present position of the Country*, Volume 2 (Tokyo: Charles E. Tuttle Co. Publishers, 1986), p. 281.

30 Ibid., pp. 281-282.

31 Myoung-Soo Kim, "Regulation and Corruption", in Yong Hyo Cho and H. George Frederickson (eds.), *The White House and the Blue House: Government Reform in the United States and Korea* (Lanham: University Press of America, 1997), pp. 253-254.

32 Robert Klitgaard, *Controlling Corruption* (Berkeley: University of California Press, 1988), p. 134.

33 Ibid., pp. 138-139.

34 Ibid., pp. 134-135 and 149.

35 Rahman, "Legal and Administrative Measures Against Bureaucratic Corruption in Asia", p. 119.

36 Manwoo Lee, *The Odyssey of Korean Democracy: Korean Politics 1987-1990* (New York: Praeger Publishers, 1990), p. 73.

37 Ibid., p. 74.

38 Ibid., p. 101.

39 Ibid., p. 102.

40 Yang, "An Analysis of South Korea's Political Process and Party Politics", p. 29, Table 2.5.

41 Ibid., p. 29, Table 2.6.

42 Quoted in KeeChul Hwang, "Administrative Corruption in the Republic of Korea", (Ph.D. dissertation, University of Southern California, 1996), p. 161.

43 Quoted in ibid., p. 161.

44 Ibid., p. 180.

45   Ibid., pp. 180-181.

46   Ibid., pp. 158-159.

47   Jong S. Jun and Myung S. Park, "Crisis and Organisational Paralysis: The Lingering Problem of Korean Public Administration", *Journal of Contingencies and Crisis Management*, Vol. 9, No. 1 (March 2001), pp. 8-9.

48   Ibid., p. 9.

49   Kim, *Bureaucratic Corruption*, p. 222.

50   Pan-Suk Kim, "The Politics of Rewards for High Public Office in Korea", in Christopher Hood and B. Guy Peters with Grace O. M. Lee (eds.), *Reward for High Public Office: Asian and Pacific Rim States* (London: Routledge, 2003), p. 125.

51   John Kie-Chiang Oh, *Korean Politics: The Quest for Democratization and Economic Development* (Ithaca: Cornell University Press, 1999), p. 165.

52   Christine A. Genzberger *et al.*, *Korea Business: The Portable Encyclopedia for Doing Business with Korea* (San Rafael: World Trade Press, 1994), p. 25.

53   Kim, "Regulation and Corruption", pp. 261-262.

54   Wank-Ki Paik, "Merits and Demerits of Public Administration in Korea's Modernization", in Gerald E. Caiden and B.W. Kim (eds.), *A Dragon's Progress: Development Administration in Korea* (West Hartford: Kumarian Press, 1991), p. 131.

55   "Graft blamed for Korean bar fire", *Straits Times* (Singapore), Novemver 2, 1999, p. 22.

56   *The Board of Audit and Inspection Annual Report for 1998* (Seoul: BAI, 1999), p. 4.

57   Han Sung Joo, "South Korea: Politics in Transition", in Larry Diamond *et al.* (eds.), *Democracy in Developing Countries: Asia* (Boulder: Lynne Rienner Publishers, 1989), p. 273.

58   *The Board of Audit and Inspection Annual Report 1998*, p.5; and Martin Hart-Landberg, *The Rush to Development: Economic Change and Political Struggle in South Korea* (New York: Monthly Review Press, 1993), p. 54.

59   For more details, see Oh Suek-Hong, "The Counter-Corruption Campaign of the Korean Government (1975-1977): Administrative Anti-Corruption Measures of the *Seojungshaeshin*", in Bun Woong Kim and Wha Joon Rho (eds.), *Korean Public Bureaucracy* (Seoul: Kyobo Publishing, 1982), p. 324.

60   Rahman, "Legal and Administrative Measures Against Bureaucratic Corruption", p. 122.

61   Jong Sup Jun, "The Paradoxes of Development: Problems of Korea's Transformation", in Bun Woong Kim *et al.* (eds.), *Administrative Dynamics and Development: The Korean Experience* (Seoul: Kyobo Publishing, 1985), p. 63.

62   Han, "South Korea: Politics in Transition", pp. 282-284.

63   Gerald E. Caiden and Jung H. Kim, "A New Anti-Corruption Strategy for Korea", *Asian Journal of Political Science*, Vol. 1, No. 1 (June 1993), pp. 137-139.

173

64   Lee, *The Odyssey of Korean Democracy*, Appendix A, "Excerpts of Chun's Statement of Apology to the Nation", p. 156.

65   Mark L. Clifford, *Troubled Tiger: Businessmen, Bureaucrats, and Generals in South Korea*, rev. ed. (Armonk: M.E. Sharpe, 1998), p. 287, emphasis added.

66   "South Korea", *Asia Yearbook 1992* (Hong Kong: Far Eastern Economic Review, 1992), p. 138.

67   Macdonald, *The Koreans*, pp. 159-160.

68   Oh, *Korean Politics*, p. 139.

69   Kim, "Regulation and Corruption", p. 255.

70   Greg Sheridan, *Tigers: Leaders of the New Asia-Pacific* (St. Leonards: Allen and Unwin, 1994), p. 15.

71   Ibid., p. 15; and Kim, "Regulation and Corruption", p. 255.

72   Dorothy M. Guerrero, "A Tiger Changing Stripes: Post-Development, Transitions and Democracy in South Korea", in Kristina N. Gaerlan (ed.), *Transitions to Democracy in East and Southeast Asia* (Quezon City: Institute for Popular Democracy, 1999), p. 77.

73   Kim, "Regulation and Corruption", p. 255.

74   *The Board of Audit and Inspection Annual Report 1998*, pp. 7-8.

75   Kim, *Bureaucratic Corruption*, p. 218.

76   "Special team to root out graft among top South Korean officials", *Straits Times* (Singapore), March 12, 1993.

77   *The Board of Audit and Inspection Annual Report 1998*, p. 12.

78   Kim, *Bureaucratic Corruption*, p. 219.

79   *Korea's Comprehensive Anti-Corruption Programs* (Seoul: Office of the Prime Minister, 1999), p. 6.

80   Ibid., pp. 9-22.

81   Kim, "Regulation and Corruption", pp. 261-262.

82   For more details on the OPEN system, see *Online Procedures Enhancement for Civil Applications* (Seoul: Seoul Metropolitan Government, July 2001), pp. 6-13. See also: http://open.metro.seoul.kr.

83   Genzberger *et al.*, *Korea Business*, p. 25.

84   Kim, *Bureaucratic Corruption*, p. 207.

85   He was released in August 2000 because of a presidential amnesty to celebrate the Korean national holiday. See *Korea Herald*, August 3, 2000, quoted in Verena Blechinger; *Report on Recent Bribery Scandals, 1996-2000* (Berlin: Transparency International Working Paper, October 2000), p. 7. See http://www.transparency.org/documents/work-papers/s_korea_paper.html.

86   Kim, "Regulation and Corruption", p. 255.

87   Doh C. Shin, *Mass Politics and Culture in Democratizing Korea* (Cambridge: Cambridge University Press, 1999), p. 212.

88   Ibid., pp. 212-214.

89   Ibid., p. 214.

90　Myoung-Soo Kim, "Causes of Corruption and Irregularities", *Korea Focus*, Vol. 8, No. 1 (January-February 2000), pp. 2-3. See http:///www.kf.or.kr/ koreafocus/focus_detail.asp?no=143&title=VOL0801&category=ess.

91　Jon Moran, "Patterns of Corruption and Development in East Asia", *Third World Quarterly*, Vol. 20, No. 3 (June 1999), p. 575.

92　Ibid., p. 576.

93　Guerrero, "A Tiger Changing Stripes", p. 77.

94　*Progress and Prospect of Regulation Reform* (Seoul: Office of the Prime Minister, 1998), quoted in Yong Hyo Cho, "Regulatory Reform in Korea", (Seoul: unpublished paper, 1999), p. 3.

95　Sin-Yong Moon, "The Utilization of the Internet Technology in the Public Services of Korea", *Asian Review of Public Administration*, Vol. 13, No. 1 (January-June 2001), p. 41.

96　Republic of Korea, *Anti-Corruption Act* (Seoul: Office for Government Policy Coordination, 2001), p. 1.

97　Paul Shin, "South Korean President laments corruption scandals involving his sons", *Yahoo!News*, July 15, 2002, p. 1. See: http://story.news.yahoo.com/ new?tmpl=story&u=/ap/20020715/ap_wo_en_po/skorea.

98　Republic of Korea, *Combating Corruption in Korea* (Seoul: Office of the Prime Minister, October 2001), p. 17.

99　Ibid., p. 18.

100　Ibid., p. 18.

CHAPTER 8

Minimising Corruption: An Impossible Dream?

INTRODUCTION

The preceding six chapters analysed respectively how Mongolia, India, the Philippines, Singapore, Hong Kong, and South Korea combated corruption. These six countries demonstrated between them the three patterns of controlling corruption. Chapters 5 and 6 have shown that the third pattern of corruption control practised by Singapore and Hong Kong is more effective than Mongolia (Pattern 1) and India and the Philippines (Pattern 2).

The purpose of this concluding chapter is fourfold: to summarise the major findings of our comparative analysis of the anti-corruption strategies in the six countries; to explain why Pattern 3 is more effective than the other two patterns of corruption control; to identify the key ingredients for an effective anti-corruption strategy; and to ascertain whether minimising corruption in Asian countries is an impossible dream.

ANTI-CORRUPTION STRATEGIES IN SIX ASIAN COUNTRIES

Of the six Asian countries discussed in this book, Singapore is the most effective and India the least effective, judging from their CPI rankings from 1995-2002. Table 8.1 provides details of the average CPI ranking and scores for the six Asian countries from 1995-2002. More specifically, Singapore's average ranking on the CPI from 1995-2002 is 6th, followed by Hong Kong (ranked 16th), South Korea (ranked 39th), Mongolia (ranked 43rd in 1999), the Philippines (ranked 55th), and India (ranked 59th).

Corruption was first made an offence in Singapore in 1871 but it was only in December 1937 that the first anti-corruption law, the Prevention of Corruption Ordinance (POCO), was enacted. However, as discussed in Chapter 5, the POCO was ineffective in curbing corruption because of its limited powers and penalties and its implementation by the Anti-Corruption Branch (ACB) of the Criminal Investigation Department of the Singapore Police Force (SPF). The ACB failed to curb corruption because of its limited manpower and resources, its priority in fighting serious crimes like homicide instead of corruption, and the prevalence of police corruption. The incident that triggered the British colonial government's decision to transfer the task of controlling corruption from the SPF to an independent anti-corruption agency was the revelation that senior police officers were involved in the robbery of S$400,000 worth of opium in October 1951. The Corrupt Practices Investigation Bureau (CPIB) was established as Asia's first independent anti-corruption agency in October 1952.

TABLE 8.1 AVERAGE CPI RANKINGS AND SCORES OF SIX ASIAN COUNTRIES, 1995-2002

Country	Average CPI Ranking	Average CPI Score
Singapore	6th	9.06
Hong Kong	16th	7.58
South Korea	39th	4.28
Mongolia*	43rd	4.30
Philippines	55th	2.96
India	59th	2.77

*Mongolia's average ranking and score is based on the 1999 CPI only as it was excluded from the CPI for the other seven years.

However, the POCO and CPIB were ineffective in curbing corruption because of their limited powers and resources. Accordingly, the People's Action Party (PAP) government, which assumed power in June 1959 after winning the May 1959 general election, demonstrated its commitment to fighting corruption by replacing the weak POCO in 1960 with the Prevention of Corruption Act (POCA), which enhanced the penalties for corrupt offences and strengthened the CPIB's powers. The CPIB's ability to enforce the POCA impartially even against the rich and famous is responsible for Singapore's success in minimising corruption as corruption is perceived as a "low-reward, high-risk" activity.

Singapore's innovative approach in fighting corruption by relying on an anti-corruption agency independent of the police was adopted by Hong Kong in February 1974, when the Independent Commission Against Corruption (ICAC) was formed. A study team of Hong Kong civil servants, who visited Singapore and Sri Lanka in 1968 to examine their anti-corruption laws, had recommended, *inter alia*, that the task of curbing corruption should be transferred from the Royal Hong Kong Police Force (RHKPF) to another independent agency. However, this recommendation was rejected by the RHKPF and was only accepted by Governor MacLehose after the June 1973 escape of a corruption suspect, Chief Superintendent Peter Godber, to the United Kingdom.

Unlike the CPIB, which focuses mainly on investigating corruption cases and enforcing the POCA, the ICAC initiated a three-pronged strategy of emphasising investigation, education, and prevention. Accordingly, it is not surprising that the ICAC has 15 times more staff than the CPIB, and is organised in terms of the Operations Department, the Community Relations Department, and the Corruption Prevention Department, to handle its three main functions.

In short, Singapore and Hong Kong have adopted the third pattern of corruption control by relying on the CPIB and ICAC to enforce their comprehensive anti-corruption laws impartially.

India and the Philippines rely on more than one agency to combat corruption. India began her fight against corruption in 1941 with the creation of the Delhi Special Police Establishment (DSPE). The enactment of the Prevention of Corruption Act (POCA) in 1947 was followed by the establishment of the Central Bureau of Investigation (CBI) in April 1963 and the Central

Vigilance Commission (CVC) in February 1964. In addition to the CBI and CVC, there are also anti-corruption bureaux (ACBs) at the state level for handling vigilance and anti-corruption work. As the CBI is a police organisation and the ACBs derive their investigation powers from the Police Act, India has not learnt the lesson of Singapore's and Hong Kong's success in curbing corruption, namely, do not make the police responsible for fighting corruption especially when it is corrupt.

The Philippines has the most number of anti-corruption laws and agencies in Asia. In my 1982 survey of anti-corruption measures in Indonesia, Malaysia, the Philippines, Singapore and Thailand, I found that the Philippines had relied on seven anti-corruption laws and ten anti-corruption agencies since its battle against corruption began in the 1950s.[1] Since then, three additional agencies were created, increasing the total number of anti-graft agencies to 13. In spite of the record number of anti-corruption measures, the Philippines has failed to implement these measures impartially. The lack of policing in the Philippines is reflected in a comparative analysis of those arrested for corruption offences which shows an individual is 35 times more likely to be arrested for a corrupt offence in Hong Kong than in the Philippines.

Unfortunately, the many anti-corruption agencies in India and the Philippines are ineffective in curbing corruption because of their limited powers and resources and their inability to enforce impartially the anti-corruption laws. In other words, the critical factor for success is not the number of anti-corruption measures but whether these measures are impartially implemented.

South Korea began her battle against corruption in 1963, when President Park Chung Hee formed the Board of Audit and Inspection (BAI) as a *de facto* anti-corruption agency by merging the Board of Audit and the Commission on Inspection. However, the BAI is not a specialised anti-corruption agency as it is more concerned with its auditing and inspection duties. The BAI was strengthened under President Kim Young Sam's administration (1993-1998) as he introduced new laws to reduce corruption and increased the BAI's staff. President Kim Dae Jung should be credited for initiating comprehensive anti-corruption reforms which resulted in the enactment of the Anti-Corruption Act (ACA) in July 2001 and the establishment of the Korean Independent Commission Against Corruption (KICAC) in January 2002. The creation of the KICAC to implement the ACA is a clear demonstration that South Korea has adopted the third pattern of corruption control.

Mongolia is the only one among the six countries analysed in this book that was under communist rule for 70 years (1921-1991). The legacy of communist rule was not positive as the transition from a command economy to a market economy not only increased the opportunities for corruption, but also added new forms of corruption to those cultivated under communist rule. After holding democratic elections in 1992, the Law of Anti-Corruption was enacted by the government in April 1996. The absence of an independent anti-corruption agency in Mongolia means that it is still relying on the police to investigate corrupt offences. This method is ineffective as the low salaries of civil servants and political leaders have contributed to corruption in many government departments, including the police. In short, Mongolia's first pattern of corruption control (anti-corruption laws without an independent anti-corruption agency) is ineffective.

THE IMPORTANCE OF POLITICAL WILL

Which of the three patterns of corruption control is the most effective and why? To answer these questions, it is necessary to explain why the third pattern is more effective than the first two patterns.

The experiences of Singapore and Hong Kong discussed in Chapters 5 and 6 have demonstrated clearly the critical importance of political will in curbing corruption. If political will is defined as "the demonstrated credible intent of political actors (elected or appointed leaders, civil society watchdogs, stakeholder groups, etc.) to attack perceived causes or effects of corruption at a systemic level", Sahr J. Kpundeh contends that it is "a critical starting point for sustainable and effective programmes" as "without it, governments' statements to reform civil service, strengthen transparency and accountability and reinvent the relationship between government and private industry remain mere rhetoric".[2]

The political leadership in a country must be sincerely committed to the eradication of corruption by demonstrating exemplary conduct and adopting a modest lifestyle themselves. Those found guilty of corruption must be punished, regardless of their position or status in society. Political will is absent or lacking when the "big fish" (rich and famous) are protected from prosecution for corruption, and only the "small fish" (ordinary people) are caught. Under these circumstances, the anti-corruption strategy lacks credibility and is doomed to failure.

Political will is the most important prerequisite as a comprehensive anti-corruption strategy will fail if it is not supported by the political leadership in a country. For example, as shown in Chapter 4, the Philippines has the most anti-corruption laws and agencies in Asia, but it has been ineffective in curbing corruption because of the absence of political will among the political leaders. Indeed, even though President Corazon Aquino was more honest than her predecessor, President Ferdinand Marcos, she lacked the political will to punish her corrupt relatives. In short, the commitment of the political leaders in fighting corruption ensures the allocation of adequate personnel and resources to the anti-corruption effort, and the impartial enforcement of the anti-corruption laws by the anti-corruption agency.

Pattern 3 is also more effective because the anti-corruption agency is a specialised agency concerned solely with minimising corruption. The agency's specific focus on combating corruption is an advantage as it is not distracted by other priorities. Thus, the CPIB in Singapore and the ICAC in Hong Kong focus their energies and resources on curbing corruption unlike India's CBI, which is concerned also with tackling terrorism and organised crime in addition to corruption.

Pattern 3 is the most effective in combating corruption because of the presence of political will, which ensures the impartial enforcement of the anti-corruption laws by an independent agency. In contrast, Patterns 1 and 2 are ineffective in curbing corruption because of the absence of political will. For both India and the Philippines, which have adopted Pattern 2, there are many agencies and laws to combat corruption. However, the political leaders in these two countries lacked the political will to implement these measures effectively. Pattern 1 is also ineffective as both political will and an independent anti-corruption agency are absent.

THE IMPORTANCE OF POLICY CONTEXT

If Pattern 3 is the most effective, why has it not been adopted in more Asian countries other than Singapore, Hong Kong, Malaysia, South Korea and Thailand? Being the two least corrupt countries in Asia, the experiences of Singapore and Hong Kong have been publicised widely as "best practices" at various international conferences and workshops. However, their effective method of corruption control is not widely practised in more Asian countries for two reasons: the absence of political will in these countries to implement the necessary anti-corruption reforms (as discussed above) and the differences in policy context.

Table 8.2 shows that Singapore and Hong Kong are city-states and the smallest of the 16 Asian countries examined. Thus, the first contextual difference is that, unlike the two city-states, the other 14 countries are much larger. China is the largest Asian country, followed by India (third), Indonesia (fifth), Mongolia (sixth), Pakistan (seventh), Thailand (10th), Japan (14th), Malaysia (15th), Vietnam (16th), the Philippines (17th), Bangladesh (23rd), South Korea (26th), Sri Lanka (27th), and Taiwan (29th).[3]

Secondly, in terms of population, China and India have the two largest populations in the world with 1,275.1 million and 1,008.9 million respectively. Indonesia is next with 212.1 million, followed by Pakistan (141.3 million), Bangladesh (137.4 million), Japan (127.1 million), Vietnam (78.1 million), the Philippines (75.7 million), Thailand (62.8 million), South Korea (46.7 million), Malaysia and Taiwan (22.2 million), Sri Lanka (18.9 million), Hong Kong (6.9 million), Singapore (4 million), and Mongolia (2.5 million).[4]

182

TABLE 8.2 POLICY CONTEXTS OF 16 ASIAN COUNTRIES

Country	Land Area (sq. km)	Population (million)	GDP per capita	Political System	2002 CPI Ranking
Singapore	682.3	4.01	US$22,960	Democracy	5th
Hong Kong	1,075	6.90	US$23,930	Democracy SAR, China	14th
Japan	377,727	127.10	US$38,160	Constitutional monarchy	20th
Taiwan	36,179	22.20	US$13,950	Democracy	29th
Malaysia	332,665	22.20	US$3,850	Constitutional monarchy	33rd
South Korea	99,274	46.70	US$9,670	Democracy	40th
Mongolia	1,565,000	2.50	US$400	Democracy	43rd*
Sri Lanka	65,610	18.90	US$840	Democracy	52nd
China	9,560,900	1,275.10	US$850	Communist	59th
Thailand	513,115	62.8	US$2,010	Constitutional monarchy	64th
India	3,287,263	1,008.9	US$450	Democracy	71st
Pakistan	803,940	141.3	US$450	Military regime	77th
Philippines	300,000	75.70	US$990	Democracy	77th
Vietnam	329,566	78.10	US$400	Communist	85th
Indonesia	1,904,443	212.10	US$730	Democracy	96th
Bangladesh	143,998	137.4	US$360	Democracy	102nd

*   Mongolia's ranking is based on the 1999 CPI as this was the only year that
       it was included in the CPI.
Source: John Andrews, *Pocket Asia*, 7th edition (London: The Economist
Newspaper Ltd. and Profile Books Ltd., 2002), pp. 34, 48, 62, 70, 80, 88, 110,
121, 142, 152, 162, 172, 182, 188, 198, 210.

Third, the variations in GDP per capita are wide, with Japan
leading the pack, followed by Hong Kong (second), Singapore (third),
Taiwan (seventh), South Korea (ninth), Malaysia (10th), Thailand (11th),
the Philippines (15th), China (17th), Sri Lanka (19th), Indonesia (22nd),
India and Pakistan (24th), Mongolia and Vietnam (26th), and
Bangladesh (28th).[5] Thus, Bangladesh, which is perceived to be the
most corrupt country in the world, is also the poorest of the 16 Asian
countries listed in Table 8.2.

The final difference in policy context is the nature of the political system. China and Vietnam are communist while Mongolia, which was communist for 70 years, became democratic in 1991. India is the world's largest democracy with the second largest population, a GDP per capita of US$450 (24th), and ranked 71st in the 2002 CPI. Pakistan is the only Asian country under a military regime since October 1999, when General Pervez Musharraf ousted the government of Prime Minister Nawaz Sharif in a military coup.

The remaining 11 countries have democratic political systems with significant variations. Japan, Malaysia and Thailand are constitutional monarchies with the Emperor, *Yang di Pertuan Agung* (Malay for King), and King respectively as the Head of State. Singapore is a parliamentary democracy with a one-party dominant system as the People's Action Party government has been in power since June 1959. Hong Kong was a British colony until July 1997 when it became a special administrative region of China.

The Philippines was under martial law from 1972-1986 and reverted to democracy in February 1986, after Corazon Aquino used "people power" to replace President Ferdinand Marcos. South Korea's political system was transformed from authoritarianism to democracy in 1988 when President Roh Tae Woo assumed power. Taiwan followed suit when martial law was lifted in July 1987 and opposition political parties were allowed to campaign openly in December 1989.[6] Soon after its attainment of independence, Bangladesh became a one-party state in February 1975 and parliamentary democracy was only restored in 1991.[7] Similarly, Indonesia became democratic in May 1998, after President Suharto resigned after 32 years of authoritarian rule. Finally, Sri Lanka became a republic in 1972, but its democratic system has been plagued by constant ethnic strife and terrorism by the Tamil Tigers.[8]

KEY INGREDIENTS FOR AN EFFECTIVE ANTI-CORRUPTION STRATEGY

Apart from the critical factor of political will, there are four other ingredients for an effective anti-corruption strategy.

An Incorruptible and Independent Anti-Corruption Agency

Singapore and Hong Kong are effective in minimising corruption because of their reliance on a single agency solely dedicated to the task of corruption control. In contrast, the task of combating corruption in India and the Philippines is shared among many agencies. The CBI is the most important anti-corruption agency in India but it is not concerned mainly with fighting corruption as it is also responsible for dealing with terrorism and organised crime. Unlike the other former British colonies like Singapore, Hong Kong and Malaysia, which have rejected the inherited British method of employing the police to curb corruption, India has continued to rely on the CBI and the state anti-corruption bureaux, which are all police units.

The anti-corruption agency must be incorruptible for two reasons. First, if its personnel is corrupt, this erodes its legitimacy and public image as its officers have broken the law by being corrupt. Second, corruption among its staff prevents them from performing their tasks impartially and effectively. For example, as shown in Chapter 3, President Aquino's creation of the Presidential Commission on Good Government (PCGG) to retrieve the money stolen by the Marcos family and his cronies was viewed critically by the public as two of her Cabinet members and her relatives were accused of corruption. In June 1988, five PCGG agents were accused of graft and 13 more were under investigation.

To ensure its incorruptibility, the anti-corruption agency must be controlled or supervised by honest and incorruptible political leaders. In Singapore, the CPIB comes under the jurisdiction of the Prime Minister's Office (PMO) and its director reports directly to the Prime Minister. For example, on November 21, 1986, the CPIB's

Director informed then Prime Minister Lee Kuan Yew that a complaint of corruption had been made against the Minister for National Development, Teh Cheang Wan. Lee authorised the CPIB's Director to pursue the case. Teh was interviewed by a senior CPIB officer on December 2, 1986 for 16 hours. Three days later, Teh was required by the Attorney-General's Office to provide the CPIB within two weeks with a sworn statement of assets belonging to him and his family and details of money or property sent out of Singapore during 1979-1986. On December 14, Teh committed suicide without furnishing the CPIB with a list of his assets. During the hearings held by the Commission of Inquiry, Prime Minister Lee Kuan Yew, stressed that: "there is no way a Minister can avoid investigations, and a trial if there is evidence to support one. Teh Cheang Wan chose death rather than face a trial on the charges of corruption which the Attorney-General had yet to settle".[9]

The CPIB will continue to investigate allegations of political corruption in Singapore as long as the incumbent government remains committed to minimising corruption. However, if the CPIB's Director does not have the Prime Minister's consent to investigate complaints of corruption against a minister, article 22G of the Constitution of the Republic of Singapore empowers him to continue his investigations if he obtains the support of the elected President.[10]

Hong Kong's ICAC is scrutinised by several independent committees made up of citizens from different sectors of the community, who were appointed by the Governor before July 1997 and by the Chief Executive after that. The Advisory Committee on Corruption reviews the ICAC's overall policy and reviews the work of the Operations Department, the Community Relations Department, the Corruption Prevention Department, and the Administration Branch. The work of each department is also examined by an advisory committee. The Operations Review Committee focuses on the Operations Department, the Corruption Prevention Advisory Committee examines the work of the Corruption Prevention Department, and the Citizens Advisory Committee on Community Relations deals with the Community Relations Department.[11]

The anti-corruption agency must be staffed by honest and competent personnel. Overstaffing should be avoided, and any staff member found guilty of corruption must be punished and dismissed. Details of such punishment must be widely publicised in the mass media to deter others and to demonstrate the anti-corruption agency's integrity and credibility to the public. In contrast to the CPIB's 84 staff members, the ICAC is much larger and has 1,286 staff members.

Making Corruption a High-Risk, Low-Reward Activity by Punishing the Guilty

As corruption is an illegal activity, corrupt individuals should be punished. However, the probability of detection and punishment of corrupt offences varies in Asian countries. Corruption thrives where the public perceives it to be a "low-risk, high-reward" activity as the probability of detecting and punishing corrupt offenders is low. Consequently, corruption can only be minimised when it is perceived by the population to be a "high-risk, low-reward" activity i.e., when corrupt individuals are likely to be caught and severely punished.

As discussed in Chapter 4, a comparison of successful prosecution of corrupt offenders in Hong Kong and the Philippines has shown that a person involved in corrupt behaviour in Hong Kong is 35 times more likely to be detected and punished than his or her counterpart in the Philippines. In his memoirs, Singapore's Senior Minister Lee Kuan Yew blamed the "soft, forgiving culture" of the Philippines for the lack of punishment meted to Marcos and his family and cronies for their corrupt activities.

In his 1969 survey of regional economic planners in Indonesia, Theodore M. Smith found that apart from the lack of incentives for correct behaviour, sanctions were also absent or rarely applied to those officials who were under-performing as "cultural norms effectively preclude punitive denial of the perquisites, however minor, that attend each position".[12] He indicated that "the common procedure for dealing with officials whose corrupt practices became open knowledge is to transfer them to new jobs before their activities gain wide attention".[13] In 1970, President Suharto accepted the Commission of Four's recommendation that civil servants should submit an annual return of their personal assets and issued an Instruction requiring all public officials to do so. However, the civil servants ignored this requirement for nine years as it was only in 1979 that 90% of the officials submitted their annual returns.[14]

Indeed, the weak disciplinary control in the Indonesian Civil Service is clearly manifested in the ineffective policing of the corrupt civil servants. According to a senior official:

> The just law applying sanction to corruptors is not consistently enforced, with the consequence that corruption is rife ... a substantial portion of the officers, especially those in the upper echelons, have been dishonest, thus facilitating corruption....[15]

Palmier found that corruption was rampant in Indonesia because it was tolerated as corrupt officials were seldom punished. He concluded that while there was strong policing against corruption in Hong Kong, "policing is very poor in Indonesia, and insufficient in India".[16]

For corruption to be perceived as a high-risk, low-reward activity, the governments in Asian countries must publicise through the mass media the detection of corrupt behaviour among civil servants and political leaders, and their punishment according to the law if they are guilty. The mass media reduce corruption by exposing it, as corruption "thrives in secrecy, and withers in the light".[17] Negative publicity is an effective deterrent against corruption. In this context, Prime Minister Lee Kuan Yew of Singapore had contended in 1987 that "the strongest deterrent [against corruption] is in a public opinion which censures and condemns corrupt persons, in other words, in attitudes which make corruption so unacceptable that the stigma of corruption cannot be washed away by serving a prison sentence".[18] Conversely, governments that "shackle the media," as in Indonesia under President Soeharto or in India during the emergency of the 1970s, "in effect [encourage] the corrupt".[19]

Reducing Opportunities for Corruption in Vulnerable Government Departments

The expanding role of the civil service in Asian countries has increased the opportunities for administrative discretion and corruption as "regulations governing access to goods and services can be exploited by civil servants in extracting 'rents' from groups vying for access to such goods and services".[20] For example, as discussed in Chapter 6, the regulation, control and prohibition of certain activities by the government in Hong Kong provided ample opportunities for corruption in construction, import and export, health, prostitution, gambling, drugs, and immigration.

As discussed in Chapter 1, Indonesian civil servants distinguished between "wet" and "dry" agencies in terms of the opportunities for corruption. "Wet" agencies are preferred by them as civil servants in such agencies have larger budgets and access to the fee-paying public while those in "dry" agencies are denied such access. According to Indonesia's co-ordinating minister from 1989 to 1993, Radius Prawiro, the tax office and customs service are the most lucrative of the "wet" government agencies because of the abundant opportunities for corruption in these agencies. Similarly, in the Philippines, the Bureau of Immigration, Bureau of Internal Revenue, Department of Education, Culture and Sports, Department of Public Works and Highways, and the Police are "wet" agencies because of their large budgets and access to the public.

Vulnerable or "wet" government agencies must review their procedures periodically to reduce opportunities for corruption. Unnecessary regulations and excessive red tape should be reduced and cumbersome administrative procedures streamlined.

Reducing Temptation by Paying Political Leaders and Civil Servants Adequate Salaries

An important cause for corruption in India, Mongolia, Philippines and South Korea was the low salaries of its civil servants and political leaders. Low salaries in Asian countries contribute to corruption as poorly paid bureaucrats and politicians will be tempted to be corrupt.

As discussed in Chapter 2, the major cause of corruption in contemporary Mongolia is the extremely low wages of its civil servants and politicians. The highest monthly salary is that of the President, who earns US$71 per month, while the lowest monthly salary for a civil servant is US$35. The salaries of civil servants and politicians in India are higher than those in Mongolia but lower than their counterparts in the Philippines, South Korea, Hong Kong, and Singapore. For example, as shown in Chapter 3, the monthly salary of the Indian Prime Minister is 162 times lower than of his Singaporean counterpart. In the Philippines, civil servants describe their salaries as "starvation wages" which are inadequate to meet the needs of their families. As civil service salaries in South Korea are equivalent to 70% of private sector wages, some scholars have suggested that bureaucratic corruption can be reduced by improving the salaries of civil servants.

The salaries of civil servants and political leaders in Singapore and Hong Kong are among the highest in the world, and certainly higher than those in Mongolia, India, the Philippines, and South Korea. The low salaries of police officers in Singapore during the British colonial period was a major cause of police corruption. However, Singapore did not solve the problem of corruption by increasing civil service salaries as it could not afford to do so when it attained self-government in 1959. Indeed, the salaries of civil servants were only raised in 1972 to minimise the brain drain from the civil service and only after corruption had been minimised through the impartial implementation of the POCA by the CPIB.[21]

Robert S. Leiken has recommended that "when the people pay government functionaries decent salaries, they are buying a layer of insulation against patronage and bribery".[22] Singapore's experience, as recounted in Chapter 5, demonstrates "the importance of reducing the incentive for corruption by keeping the salaries of civil servants and political leaders competitive with the private sector" for they will be more vulnerable to corruption if their salaries are low.[23]

However, this strategy of reducing corruption through salary increase is expensive and many governments in Asian countries cannot afford to raise salaries. More importantly, raising salaries alone will not solve the problem of corruption if the government does not have the political will to minimise corruption and ensure the incorruptibility of the anti-corruption agency, and if it does not punish corrupt officials or reduce opportunities for corruption in vulnerable agencies. In short, raising salaries of civil servants and political leaders is a necessary but insufficient prerequisite for an effective anti-corruption strategy.

CONCLUSION

The successful experiences of Singapore and Hong Kong in curbing corruption demonstrate that minimising corruption in Asian countries is not an impossible dream if there is political will. Singapore and Hong Kong have adopted the effective third pattern of corruption control of relying on an independent anti-corruption agency to implement the anti-corruption legislation. Corruption was a way of life in these two city-states during the British colonial period. However, the establishment of the CPIB as an independent anti-corruption agency in 1952 and the enactment of the POCA in 1960 strengthened the CPIB's powers and enhanced its effectiveness in minimising corruption. Similarly, the fight against corruption in Hong Kong only made progress after the creation of the ICAC in 1974.

Of the six countries discussed in this book, Singapore and Hong Kong are the smallest in terms of land area and population, but also the richest in terms of GDP per capita. In contrast, South Korea, the Philippines, Mongolia and India, are larger countries with larger populations with the exception of Mongolia. India is a sub-continent with a federal system, while the Philippines is an archipelago. Mongolia is also much larger than Singapore and Hong Kong, but has fewer people and a much lower population density. As former British colonies, both have benefited from the legacy of meritocracy and clean government on the one hand, and suffered from relying on the British method of using the police to curb corruption on the other.

The policy contexts of the other 14 Asian countries listed in Table 8.2 are quite different from the more favourable policy contexts of Singapore and Hong Kong. Apart from being city-states with smaller populations, Singapore and Hong Kong are also richer than the other Asian countries except Japan and can therefore devote the required resources for their anti-corruption strategies and to pay competitive salaries to their civil servants and political leaders. In the final analysis, whether the effective anti-corruption strategies of Singapore and Hong Kong can be successfully transplanted to the other Asian countries depends on two important factors: the nature of their policy context, and whether their political leaders have the political will to implement the required reforms.

Given the contextual differences between the two city-states and the other Asian countries, and the absence of political will, it is unlikely that many Asian countries can successfully transplant the effective anti-corruption strategies of Singapore and Hong Kong. Indeed, according to Michael Johnston, while Independent Commissions Against Corruption "are unlikely to be right for every country", they do demonstrate that "permanent, independent agencies addressing corruption as a deep-rooted problem, making society a partner in reform, and developing careful strategies for prevention may be a promising way to confront serious corruption".[24]

Nevertheless, in view of the different policy contexts, other Asian countries can emulate and adapt some features of Singapore's and Hong Kong's anti-corruption strategy to suit their own needs, provided that their political leaders, civil servants, and the population are prepared to support and implement the required reforms. The establishment of the Korean Independent Commission Against Corruption (KICAC) in South Korea in January 2002 is a good example as the KICAC is the Korean version of Hong Kong's ICAC.

Finally, as was discussed in Chapter 3 on India, the $64,000 question is: If political will is the critical factor responsible for ensuring the effectiveness of an anti-corruption strategy, how can it be nurtured in those countries where there is no political will to fight corruption? As suggested in Chapter 3, to enhance the political will to minimise corruption in other Asian countries like Mongolia, India and the Philippines, the citizens in these three countries must elect to public office honest and incorruptible political leaders who will strengthen or improve the existing anti-corruption measures and enforce these measures impartially. This is the critical first step as the role of the political leaders is to serve as a catalyst to change the population's tolerant attitude towards corruption by introducing more effective anti-corruption measures and enforcing such measures fairly.

Robert Klitgaard has suggested three "almost psychological steps" for generating the political will to fight corruption. First, "leaders must see that improvements are possible without political suicide". Second, "leaders must develop a strategy that recognises that not everything can be done at once". Third, "leaders need political insulation".[25] All three steps can be provided by international collaboration with other countries and international agencies like the Asian Development Bank, the Inter-American Development Bank, the Organisation for Economic Cooperation and Development, the United Nations Development Programme, and the World Bank.

Thus, Singapore and Hong Kong can assist other Asian countries interested in improving the effectiveness of their anti-corruption strategies by sharing their experiences and "best practices" at international conferences, seminars and workshops and on-site visits to the CPIB and ICAC.

ENDNOTES

1   Jon S.T. Quah, "Bureaucratic Corruption in the ASEAN Countries: A Comparative Analysis of Their Anti-Corruption Strategies", *Journal of Southeast Asian Studies*, Vol. 13, No. 1 (March 1982), pp. 166-169.

2   Sahr J. Kpundeh, "Political Will in Fighting Corruption", in *Corruption and Integrity Improvement Initiatives in Developing Countries* (New York: United Nations Development Programme, 1998), p. 92.

3   John Andrews, *Pocket Asia*, 7th edition (London: The Economist Newspaper Ltd. and Profile Books Ltd., 2002), p. 14.

4   Ibid., p. 14.

5   Ibid., p. 19.

6   Ibid., p. 189.

7   Ibid., pp. 34-35.

8   Ibid., p. 183.

9   *Report of the Commission of Inquiry on Investigations Concerning the late Mr Teh Cheang Wan* (Singapore: Singapore National Printers, 1987), pp. 27-30.

10   Thio Li-Ann, "The Elected President and the Legal Control of Government: *Quis Custodes Ipsos Custodes?*" in Kevin Y.L. Tan and Lam Peng Er (eds.), *Managing Political Change in Singapore: The Elected Presidency* (London: Routledge, 1997), p. 114.

11   Peter Allan, *Annual Report on the Activities of the Independent Commission Against Corruption for 1991* (Hong Kong: Government Printer, 1992), pp. 5-6.

12   Theodore M. Smith, "Culture, Tradition and Change", *Indonesia*, Vol. 11 (April 1971), p. 30.

13   Ibid., p. 30.

14   Leslie Palmier, *The Control of Bureaucratic Corruption: Case Studies in Asia* (New Delhi: Allied Publishers, 1985), pp. 257-258.

15   S.L.S. Danuredjo, "The Declining Trend of Legal and Administrative Performance in Indonesia: Some Remedial Actions Suggested", *International Review of Administrative Sciences*, Vol. 34, No. 2 (1968), pp. 165-166.

16   Palmier, *The Control of Bureaucratic Corruption*, p. 280.

17   Ibid., p. 279.

18   Quoted in *Report of the Commission of Inquiry on Investigations Concerning the Late Mr Teh Cheang Wan*, p. 2.

19   Palmier, *The Control of Bureaucratic Corruption,*, p. 279.

20   David J. Gould and Jose A. Amaro-Reyes, *The Effects of Corruption on Administrative Performance: Illustrations from Developing Countries* (Washington, D.C.: World Bank Staff Working Papers No. 580, 1983), p. 17.

21   Jon S.T. Quah, "Paying for the 'Best and Brightest': Rewards for High Public Office in Singapore", in Christopher Hood and B. Guy Peters with Grace O.M. Lee (eds.), *Reward for High Public Office: Asian and Pacific Rim States* (London: Routledge, 2003), p. 159.

22   Robert S. Leiken, "Controlling the Global Corruption Epidemic", *Foreign Policy*, No. 105 (Winter 1996-97), p. 68.

23   Jon S.T. Quah, "Singapore's Experience in Curbing Corruption", in Arnold J. Heidenheimer, Michael Johnston, and Victor LeVine (eds.), *Political Corruption: A Handbook* (New Brunswick: Transaction Publishers, 1989), p. 850.

24   Michael Johnston, "A Brief History of Anti-Corruption Agencies", in Andreas Schedler, Larry Diamond and Marc F. Plattner (eds.), *The Self-Restraining State: Power and Accountability in New Democracies* (Boulder: Lynne Rienner, 1999), p. 225.

25   Robert Klitgaard, "Cleaning Up and Invigorating the Civil Service", *Public Administration and Development*, Vol. 17, No. 5 (December 1997), p. 502.

Corruption in Asian Countries: A Selected Bibliography

COUNTRY STUDIES

China

Blackman, Carolyn. *China Business: The Rules of the Game*. St. Leonards: Allen and Unwin, 2000. Chapter 3, "Corruption: 'Legitimate Loot'", pp. 24-39; and Chapter 7, "Corrupt Practices", pp. 83-93.

Burns, John P. "Rewarding Comrades at the top in China". In Christopher Hood *et al.* (eds.), *Reward for High Public Office: Asian and Pacific Rim States*. London: Routledge, 2003. Chapter 3, pp. 49-69.

Chan, Anita and Jonathan Unger. "Grey and Black: The Hidden Economy of Rural China". *Pacific Affairs*, Vol. 55, No. 3 (1982), pp. 452-471.

Chan, Kin-Man. "Popular Perception of Corruption in Post-Mao China". Ph.D. dissertation, Yale University, 1995.

Chan, Kin-Man. "Corruption in China: A Principal-Agent Perspective". In Hoi-Kwok Wong and Hon S. Chan (eds.), *Handbook of Comparative Public Administration in the Asia-Pacific Basin*. New York: Marcel Dekker, 1999. Chapter 14, pp. 299-324.

Chan, Kin-Man. "Toward an Integrated Model of Corruption: Opportunities and Control in China". *International Journal of Public Administration*, Vol. 23, No. 4 (2000), pp. 507-551.

Chen, Fang. *The Wrath of Heaven: Scandal at the Top in China*. Hong Kong: Edko Publishing, 2000. Translated by Pang Sing-Hong.

Chen, Kang, Arye L. Hillman and Gu Qingyang. "From the Helping Hand to the Grabbing Hand: Fiscal Federalism and Corruption in China". In John Wong and Lu Ding (eds.), *China's Economy into the New Century: Structural Issues and Problems*. Singapore: Singapore University Press and World Scientific, 2002. Chapter 8, pp. 193-218.

Chu, Huaizhi. "Perfecting China's Legal System to Fight Crimes of Bribery". In Wang Guiguo and Wei Zhenying (eds.), *Legal Developments in China: Market Economy and Law*. Hong Kong: Sweet and Maxwell, 1996, pp. 325-335.

Damon, Francois-Yves. "Corruption in Mainland China Today: Data and Law in a Dubious Battle". In John Kidd and Frank-Jurgen Richter (eds.), *Fighting Corruption in Asia: Causes, Effects and Remedies*. Singapore: World Scientific Publishing, 2003. Chapter 7, pp. 175-201.

Dickson, Bruce J. "Political Instability at the Middle and Lower Levels: Signs of a Decaying CCP, Corruption, and Political Dissent". In David Shambaugh (ed.), *Is China Unstable?: Assessing the Factors*. Armonk: M.E. Sharpe, 2000. Chapter 4, pp. 40-56.

Einwalter, Dawn. "The Limits of the Chinese State: Public Morality and the Xu Honggang Campaign". In Suisheng Zhao (ed.), *China and Democracy: Reconsidering the Prospects for a Democratic China*. New York: Routledge, 2000. Chapter 8, pp. 173-186.

Gong, Ting. *The Politics of Corruption in Contemporary China: An Analysis of Policy Outcomes*. Westport: Praeger, 1994.

Gong, Ting. "Forms and Characteristics of China's Corruption in the 1990s: Change with Continuity". *Communist and Post-Communist Studies*, Vol. 30, No. 3 (1997), pp. 277-288.

Goodman, David S.G. "Corruption in the People's Liberation Army". In Gerald Segal and Richard H. Yang (eds.), *Chinese Economic Reform: The Impact on Security*. London: Routledge, 1996. Chapter 3, pp. 35-52.

Hao, Yufan and Michael Johnston. "Reform at the Crossroads: An Analysis of Chinese Corruption". *Asian Perspective*, Vol. 19, No. 1 (Spring-Summer 1995), pp. 117-149.

Hao, Yufan and Michael Johnston. "Corruption and the Future of Economic Reform in China". In Arnold J. Heidenheimer and Michael Johnston (eds.), *Political Corruption: Concepts and Contexts* 3rd ed. New Brunswick: Transaction Publishers, 2002. Chapter 31, pp. 583-604.

He, Zengke. "Corruption and Anti-Corruption in Reform China". *Communist and Post-Communist Studies*, Vol. 33, No. 2 (June 2000), pp. 243-270.

Hsu, Carolyn L. *Corruption and Morality in the People's Republic of China*. Bloomington: East Asian Studies Center, Indiana University Working Paper No. 8, 1996.

Hu, Angang and Guo Yong. "Administrative Monopoly, Corruption, and China's Economic Transformation". In Pamela C.M. Mar and Frank-Jurgen Richter (eds.), *China: Enabling a New Era of Changes*. Singapore: John Wiley and Sons (Asia), 2003, pp. 97-115.

Huang, Weiding. "Fighting Corruption Amidst Economic Reform". In Laurence J. Brahm (ed.), *China's Century: The Awakening of the Next Economic Powerhouse*. Singapore: John Wiley & Sons (Asia), 2001, pp. 39-55.

Jensen, Lionel M. "Everyone's a Player, but the Nation's a Loser: Corruption in Contemporary China". In Timothy B. Weston and Lionel M. Jensen (eds.), *China Beyond the Headlines*. Lanham: Rowan and Littlefield Publishers, 2000. Chapter 2, pp. 37-67.

197

Johnston, Michael and Yufan Hao. "China's Surge of Corruption". *Journal of Democracy*, Vol. 6, No. 4 (1995), pp. 80-94.

Kipnis, Andrew B. *Producing Guanxi: Sentiment, Self, and Subculture in a North China Village*. Durham: Duke University Press, 1997.

Kiser, Edgar and Tong Xiaoxi. "Determinants of the Amount and Type of Corruption in State Fiscal Bureaucracies: An Analysis of Late Imperial China". *Comparative Political Studies*, Vol. 25, No. 3 (1992), pp. 300-331.

Kwong, Julia. *The Political Economy of Corruption in China*. Armonk: M.E. Sharpe, 1997.

Lee, Peter Nan-Shong. "Bureaucratic Corruption during the Deng Xiaoping Era". *Corruption and Reform*, Vol. 5, No. 1 (1990), pp. 29-47.

Levy, Richard. "Corruption, Economic Crime, and Social Transformation since the Reforms: The Debate in China". *Australian Journal of Chinese Affairs*, Vol. 33, No. 1 (January 1995), pp. 1-25.

Levy, Richard. "*Fubai*: Differing Chinese Views on Corruption since Tiananmen". *International Journal of Public Administration*, Vol. 24, No. 1 (January 2001).

Levy, Richard. "Corruption in Popular Culture". In Perry Link, Richard P. Madsen and Paul G. Pickowicz (eds.), *Popular China: Unofficial Culture in a Globalizing Society*. Lanham: Roman and Littlefield Publishers, 2002. Chapter 2, pp. 39-56.

Li, Boyuan. *Officialdom Unmasked*. Hong Kong: Hong Kong University Press, 2001. Translated and abridged by T.L. Yang.

Li, Jinyan. "China: Countering Corruption in the Tax Administration in Transitional Economies: A Case Study of China". *Bulletin for International Fiscal Documentation*, Vol. 51, No. 11 (November 1997), pp. 474-492.

Liu, Alan P.L. "The Politics of Corruption in the People's Republic of China". *American Political Science Review*, Vol. 77, No. 3 (September 1983), pp. 602-623.

Lo, Jack Man Keung. "Bureaucratic Corruption in China during the Reform Era: Current Issues and Future Directions". *Philippine Journal of Public Administration*, Vol. 38, No. 1 (January 1994), pp. 17-30.

Lo, Sonny Shiu Hing. "Public Maladministration and Bureaucratic Corruption". In David C.B. Teather and Herbert S. Yee (eds.), *China in Transition: Issues and Politics*. New York: St. Martin's Press, 1999. Chapter 3, pp. 47-68.

Lu, Xiaobo. "From Rank-Seeking to Rent-Seeking: Changing Administrative Ethos and Corruption in Reform China". *Crime, Law and Social Change*, Vol. 32, No. 4 (December 1999), pp. 347-370.

Lu, Xiaobo. *Cadres and Corruption: The Organizational Involution of the Chinese Communist Party*. Stanford: Stanford University Press, 2000.

Lu, Xiaobo. "Booty Socialism, Bureau-preneurs, and the State in Transition: Organizational Corruption in China". *Comparative Politics*, Vol. 32, No. 3 (April 2000), pp. 273-294.

198

Lu, Yadong. *Guanxi and Business.* Singapore: World Scientific Publishing, 2000.

Lui, Adam Y.C. *Corruption in China during the Early Ch'ing Period, 1644-1660.* Hong Kong: Hong Kong University Press, 1979.

Ma, Stephen K. "Reform Corruption: A Discussion on China's Current Developments". *Pacific Affairs*, Vol. 62, No. 1 (Spring 1989), pp. 40-52.

Ma, Stephen K. "The Culture of Corruption in Post-Mao China". In Gerald E. Caiden *et al.* (eds.), *Where Corruption Lives.* Bloomfield: Kumarian Press, 2001. Chapter 11, pp. 145-157.

Madsen, Richard. *Morality and Power in a Chinese Village.* Berkeley: University of California Press, 1984.

Manion, Melanie. "Corruption by Design: Bribery in Chinese Enterprise Licensing". *Journal of Law, Economics and Organisation*, Vol. 12, No. 1 (April 1996), pp. 167-195.

Manion, Melanie. "Issues in Corruption Control in Post-Mao China". *Issues and Studies*, Vol. 34, No. 9 (1998), pp. 1-21.

Marsh, Robert M. "The Venality of Provincial Office in China and in Comparative Perspective". *Comparative Studies in Society*, Vol. 4, No. 4 (1962), pp. 454-466.

Meaney, Connie Squires. "Market Reform and Corruption in Urban China". In Richard Baum (ed.), *Reform and Reaction in Post-Mao China.* New York: Routledge, 1991. Chapter 7, pp. 124-142.

Miles, James A.R. *The Legacy of Tiananmen: China in Disarray.* Ann Arbor: University of Michigan Press, 1996. Chapter 5, "The Virus of Corruption", pp. 147-168.

Myers, James T. "China's Modernization and 'Unhealthy Tendencies'", *Comparative Politics*, Vol. 21, No. 2 (January 1989), pp. 193-214.

Nimerius, Peter. "Daring to Fight Tigers?: Anti-Corruption Work in Contemporary China". M.A. thesis, Stockholm University, June 1997.

Nojonen, Matti. "The Competitive Advantage with Chinese Characteristics: The Sophisticated Choreography of Gift-Giving". In John B. Kidd and Frank-Jurgen Richter (eds.), *Corruption and Governance in Asia.* Basingstoke: Palgrave Macmillan, 2003. Chapter 6, pp. 107-130.

Oi, Jean. "Market Reforms and Corruption in Rural China". *Studies in Comparative Communism*, Vol. 22, Nos. 2-3 (1989), pp. 221-233.

Oi, Jean. "Partial Market Reform and Corruption in Rural China". In Baum (ed.), *Reform and Reaction in Post-Mao China.* Chapter 8, pp. 143-161.

Ostergaard, C.S. "Explaining China's Recent Political Corruption: Patterns, Remedies, and Counter-Strategies at the Local Level". *Corruption and Reform*, Vol. 1, No. 3 (1986), pp. 209-233.

Park, Nancy Elizabeth. "Corruption and Its Recompense: Bribes, Bureaucracy, and the Law in Late Imperial China". Ph.D. dissertation, Harvard University, 1993.

199

Perry, Elizabeth J. "Crime, Corruption, and Contention". In Merle Goodman and Roderick MacFarquhar (eds.), *The Paradox of China's Post-Mao Reforms*. Cambridge: Harvard University Press, 1999. Chapter 14, pp. 308-329.

Reed, Bradly W. *Talons and Teeth: County Clerks and Runners in the Qing Dynasty.* Stanford: Stanford University Press, 2000. Chapter 1, "Illicit Bureaucrats", pp. 1-30.

Rocca, Jean-Louis. "Corruption and Its Shadow: An Anthropological View of Corruption in China". *The China Quarterly*, Vol. 130 (1992), pp. 402-416.

Rocca, Jean-Louis. *Power, Wealth and Corruption in Mainland China.* Lyon: Maison Rhone-Alpes des Sciences de l'Homme, 1993.

Root, Hilton. "Corruption in China: Has it become Systemic?" *Asian Survey*, Vol. 36, No. 8 (August 1996), pp. 741-757.

Sands, Barbara N. "Market-Clearing by Corruption: The Political Economy of China's Recent Economic Reforms". *Journal of Institutional and Theoretical Economics*, Vol. 145, No. 1 (March 1989), pp. 116-126.

Sands, Barbara N. "Decentralizing an Economy: The Role of Bureaucratic Corruption in China's Economic Reforms". *Public Choice*, Vol. 65 (April 1990), pp. 85-91.

Schramm, Matthias and Markus Taube. "The Institutional Economics of Legal Institutions, *Guanxi*, and Corruption in the People's Republic of China". In Kidd and Richter (eds.), *Fighting Corruption in Asia: Causes, Effects and Remedies*, Singapore: World Scientific Publishing, 2003. Chapter 11, pp. 271-296.

Seligman, Scott D. *Chinese Business Etiquette.* New York: Warner Books, 1999. Chapter 10, "*Guanxi*: Grease for the Wheels of China", pp. 180-196.

Solinger, Dorothy J. *Chinese Business Under Socialism: The Politics of Domestic Commerce, 1949-1980.* Berkeley: University of California Press, 1991. Chapter 3, "Technological Underdevelopment: A Case Study of Corruption in the Southwest Countryside, 1949-1952", pp. 124-153.

Steidlmeier, P. "Gift-giving, Bribery and Corruption: Ethical Management of Business Relationships in China". *Journal of Business Ethics*, Vol. 20 (1999), pp. 121-132.

Sun, Yan. "The Chinese Protests of 1989: The Issue of Corruption". *Asian Survey*, Vol. 31, No. 8 (August 1991), pp. 762-782.

Tang, Shengming. "Official Corruption in a Developing Economy: The Case of the People's Republic of China". *Humanity and Society*, Vol. 20, No. 2 (1996), pp. 58-71.

White, Gordon. "Corruption and the Transition from Socialism in China". In Michael Levi and David Nelken (eds.), *The Corruption of Politics and the Politics of Corruption*. Oxford: Blackwell Publishers, 1996, pp. 149-169.

White, Gordon. "Corruption and Market Reform in China". *IDS Bulletin*, Vol. 27, No. 2 (1996), pp. 40-47.

White, Lynn T. "Changing Concepts of Corruption in Communist China". *Issues and Studies*, Vol. 24, No. 1 (January 1988), pp. 49-95.

Xie, Baogui. "The Function of the Chinese Procuratorial Organ in the Combat Against Corruption". *Asian Journal of Public Administration*, Vol. 10, No. 1 (June 1988), pp. 71-79.

Yan, Geng. "Corruption and the Clean-Government Drive in China". In G.B.N. Pradhan and Mila A. Reforma (eds.), *Public Administration in the 1990s: Challenges and Opportunities*. Manila: EROPA Secretariat General, 1991. Chapter 16, pp. 201-211.

Yan, Yunxiang. *The Flow of Gifts: Reciprocity and Social Networks in a Chinese Village*. Stanford: Stanford University Press, 1996.

Yan, Yunxiang. "The Culture of *Guanxi* in a North China Village". *China Journal*, Vol. 35 (1996), pp. 1-25.

Yang, Mayfair Mei-Hui. *Gifts, Favors, and Banquets: The Art of Social Relationships in China*. Ithaca: Cornell University Press, 1994.

Ye, Feng. "The Chinese Procuratorates and the Anti-Corruption Campaigns in the People's Republic of China". In Jianfu Chen, Yuwen Li, and Jan Michiel Otto (eds.), *Implementation of Law in the People's Republic of China*. The Hague: Kluwer Law International, 2002. Chapter 6, pp. 113-124.

Yeh, Milton D. "Modernization and Corruption in Mainland China". *Issues and Studies*, Vol. 23, No. 11 (November 1987), pp. 11-27.

Zhang, Lening. "White-Collar Crime: Bribery and Corruption in China". In Jianhong Liu *et al.* (eds.), *Crime and Social Control in a Changing China*. Westwood: Greenwood Press, 2001. Chapter 2, pp. 23-35.

Zhang, Wei-Wei. *Transforming China: Economic Reforms and its Political Implications*. New York: St. Martin's Press, 1999. Chapter 14, "Corruption", pp. 132-140.

Zhang, Xiaoqin. "The Present Situation of Corruption in China and Anti-Corruption Countermeasures". In Wang Guigo and Wei Zhenying (eds.), *Legal Developments in China: Market Economy and Law*. Hong Kong: Sweet and Maxwell, 1996, pp. 352-360.

Zhao, Yuezhi. *Media, Market, and Democracy in China: Between the Party Line and the Bottom Line*. Urbana: University of Illinois Press, 1998. Chapter 4, "Corruption: The Journalism of Decadence", pp. 72-93.

Zhou, Keyuan. *Why China's Rampant Corruption Cannot be Checked by Laws Alone*. Singapore: East Asian Institute, National University of Singapore, EAI Background Brief No. 74, 2000.

Hong Kong

Chan, Thomas. "Corruption Prevention: The Hong Kong Experience". In *Resource Material Series No. 56*. Tokyo: UNAFEI, December 2000, pp. 365-377.

Chua, Anthony C.H. "Whistleblowing, Red Chips, and the Provisional Legislature in Hong Kong". *Public Administration Review*, Vol. 58, No. 1 (January-February 1998), pp. 1-7.

Clark, David. "Review Article: Corruption in Hong Kong, The ICAC Story". *Corruption and Reform*, Vol. 1, No. 1 (1986), pp. 57-62.

Clark, David. "Ten Years After: Corruption and Anti-Corruption in Hong Kong", *Asian Journal of Public Administration*, Vol. 8 (1986), pp. 113-132.

Clark, David. "A Community Relations Approach to Corruption: The Case of Hong Kong". *Corruption and Reform*, Vol. 2, No. 3 (1987), pp. 235-257.

De Speville, Bertrand. *Hong Kong: Policy Initiatives Against Corruption*. Paris: Organisation for Economic Co-operation and Development, 1997.

De Speville, Bertrand. "Hong Kong's Quiet Revolution". *Governance*, Vol. 1, No. 1 (January 1998), pp. 29-36.

De Speville, Bertrand. "The Experience of Hong Kong, China, in Combating Corruption". In Rick Stapenhurst and Sahr J. Kpundeh (eds.). *Curbing Corruption: Toward a Model for Building National Integrity*. Washington, D.C.: The World Bank, 1999. Chapter 3, pp. 51-58.

Downey, Bernard. "Combating Corruption: The Hong Kong Solution". *Hong Kong Law Journal*, Vol. 6, No. 1 (1976), pp. 27-66.

Faure, David. "Paying for Convenience: An Aspect of Corruption that Arise from Revenue Spending". *Philippine Journal of Public Administration*, Vol. 24, No. 2 (April 1980), pp. 127-144.

Independent Commission Against Corruption. *Fighting Corruption: The Mission Continues*. Hong Kong: ICAC, 1999.

Independent Commission Against Corruption. *2000 Annual Report by the Commissioner of the ICAC Hong Kong SAR*. Hong Kong: ICAC, 2001.

Independent Commission Against Corruption. *2001 Annual Report by the Commissioner of the ICAC Hong Kong SAR*. Hong Kong: ICAC, 2002.

Independent Commission Against Corruption. *An Introduction to the Independent Commission Against Corruption*. Hong Kong: ICAC, 2002.

King, Ambrose Yeo-Chi. "An Institutional Response to Corruption: The ICAC of Hong Kong". In Leung Chi-Keung, J.W. Cushman and Wang Gungwu (eds.), *Hong Kong: Dilemmas of Growth*. Canberra: Research School of Pacific Studies, 1980, pp. 115-142.

Lai, Alan N. "Keeping Hong Kong Clean: Experiences of Fighting Corruption post 1997". *Harvard Asia Pacific Review*, Vol. 5, No. 2 (Fall 2001), pp. 51-54.

Lee, Rance P.L. "The Folklore of Corruption in Hong Kong". *Asian Survey*, Vol. 21, No. 3 (March 1981), pp. 355-368.

Lee, Rance P.L. (ed.). *Corruption and Its Control in Hong Kong*. Hong Kong: The Chinese University Press, 1981.

Lethbridge, Henry J. "The Emergence of Bureaucratic Corruption as a Social Problem in Hong Kong". *Journal of Oriental Studies*, Vol. 12 (1974), pp. 16-29.

Lethbridge, Henry J. *Hard Graft in Hong Kong: Scandal, Corruption, the ICAC*. Hong Kong: Oxford University Press, 1985.

Lo, Jack M.K. "Controlling Corruption in Hong Kong: From Colony to Special Administrative Region", *Journal of Contingencies and Crisis Management*, Vol. 9, No. 1 (March 2001), pp. 21-28.

Manion, Melanie. "Policy Instruments and Political Context: Transforming a Culture of Corruption in Hong Kong". Paper presented at the Annual Meeting of the Association of Asian Studies, in Honolulu, Hawaii, 1996.

McDonald, Gael M. "Value Modification Strategies on a National Scale: The Activities of the Independent Commission Against Corruption in Hong Kong". In W. Michael Hoffman *et al.* (eds.), *Emerging Global Business Ethics.* Westport: Quorum Books, 1994. Chapter 2, pp. 14-35.

Moran, Jonathan. "The Changing Context of Corruption Control: The Hong Kong Special Administrative Region, 1997-99". In Alan Doig and Robin Theobald (eds.), *Corruption and Democratisation.* London: Frank Cass, 2000, pp. 98-116.

Rooke, Peter and Michael H. Wiehen. *Hong Kong: The Airport Core Programme and the Absence of Corruption.* Berlin: Transparency International Working Paper, December 1999.

Scott, Tony *et al.* "Corruption Prevention: The Hong Kong Approach". *Asian Journal of Public Administration*, Vol. 10, No. 1 (June 1988), pp. 110-119.

Skidmore, Max J. "Promise and Peril in Combating Corruption: Hong Kong's ICAC". *The Annals of the American Academy*, Vol. 547 (September 1996), pp. 118-130.

Thomas, Michael. "Prosecution of Corruption Cases in Hong Kong". *Asian Journal of Public Administration*, Vol. 10, No. 1 (June 1988), pp. 99-109.

Wong, Jeremiah K.H. "The ICAC and Its Anti-Corruption Measures". In Lee (ed.), *Corruption and Its Control in Hong Kong.* Chapter 2, pp. 45-72.

India

Agarwal, U.C. "Politics of Crime, Corruption and Waste, Caste and Creed". *Indian Journal of Public Administration*, Vol. 41, No. 3 (1995), pp. 462-471.

Agarwal, U.C. "Galloping Corruption: Need for Effective Vigilance". In T.N. Chaturvedi (ed.), *Fifty Years of Indian Administration: Retrospect and Prospect.* New Delhi: Indian Institute of Public Administration, 1998, pp. 174-180.

Agrawala, S.K. "Public Servants' Offence of Corruption and Sentencing by the Supreme Court of India". *Indian Journal of Public Administration*, Vol. 26, No. 4 (October-December 1980), pp. 932-986.

Bayley, David H. "Effects of Corruption in a Developing Nation". *Western Political Quarterly*, Vol. 19 (December 1966), pp. 719-732.

Bhatia, L.M. "Central Vigilance Commission: Its Role in Administrative Vigilance". *Indian Journal of Public Administration*, Vol. 17 (January-March 1971), pp. 65-75.

Bhatnagar, S. and S.K. Sharma. *Corruption in Indian Politics and Bureaucracy.* New Delhi: Ess Ess Publisher, 1991.

Central Vigilance Commission. *The Citizen's Guide to Fighting Corruption.* New Delhi: CVC, 2001.

Central Vigilance Commission. *The Indian Administrative Service: A Study of the Current State of Punitive and Preventive Vigilance Mechanisms.* New Delhi: CVC, October 2001.

Corruption in India: An Empirical Study. New Delhi: Transparency International and Org-Marg Research Private Ltd., 2002.

Dwivedi, O.P. and R.B. Jain. "Bureaucratic Morality in India". *International Political Science Review*, Vol. 9, No. 3 (July 1988), pp. 205-214.

Dwivedy, Surendranath. *Political Corruption in India.* New Delhi: Popular Book Services, 1967.

Gill, S.S. *The Pathology of Corruption.* New Delhi: HarperCollins Publishers, 1998.

Gopinath, Krishna P. "Corruption in Political and Public Offices: Causes and Cure". *Indian Journal of Public Administration*, Vol. 28, No. 4 (October-December 1982), pp. 897-918.

Gopinath, P.K. "Central Vigilance Commission: A Profile". In Chaturvedi (ed.), *Fifty Years of Indian Administration: Retrospect and Prospect.* New Delhi: Indian Institute of Public Adminstration, 1998, pp. 161-173.

Guhan, S. and Samuel Paul. (eds.). *Corruption in India: Agenda for Action.* New Delhi: Vision Books, 1997.

Gupta, Suraj B. *Black Income in India.* New Delhi: Sage Publications, 1992.

Hager, L. Michael. "Bureaucratic Corruption in India: Legal Control of Maladministration". *Comparative Political Studies*, Vol. 6, No. 2 (July 1973), pp. 197-219.

Halan, Monika. "Ungreasing Palms in India: An Anticorruption Crusader Discovers the Internet Cuts Bureaucracy and Bribes". *The Industry Standard*, June 29, 2000.

Jain, R.B. "Fighting Political Corruption: The Indian Experience". *Indian Political Science Review*, Vol. 17, No. 2 (July 1983), pp. 215-228.

Kashyap, Subhash C. (ed.). *Crime and Corruption to Good Governance.* New Delhi: Uppal Publishing House, 1997.

Kashyap, Subhash C. (ed.). *Eradication of Corruption and Restoration of Values.* New Delhi: Sterling Publishers, 2001.

Kaura, Mohinder N. "Administrative and Financial Accountability in India". In Sirajuddin H. Salleh and Arabinda Kar (eds.), *Administrative and Financial Accountability: The ASEAN-SAARC Experience.* Kuala Lumpur: Asian and Pacific Development Centre, 1995. Chapter 11, pp. 317-343.

Kohli, Suresh (ed.). *Corruption in India.* New Delhi: Chetana Publications, 1975.

Mansukhani, H.L. *Corruption and Public Servants.* New Delhi: Vikas Publishing House, 1979.

Mishra, Girish and Braj Kumar Pandey. *White Collar Crimes*. New Delhi: Gyan Publishing House, 1998. Chapter 8, "Corruption and Bureaucracy", pp. 159-183; and Chapter 9, "Corruption in Political Sphere", pp. 185-230.

Mitra, Chandan. *The Corrupt Society: The Criminalization of India from Independence to the 1990s*. New Delhi: Penguin Books India, 1998.

Monteiro, John B. *Corruption: Control of Maladministration*. Bombay: Manaktalas, 1966.

Narayanasamy, N., M.P. Boruian and M.A. Jeyaraju (eds.). *Corruption at the Grassroots: The Shade and Shadows*. New Delhi: Concept Publisher, 2000.

Oldenburg, Philip. "Middlemen in Third-World Corruption: Implications of an Indian Case". *World Politics*, Vol. 39, No. 4 (1987), pp. 508-535.

Oza, B.M. *Bofors: The Ambassador's Evidence*. New Delhi: Konark Publishers, 1997.

Padhy, Krushna Singh and P.K. Muni. *Corruption in Indian Politics: A Case Study of an Indian State*. Delhi: Discovery Publishing House, 1987.

Palmier, Leslie. "Corruption in India". *New Society*, No. 5 (June 1975), pp. 577-579.

Paul, Samuel. "Corruption in India: Who Will Bell the Cat?" *Asian Journal of Political Science*, Vol. 6, No. 1 (June 1998), pp. 1-15.

Paul, Samuel. *Holding the State to Account: Citizen Monitoring in Action*. Bangalore: Books for Change, 2002.

Pavarala, Vinod. *Interpreting Corruption: Elite Perspectives in India*. New Delhi: Sage Publications, 1996.

Raghavan, R.K. "Recent Innovations in Tackling Corruption in the Civil Services in India". In *Research Material Series No. 56*. Tokyo: UNAFEI, December 2000, pp. 378-385.

Santhanam Committee. *Report of the Committee on Prevention of Corruption*. New Delhi: Ministry of Home Affairs, 1964.

Shunglu, Vijay K. "India's Anti-Corruption Strategy". In *Combating Corruption in Asian and Pacific Economies*. Manila: Asian Development Bank, 2000, pp. 13-18.

Singh, Gurharpal. "Understanding Political Corruption in Contemporary Indian Politics". In Paul Heywood (ed.), *Political Corruption*. Oxford: Blackwell Publishers, 1997, pp. 210-222.

Singh, Joginder. *Inside the CBI*. New Delhi: Chandrika Publications, 1999.

Singh, Joginder. *Outside CBI*. New Delhi: Gyan Publishing House, 1999.

Singh, N.K. *The Politics of Crime and Corruption: A Former CBI Officer Speaks*. New Delhi: HarperCollins Publishers, 1999.

Singh, Shekar. "Ethics and Administration". In Chaturvedi (ed.), *Fifty Years of Indian Administration: Retrospect and Prospect*. New Delhi: Indian Institute of Public Administration, 1998, pp. 71-83.

Somjee, A.H. "Social Perspectives on Corruption in India". *Political Science Review*, Vol. 13, Nos. 1-4 (1974), pp. 180-186.

Srivastava, C.P. *Corruption: India's Enemy Within.* New Delhi: Macmillan India, 2001.

Taub, Richard P. *Bureaucrats under Stress: Administrators and Administration in an Indian State.* Berkeley: University of California Press, 1969. Chapter 8, "Sources of Strain: The Impact of Democratization on Income", pp. 136-151.

Thakur, Upendra. *Corruption in Ancient India.* New Delhi: Abhinava Publications, 1979.

Thomas, K.T. "Anatomy and Epidemic of Corruption". D.P. Kohli Memorial Lecture, 2001. See http://www.cbi.nic.in/lecture.htm

Tummala, Krishna K. "Corruption in India: Control Measures and Consequences". *Asian Journal of Political Science*, Vol. 10, No. 2 (December 2002), pp. 43-69.

Upadhyay, R. "Political Corruption in India: An Analysis". New Delhi: South Asia Analysis Group Paper No. 219, March 2001. See http://www.saag.org/paper3/paper219.htm.

Vanhanen, Tatu. "Politics of Ethnic Nepotism in India." In Diethelm Weidemann (ed.), *Nationalism, Ethnicity and Political Development in South Asia.* New Delhi: Manohar, 1991, pp. 69-92.

Varma, S.P. "Corruption and Political Development in India". *Political Science Review*, Vol. 13, Nos. 1-4 (1974), pp. 157-179.

Verma, Arvind. "Cultural Roots of Police Corruption in India". *Policing*, Vol. 22, No. 3 (1999), pp. 264-279.

Visvanathan, Shiv and Harsh Sethi (eds.). *Foul Play: Chronicles of Corruption, 1947-97.* New Delhi: Banyan Books, 1998.

Vittal, N. "Applying Zero Tolerance to Corruption". New Delhi: CVC, 1999. See http://cvc.nic.in/vscvc/note.html.

Vittal, N. and S. Mahalingam. *Fighting Corruption and Restructuring Government.* New Delhi: Manas Publications, 2000.

Wade, Robert. "The System of Administrative and Political Corruption: Canal Irrigation in South India". *Journal of Development Studies*, Vol. 18, No. 3 (April 1982), pp. 287-328.

Wade, Robert. "Irrigation Reform in Conditions of Populist Anarchy: An Indian Case". *Journal of Development Economics*, Vol. 14, No. 3 (1984), pp. 285-303.

Wade, Robert. "The Market for Public Office: Why the Indian State is Not Better at Development". *World Development*, Vol. 13, No. 4 (1985), pp. 467-497.

Indonesia

A National Survey of Corruption in Indonesia. Jakarta: Partnership for Governance Reform, Final Report, December 2001.

Abbott, Jason. *Developmentalism and Dependency in Southeast Asia: The Case of the Automotive Industry.* London: Routledge, 2003. Chapter 3, "Indonesia: Soeharto and the Neo-patrimonial State", pp. 57-79.

Abimanyu, Anggito. "Challenge Toward Good Governance and Anti-Corruption: The Case of Indonesia". Paper presented at the "Second Intellectual Dialogue on Building Asia's Tomorrow: Promoting Sustainable Development and Human Security", co-organised by Japan Centre for International Exchange and the Institute of Southeast Asian Studies in Singapore, 12-13 July 1999.

Assegaf, Ibrahim. "Legends of the Fall: An Institutional Analysis of Indonesian Law Enforcement Agencies Combating Corruption". In Tim Lindsey and Howard Dick (eds.), *Corruption in Asia: Rethinking the Governance Paradigm.* Annandale: The Federation Press, 2002. Chapter 8, pp. 127-146.

Backman, Michael. *Asian Eclipse: Exposing the Dark Side of Business in Asia.* Rev. edition. Singapore: John Wiley and Sons (Asia), 2001. Chapter 1, "Bureaucrats, Bribery, and Bankruptcy", pp. 7-21; and Chapter 13, "President of the Country; Chairman of the Board", pp. 234-264.

Bresnan, John. *Managing Indonesia: The Modern Political Economy.* New York: Columbia University Press, 1993. Chapters 4, 6 and 7.

Clark, David H. and Mayling Oey-Gardiner. "How Indonesian Lecturers Have Adjusted to Civil Service Compensation". *Bulletin of Indonesian Economic Studies,* Vol. 27, No. 3 (December 1991), pp. 129-141.

Colmey, John and David Liebhold. "The Family Firm". *Time,* 24 May 1999, pp. 15-29.

Crouch, Harold. "Generals and Business in Indonesia". *Pacific Affairs,* Vol. 48, No. 4 (1975), pp. 519-540.

Crouch, Harold. *The Army and Politics in Indonesia.* Ithaca: Cornell University Press, 1988.

Danuredjo, S.L.S. "The Declining Trend of Legal and Administrative Performance in Indonesia: Some Remedial Actions Suggested". *International Review of Administrative Sciences,* Vol. 34 (1968), pp. 164-172.

Eklof, Stefan. "Politics, Business, and Democratization in Indonesia". In Edmund Terence Gomez (ed.), *Political Business in East Asia.* London: Routledge, 2002. Chapter 7, pp. 216-249.

Feng, Yi, Antonio C. Hsiang, and Jaehoon Lee. "Indonesia's Economic Crisis and Dilemma: Contradictions of Two Kinds of Freedom". In Kuotsai Tom Liou (ed.), *Managing Economic Development in Asia: From Economic Miracle to Financial Crisis.* Westport: Praeger, 2002. Chapter 8, pp. 187-208.

Filmer, Deon and David L. Lindauer. "Does Indonesia Have a 'Low Pay' Civil Service?" *Bulletin of Indonesian Economic Studies,* Vol. 37, No. 2 (2001), pp. 189-205.

Goodpaster, Gary. "Reflections on Corruption in Indonesia". In Lindsey and Dick (eds.), *Corruption in Asia,* Chapter 6, pp. 87-108.

Gray, Clive. "Civil Service Compensation in Indonesia". *Bulletin of Indonesian Economic Studies,* Vol. 15, No. 1 (March 1979), pp. 85-113.

Hadisumarto, D. *The Indonesian Civil Service and Its Reform Movements.* Ph.D. dissertation, University of Southern California, 1974.

207

Hamilton-Hart, Natasha. "Anti-Corruption Strategies in Indonesia". *Bulletin of Indonesian Economic Studies*, Vol. 37, No. 1 (2001), pp. 65-82.

Hanna, Willard A. "A Primer of *Korupsi*", *American Universities Field Staff Reports*, Southeast Asia Series, Vol. 19, No. 8 (1971), pp. 1-8.

Hardjono, Ratih and Stefanie Teggemann (eds.). *The Poor Speak Up: 17 Stories of Corruption*. Jakarta: Partnership for Governance Reform in Indonesia, 2002.

Harahap, Rudy M. *Strategies for Preventing Corruption in Indonesia*. Canberra: Asia Pacific School of Economics and Management Working Papers, Asia Pacific Press, 1999.

Hill, Hal. *The Indonesian Economy in Crisis: Causes, Consequences and Lessons*. Singapore: Institute of Southeast Asian Studies, 1999.

Holloway, Richard (ed.). *Stealing from the People: 16 Studies on Corruption in Indonesia*. Books 1-4. Jakarta: Aksara Foundation, 2002. The titles of the four books are: Book 1, *Corruption: From Top to Bottom*; Book 2, *The Big Feast: Soldier, Judge, Banker, Civil Servant*; Book 3, *Foreign Aid, Business, and State Enterprise: Counting the Cost*; and Book 4, *The Clampdown: In Search of New Paradigms*.

Imbaruddin, Amir. "Corruption in Indonesia: Causes, Forms and Remedies". *Development Bulletin* (Canberra), No. 42 (July 1997), pp. 12-15.

Jenkins, David. *Suharto and His Generals: Indonesian Military Politics, 1975-1983*. Ithaca: Cornell Modern Indonesia Project No. 64, Cornell University Press, 1984.

Kingsbury, Damien. *The Politics of Indonesia*. Melbourne: Oxford University Press, 1998. Chapter 11, "Corruption and the First Family", pp. 198-218.

Loveard, Keith. *Suharto: Indonesia's Last Sultan*. Singapore: Horizon Books, 1999.

MacIntyre, Andrew. *Business and Politics in Indonesia*. Sydney: Allen and Unwin, 1990.

MacIntyre, Andrew. "Power, Prosperity and Patrimonialism: Business and Government in Indonesia". In Andrew MacIntyre (ed.), *Business and Government in Industrialising Asia*. Sydney: Allen and Unwin, 1994, pp. 244-267.

MacIntyre, Andrew. "Investment, Property Rights, and Corruption in Indonesia". In J. Edgardo Campos (ed.), *Corruption: The Boom and Bust of East Asia*. Quezon City: Ateneo de Manila University Press, 2001. Chapter 2, pp. 25-44.

Mackie, J.A.C.. "The Commission of Four Report on Corruption". *Bulletin of Indonesian Economic Studies*, Vol. 6, No. 3 (November 1970), pp. 87-101.

Manning, Nick *et al*. *Pay and Patronage in the Core Civil Service in Indonesia*. Washington, D.C.: World Bank, March 2000.

Marlay, Ross and Clark Neher. *Patriots and Tyrants: Ten Asian Leaders*. Lanham: Rowman and Littlefield Publishers, 1999. Chapter 9, "Suharto: The Impassive Administrator", pp. 239-259.

Marshall, Katherine. "Combating Corruption in Indonesia: Aide Memoire of the World Bank Team". Jakarta: World Bank , 20 September 1998.

McLeod, Ross H. "Government-Business Relations in Soeharto's Indonesia". In Peter Drysdale (ed.), *Reform and Recovery in East Asia: The Role of the State and Economic Enterprise*. London: Routledge, 2000. Chapter 7, pp. 146-168.

Palmier, Leslie. "Corruption in Context". In John Kidd and Frank-Jurgen Richter (eds.), *Fighting Corruption in Asia: Causes, Effects and Remedies*. Singapore: World Scientific Publishing, 2003. Chapter 4, pp. 73-89.

Poole-Robb, Stuart and Alan Bailey. *Risky Business: Corruption, Fraud, Terrorism and Other Threats to Global Business*. London: Kogan Page, 2002. Chapter 5, "Bureaucracy, Corruption and Foreign Direct Investment". pp. 49-68.

Robertson-Snape, Fiona. "Corruption, Collusion and Nepotism in Indonesia". *Third World Quarterly*, Vol. 20, No. 3 (June 1999), pp. 589-602.

Root, Hilton L. *Small Countries, Big Lessons: Governance and the Rise of East Asia*. Hong Kong: Oxford University Press for the Asian Development Bank, 1996. Chapter 7, "Indonesia: Informality Triumphs", pp. 90-110.

Server, O.B. "Corruption: A Major Problem for Urban Management— Some Evidence from Indonesia". *Habitat International*, Vol. 20, No. 1 (1996), pp. 24-41.

Smith, Theodore M. "Corruption, Tradition and Change". *Indonesia*, Vol. 11 (April 1971), pp. 21-40.

Smith, Theodore M. "Stimulating Performance in the Indonesian Bureaucracy: Gaps in the Administrator's Tool Kit". *Economic Development and Cultural Change*, Vol. 23, No. 4 (July 1975), pp. 719-738.

Soesastro, Hadi. "Governance and the Crisis in Indonesia". In Drysdale (ed.), *Reform and Recovery in East Asia*. Chapter 6, pp. 120-145.

Soetjipto, Adi. "The Battle against Corruption in the Context of a Developing Country: The Case of Indonesia". In Cyrille Fijnaut and Leo Huberts (eds.), *Corruption, Integrity and Law Enforcement*. The Hague: Kluwer Law International, 2002. Chapter 4, pp. 59-71.

Warwick, Donald P. *Civil Service Reform in Indonesia: Problems and Possibilities*. Unpublished report, October 1978.

Warwick, Donald P. "The Effectiveness of the Indonesian Civil Service". *Southeast Asian Journal of Social Science*, Vol. 15, No. 2 (1987), pp. 40-56.

Japan

Allen, Margaret. *The Dirty Dozen: The World's Greatest Financial Disasters and Frauds*. Singapore: Times Books International, 1997. Chapter 9, "Recruit: A Case of Bribery", pp. 124-134.

Babb, James. *Tanaka: The Making of Postwar Japan*. Harlow: Longman, 2000.

Babb, James. *Business and Politics in Japan*. Manchester: Manchester University Press, 2001.

Babb, James. "Politics, Business, and the Inescapable Web of Structural Corruption in Japan". In Edmund Terence Gomez (ed.), *Political Business in East Asia*. London: Routledge, 2002. Chapter 10, pp. 324-338.

Backman, Michael. *Asian Eclipse: Exposing the Dark Side of Business in Asia*. Rev. edition. Singapore: John Wiley and Sons (Asia), 2001. Chapter 9, "What's Wrong with Japan", pp. 125-158.

Baerwald, Hans H. "Lockheed and Japanese Politics". *Asian Survey*, Vol. 16, No. 9 (September 1976), pp. 817-829.

Befu, Harumi. "Gift-Giving in a Modernizing Japan". *Monumenta Nipponica*, Vol. 23 (Winter 1968), pp. 445-456.

Befu, Harumi. *Bribery in Japan: When Law Tangles with Culture*. Berkeley: University of California Press, 1971.

Berkofsky, Axel. "Corruption and Bribery in Japan's Ministry of Foreign Affairs: The Case of Muneo Suzuki". Japan Policy Research Institute Working Paper No. 86, June 2002, pp. 1-9.

Blaker, M. "Japan: The Year of Lockheed". *Asian Survey*, Vol. 17, No. 1 (January 1977), pp. 81-90.

Blechinger, Verena. "Changes in the Handling of Corruption Scandals in Japan since 1994"v *Asia-Pacific Review*, Vol. 6, No. 2 (1999), pp. 42-64.

Blechinger, Verena. *Corruption Through Political Contributions in Japan*. Berlin: Transparency International Working Paper, October 2000.

Bouissou, Jean-Marie. "Gifts, Networks and Clienteles: Corruption in Japan as a Redistributive System". In Donatella Della Porta and Yves Meny (eds.), *Democracy and Corruption in Europe*. London: Pinter, 1997. Chapter 9, pp. 132-147.

Castberg, Anthony Didrick. "Corruption in Japan and the US". In *Resource Material Series No. 56*. Tokyo: UNAFEI, December 2000, pp. 435-439.

Dairokuno, Kosaku. "Corruption and Rewards for High Public Offices: A Japanese Experience". *Asian Review of Public Administration*, Vol. 13, No. 1 (January-June 2001), pp. 102-117.

Dixon, Karl. "Japan's Lockheed Scandal: 'Structural Corruption'". *Pacific Community*, Vol. 8 (January 1977), pp. 340-362.

Farley, Maggie. "Japan's Press and the Politics of Scandal". In Susan J. Pharr and Ellis S. Krauss (eds.), *Media and Politics in Japan*. Honolulu: University of Hawaii Press, 1996. Chapter 4, pp. 133-163.

Fisher, Larry Warren. "The Lockheed Affair: A Phenomenon of Japanese Politics". Ph.D. dissertation, University of Colorado, Boulder, 1980.

Fukuda, Kan'ichi. "Parliamentary Democracy and Political Corruption". *Japan Interpreter*, Vol. 11, No. 2 (Autumn 1976), pp. 159-166.

Goto, Hiroshi. "Business Corruption in Japan, 1996: Nothing New and Something New". In Barry Rider, Yutake Tajima, and Fiona Macmillan (eds.), *Commercial Law in a Global Context: Some Perspectives in Anglo-Japanese Law*. London: Kluwer Law International, 1998. Chapter 3, pp. 17-36.

Hasegawa, Tamotsu. "Investigation of Corruption in Japan". In *Resource Material Series No. 56*, pp. 469-475.

Hirata, Keiko. *Civil Society in Japan: The Growing Role of NGOs in Tokyo's Aid and Development Policy*. Basingstoke: Palgrave Macmillan, 2002. Chapter 3, "Domestic Crises and Pluralism"v pp. 74-96.

Hrebenar, Ronald J. "Political Money, the LDP and the Symbolic Politics of Reform". *Japan Interpreter*, Vol. 10, No. 3 (September 1976), pp. 66-73.

Hrebenar, Ronald J. *Japan's New Party System*. Boulder: Westview Press, 2000. Chapter 3, "The Money Base of Japanese Politics", pp. 59-83.

Hunziker, Steven and Ikuro Kamimura. *Kakuei Tanaka: A Political Biography of Modern Japan*. Singapore: Times Books International, 1996.

Iga, Mamoru and Morton Auerbach. "Political Corruption and Social Structure in Japan". *Asian Survey*, Vol. 17, No. 6 (June 1977), pp. 556-564.

Imazu, Hiroshi. "Power Mosaic: Hotbed of the Lockheed Case". *Japan Quarterly*, Vol. 23 (July-September 1976), pp. 228-237.

Inoguchi, Takashi. "Japanese Bureaucracy: Coping with New Challeges". In Purnedra Jain and Takashi Inoguchi (eds.), *Japanese Politics Today: Beyond Karaoke Democracy?* South Melbourne: Macmillan Education Australia, 1997. Chapter 6, pp. 92-107.

Johnson, Chalmers. "Tanaka Kakuei, Structural Corruption, and the Advent of Machine Politics in Japan". *Journal of Japanese Studies*, Vol. 12, No. 1 (1986), pp. 1-28.

Johnson, David T. "Bureaucratic Corruption in Japan". Japan Policy Research Institute Working Paper No. 76 (April 2001), pp. 1-6.

Kaplan, David E. and Alec Dubro. *Yakuza: Japan's Criminal Underworld* Expanded edition. Berkeley: University of California Press, 2003.

Kearns, Ian. "The Recruit Scandal and Corruption in Japanese Political Life". *Corruption and Reform*, Vol. 5, No. 1 (1990), pp. 63-70.

Kubota, Akira. "Big Business and Politics in Japan, 1993-95". In Jain and Inoguchi (eds.), *Japanese Politics Today*, Chapter 8, pp. 124-143.

Lintner, Bertil. *Blood Brothers: Crime, Business and Politics in Asia*. Crows Nest: Allen and Unwin, 2002. Chapter 3, "The Dark Masters of Kabuki", pp. 136-181.

Macdougall, Terry. "The Lockheed Scandal and the High Costs of Politics in Japan". In Andrei S. Markovits and Mark Silverstein (eds.), *The Politics of Scandal: Power and Process in Liberal Democracies*. New York: Holmes and Meier Publishers, 1988. Chapter 8, pp. 193-229.

Mitchell, Richard H. *Political Bribery in Japan*. Honolulu: University of Hawaii Press, 1996.

Miyake, Maiko, Kathryn Gordon and Iwao Taka. "Fighting against Corruption: The Japanese Approach to Reform Corporate Governance". In John B. Kidd and Frank-Jurgen Richter (eds.), *Corruption and Governance in Asia*. Basingstoke: Palgrave Macmillan, 2003. Chapter 9, pp. 166-179.

211

Muta, Shohei. "The Fall of the Mighty MOF? Lack of Accountability in the Japanese Bureaucracy". *NIRA Review*, Vol. 3, No. 2 (Spring 1996).

Nakamura, Akira. "A Pattern of Rewards: Corruption in Japanese Politics and the Importance of Cultural Aspects". Paper presented at the workshop on "Rewards for High Public Office in the Pacific Rim" held at the City University of Hong Kong, in Hong Kong from 15-17 July 2000.

Nakamura, Akira and Kosaku Dairokuno. "Japan's Pattern of Rewards for High Public Office: A Cultural Perspective". In Christopher Hood *et al.* (eds.), *Reward for High Public Office: Asian and Pacific Rim States.* London: Routledge, 2003. Chapter 6, pp. 105-118.

O'uchi, Minoru. "Scandals During the Occupation and After Gaining Independence". Paper presented at the International Development Research Centre and University of the Philippines College of Public Administration Project Development Meeting on "Bureaucratic Behaviour and Development" in Baguio City, Philippines, 26-31 January 1975.

O'uchi, Minoru. "Political Corruption and Japanese Corporate Donations". In Savitri Vishwanathan (ed.), *Japan: The New Challenges.* New Delhi: Allied Publishers, 1982, pp. 94-126.

O'uchi, Minoru. "Public Accountability in Japanese Politics and Administration". In Raul P. de Guzman *et al.* (eds.), *Public Administration in a Changing National and International Environment.* Manila: EROPA Secretariat General, 1989, pp. 105-114.

Pharr, Susan J. "Officials' Misconduct and Public Distrust: Japan and the Trilateral Democracies". In Susan J. Pharr and Robert D. Putnam (eds.), *Disaffected Democracies: What's Troubling the Trilateral Countries?* Princeton: Princeton University Press, 2000. Chapter 8, pp. 173-201.

Pharr, Susan J. "Public Trust and Corruption in Japan". In Arnold J. Heidenheimer and Michael Johnston (eds.), *Political Corruption: Concepts and Contexts* 3rd ed. New Brunswick: Transaction Publishers, 2002. Chapter 43, pp. 835-864.

Reed, Steven R. "Political Corruption in Japan". *International Social Science Journal*, Vol. 149 (September 1996), pp. 395-405.

Reed, Steven R. "Punishing Corruption: The Response of the Japanese Electorate to Scandals". In Ofer Feldman (ed.), *Political Psychology in Japan: Behind the Nails (that Sometimes Stick Out (and Get Hammered Down).* Commack: Nova Science Publishers, 1999. Chapter 7, pp. 131-148.

Reed, Steven R. "Impersonal Mechanisms and Personal Networks in the Distribution of Grants". In Michio Muramatsu, Farrukh Iqbal and Ikuo Kume (eds.), *Local Government Development in Post-war Japan.* New York: Oxford University Press, 2001. Chapter 5, pp. 112-131.

Rothacher, Albrecht. "Political Corruption in Japan". In Martin J. Bull and James L. Newell (eds.), *Corruption in Contemporary Politics.* Basingstoke: Palgrave Macmillan, 2003. Chapter 9, pp. 106-119.

Schlesinger, Jacob M. *Shadow Shoguns: The Rise and Fall of Japan's Postwar Political Machine*. Stanford: Stanford University Press, 1999.

Spaulding, Robert M. Jr. *Imperial Japan's Higher Civil Service Examinations*. Princeton: Princeton University Press, 1967. Chapter 24, "Fraud and Favoritism", pp. 293-305.

Sugimoto, Yoshio. *An Introduction to Japanese Society* 2nd ed. Cambridge: Cambridge University Press, 2003. Chapter 8, "Collusion and Competition in the Establishment", pp. 212-243.

Tabb, William K. *The Postwar Japanese System: Cultural Economy and Economic Transformation*. New York: Oxford University Press, 1995. Chapter 8, "Overaccumulation, Speculation, and Corruption", pp. 198-224.

Tachi, Yuichiro. "Role of Public Prosecutors in Japan". In *Taking Action Against Corruption in Asia and the Pacific*. Manila: Asian Development Bank, 2002. Chapter 11, pp. 119-126.

Wolferen, Karel van. *The Enigma of Japanese Power: People and Politics in a Stateless Nation*. New York: Alfred A. Knopf, 1989. Chapter 5, "The Administrators", pp. 109-158.

Woodall, Brian. *Japan Under Construction: Corruption, Politics, and Public Works*. Berkeley: University of California Press, 1996.

Woronoff, Jon. *Japan as—Anything But—Number One*. Tokyo: Yohan Publications, 1990. Chapter 8, pp. 141-169.

Yamaguchi, Michihiko. "The Globalisation of Economic Markets and the Corruption of Professional Ethics in Japan". In Kotaku Ishido and David Myers (eds.), *Reinventing the Old Japan*. Rockhampton: Central Queensland University Press, 2001, pp. 19-23.

Yanaga, Chitoshi. *Big Business in Japanese Politics*. New Haven: Yale University Press, 1968.

Yasko, Richard. "Bribery Cases and the Rise of the Justice Ministry in Late *Meiji*-Early *Taisho* Japan". *Law in Japan: An Annual*, Vol. 12 (1979), pp. 57-68.

Yayama, Taro. "The Recruit Scandal: Learning from the Causes of Corruption". *Journal of Japanese Studies*, Vol. 16 (Winter 1990), pp. 93-114.

Ziemba, William T. and Sandra L. Schwartz. *Power Japan: How and Why the Japanese Economy Works*. Chicago: Probus Publishing Company, 1992. Chapter 9, "Scandals and Reform: The Role of the Stock Market in Political Change", pp. 273-299.

Macau

Annual Report of the Commission Against Corruption 2000. Macau: CCAC, 2002.

Organizational Law of the Commission Against Corruption. Macau: CCAC, 2002.

10 Years of Safeguarding Honesty and Transparency in Macao. Macau: CCAC, 2002.

Lo, Shiu-Hing. "Bureaucratic Corruption and its Control in Macao". *Asian Journal of Public Administration*, Vol. 15, No. 1 (June 1993), pp. 32-58.

Lo, Shiu-Hing. *Political Development in Macau*. Hong Kong: The Chinese University Press, 1995. Chapter 6, "Administrative Modernization: Bureaucratic Corruption and Its Control"v pp. 171-196.

Malaysia

Abdul, Tunku Aziz. "International Case Study: Stamping Out Corruption in Malaysia". In *Resource Material Series No. 56*. Tokyo: UNAFEI, December 2000, pp. 393-399.

Abdullah, Abdul Rahman. "Administrative and Financial Accountability in Malaysia"v In Sirajuddin H. Salleh and Arabinda Kar (eds.), *Administrative and Financial Accountability: The ASEAN-SAARC Experience*. Kuala Lumpur: Asian and Pacific Development Centre, 1995. Chapter 6, pp. 146-167.

Anti-Corruption Agency. "Strengthening Integrity by Promoting Good Governance in the Malaysian Public Administration: Issues and Challenges". Kuala Lumpur: ACA, n.d.

The Anwar Ibrahim Judgment. Kuala Lumpur: Malayan Law Journal, 1999.

Gale, Bruce. *Politics and Public Enterprise in Malaysia*. Singapore: Eastern Universities Press, 1981.

Gomez, Edmund Terence. *Political Business: Corporate Involvement of Malaysian Political Parties*. Townsville: Centre for Southeast Asian Studies, James Cook University of North Queensland, 1994.

Gomez, Edmund Terence. "Political Business in Malaysia: Party Factionalism, Corporate Development, and Economic Crisis". In Edmund Terence Gomez (ed.), *Political Business in East Asia*. London: Routledge, 2002. Chapter 3, pp. 82-114.

Gomez, Edmund Terence and K.S. Jomo. *Malaysia's Political Economy: Politics, Patronage and Profits*. Cambridge: Cambridge University Press, 1997.

Hilley, John. *Malaysia: Mahathirism, Hegemony and the New Opposition*. London: Zed Books, 2001.

Ho, Khai Leong. "Bureaucratic Accountability in Malaysia: Control Mechanisms and Critical Concerns". In Hoi-Kwok Wong and Hon S. Chan (eds.), *Handbook of Comparative Public Administration in the Asian-Pacific Region*. New York: Marcel Dekker, 1999. Chapter 2, pp. 23-45.

Ho, Khai Leong. "The Political and Administrative Frames: Challenges and Reforms under the Mahathir Administration". In Ho Khai Leong and James Chin (eds.), *Mahathir's Administration: Performance and Crisis in Governance*. Singapore: Times Books International, 2001, pp. 7-27.

Jomo, K.S. "Governance, Rent-Seeking, and Private Investment in Malaysia". In J. Edgardo Campos (ed.), *Corruption: the Boom and Bust of East Asia*. Quezon City: Ateneo de Manila University Press, 2001. Chapter 6, pp. 131-162.

Jomo, K.S. and Edmund Terence Gomez. "Rents and Development in Multiethnic Malaysia". In M. Aoki, H. Kim and M. Okuno-Fujiwara (eds.), *The Role of Government in East Asian Economic Development*. New York: Oxford University Press, 1997. Chapter 12, pp. 342-372.

Khalid, Azmi and Harun Halim Rasip. "Corruption and the Malaysian Situation". In *Corruption*. Kuala Lumpur: Aliran Kesedaran Negara, 1981, pp. 74-82.

Lim, Hong Hai. "Public Administration: The Effects of Executive Dominance". In Francis Loh Kok Wah and Khoo Boo Teik (eds.), *Democracy in Malaysia: Discourses and Practices*. Richmond: Curzon Press, 2002. Chapter 7, pp. 165-197.

Lim, Kit Siang. *Malaysia: Crisis of Identity*. Petaling Jaya: Democratic Action Party, 1986. "On a Clean, Efficient and Democratic Government", pp. 227-364.

Lim Kit Siang. *The $62 Billion North-South Highway Scandal*. Petaling Jaya: Democratic Action Party, 1987.

Lim, Kit Siang. *Samy Vellu and Maika Scandal*. Kuala Lumpur: Democratic Action Party, 1992.

Marican, Y. Mansoor. "Combating Corruption: The Malaysian Experience". *Asian Survey*, Vol. 19, No. 6 (June 1979), pp. 597-610.

Milne, R.S. "Levels of Corruption in Malaysia: A Comment on the Case of Bumiputra Malaysia Finance". *Asian Journal of Public Administration*, Vol. 9, No. 1 (June 1987), pp. 56-73.

Nordin, Abu Samah. *Corruption and the National Bureau of Investigation*. Kuala Lumpur: Academic Exercise, Faculty of Law, University of Malaya, 1975.

Sarji, Ahmad and Mahmud Taib. *Upholding the Integrity of the Malaysian Civil Service*. Petaling Jaya: Pelanduk Publications, 1993.

Searle, Peter. *The Riddle of Malaysian Capitalism: Rent-seekers or Real Capitalists?* St. Leonards: Allen and Unwin, 1999.

Singh, Jagir. *Law of Bribery and Corruption in Malaysia with Cases and Commentaries*. Kuala Lumpur: International Law Book Services, 1994.

Sivalingam, G. "Bureaucratic Corruption in Malaysia: The Incongruence between Social and Legal Norms". *Philippine Journal of Public Administration*, Vol. 27, No. 4 (October 1983), pp. 418-435.

Sivalingam, G. and Yong Siew Peng. "The System of Political and Administrative Corruption in a West Malaysian State". *Philippine Journal of Public Administration*, Vol. 35, No. 3 (July 1991), pp. 264-286.

Stewart, Ian. *The Mahathir Legacy: A Nation Divided, A Region at Risk*. Crows Nest: Allen and Unwin, 2003.

Tharan, Sri. "Systems Corruption and the New Economic Policy". *Philippine Journal of Public Administration*, Vol. 23, No. 1 (January 1979), pp. 39-60.

Mongolia

Adiya, O. "A Beginner's Guide to Corruption". *UB Post*, 15 September 1998, p. 3.

Bikales, William G. "Capacity Building in a Transition Country: Lessons from Mongolia". In Merilee S. Grindle (ed.), *Getting Good Government: Capacity Building in the Public Sectors of Developing Countries*. Cambridge: Harvard Institute for International Development, 1997. Chapter 15, pp. 435-463.

Bruun, Ole and Ole Odgaard (eds.). *Mongolia in Transition: Old Patterns, New Challenges*. Richmond: Curzon Press, 1996.

Fitch, Christopher M. "Mongolia in 2001: Political Consolidation and Continued Economic Reform". *Asian Survey*, Vol. 42, No. 1 (January/February 2002), pp. 39-45.

Goyal, Hari D. "A Development Perspective on Mongolia". *Asian Survey*, Vol. 39, No. 4 (July/August 1999), pp. 633-655.

Lawless, Jill. *Wild East: Travels in the New Mongolia*. Toronto: ECW Press, 2000. Chapter 5, "The School for Scandal", pp. 47-65.

"Mongolia". In Adrian Karatnycky, Alexander Motyl, and Aili Piano (eds.), *Nations in Transit 1999-2000*. New York: Freedom House, 2000, pp. 464-482. See http://freedomhouse.org/pdf_docs/research/nitransit/Mongolia.PDF

Mongolian Business Development Agency. *Doing Business in Mongolia*. Ulaanbataar: MBDA, 1996.

Narayan, Francis B. and Barry Reid. *Financial Management and Governance Issues in Mongolia*. Manila: Asian Development Bank, 2000. See http://www.adb.org/Documents/Books/Financial_Mgt/Mongolia/chap6.pdf

Nixson, Frederick I. and Bernard Walters. "Administrative Reform and Economic Development in Mongolia, 1990-1997: A Critical Perspective". In Kuotsai Tom Liou (ed.), *Administrative Reform and National Economic Development*. Aldershot: Ashgate, 2000, Chapter 10, pp. 213-239.

Oquist, Paul. "Good Governance Implementation for Human Security in Mongolia". Paper presented at the conference on "Best Practices in Good Governance" in Ulaanbaatar, Mongolia, 8-10 February 2001.

Oyuntuya, J. *National Integrity Systems Country Study Report: Mongolia 2001*. Ulaanbataar: Democratic Governing Institutions Capacity Building Project, 2001.

Quah, Jon S.T. *Combating Corruption in Mongolia: Problems and Prospects*. Singapore: Department of Political Science, National University of Singapore, Working Paper No. 22, 1999.

Severinghaus, Sheldon R. "Mongolia in 1998 and 1999". *Asian Survey*, Vol. 40, No. 1 (January/February 2000), pp. 130-139.

Sneath, David. "Pastoral Adaptation and Subsistence in Mongolia's 'Age of the Market'". In Pietro P. Masina (ed.), *Rethinking Development in East Asia: From Illusory Miracle to Economic Crisis*. Richmond: Curzon Press, 2002. Chapter 14, pp. 297-317.

Tserendondov, Altanzaya. "Corruption in Privatisation and Effective Anti-Corruption Strategies in Transition Country: Mongolia". Paper presented at the 10th International Anti-Corruption Conference in Prague, Czech Republic, 7-11October 2001.

United Nations Development Programme. *Human Development Report Mongolia 1997.* Ulaanbaatar: UNDP, 1997.

Philippines

Abueva, Jose V. "What are We in Power for ? The Sociology of Graft and Corruption". *Philippine Sociological Review*, Vol. 18, Nos. 3-4 (July-October 1970), pp. 203-210.

Alfiler, Ma. Concepcion P. "Administrative Discipline and the Implementation of Anti-Graft Policies in the Philippines". *Thai Journal of Development Administration*, Vol. 17 (July 1977), pp. 406-426.

Alfiler, Ma Concepcion P. "Administrative Measures Against Bureaucratic Corruption: The Philippine Experience". *Philippine Journal of Public Administration*, Vol. 23, Nos. 3 & 4 (July-October 1979), pp. 321-349.

Angeles, Teresita N. *An Anti-Corruption Strategy for the Philippines.* Canberra: Asia Pacific School of Economics and Management Working Papers, Asia Pacific Press, 1999.

Aquino, Belinda A. *Politics of Plunder: The Philippines under Marcos.* Manila: Great Books Trading and College of Public Administration, University of the Philippines, 1987.

Aquino, Belinda A. "The Transnational Dynamics of the Marcos Plunder". *Journal of Asian and African Studies*, Vol. 5 (September 1998), pp. 37-74.

Austin, W. Timothy. *Banana Justice: Field Notes on Philippine Crime and Custom.* Westport: Praeger, 1999. Chapter 7, "Bribery and Extortion", pp. 95-116.

Batalla, Eric C. "De-institutionalising Corruption in the Philippines". Paper presented at the Conference on Institutionalising Strategies to Combat Corruption in Manila, Philippines, 12-13 August 2000.

Beschel, Robert P. Jr. "Corruption, Transparency and Accountability in the Philippines". Manila: Asian Development Bank, 1999. Unpublished report.

Bhargava, Vinay. "Combating Corruption in the Philippines". Manila: World Bank Office, 1999.

Borja, Jacinto Castel. *The Honorable Jan Abusado: The Story Behind the Corruption in Philippine Officialdom.* Manila: J. Castel Borja Co., 1961.

Carbonell-Catillo, A. "The Philippines: The Politics of Plunder". *Corruption and Reform*, Vol. 1, No. 3 (1986), pp. 235-243.

Carino, Ledivina V. "The Politicization of the Philippine Bureaucracy: Corruption or Commitment?" *International Review of the Administrative Sciences*, Vol. 51, No. 1 (1985), pp. 13-18.

Carino, Ledivina V. "Enhancing Accountability in the Philippines: The Continuing Quest". In John P. Burns (ed.), *Asian Civil Service Systems: Improving*

Efficiency and Productivity. Singapore: Times Academic Press, 1994. Chapter 5, pp. 106-125.

Castro, David. "The Presidential Commission on Good Government: A Self-Assessment". In Jose V. Abueva and Emerlina R. Roman (eds.), *Post-Edsa Constitutional Commissions: Self-Assessments and External Views and Assessments*. Quezon City: University of the Philippines Press, 1999, pp. 133-140.

Chanco, Mario P. *The Anatomy of Corruption*. Manila: Manor News Corporation, 1961.

Chua, Yvonne T. *Robbed: An Investigation of Corruption in Philippine Education*. Metro Manila: Philippine Center for Investigative Journalism, 1999.

Clemente, Wilfredo Al. *Philippine Bureaucracy and Local Development: The Case of Two Municipalities*. Ph.D. dissertation, University of Connecticut, 1974. Chapter 7, pp. 106-114.

Clemente, Wilfredo Al. and Fernandez Constanza. "Philippine Corruption at the Local Level". *Solidarity*, Vol. 7, No. 6 (June 1972), pp. 73-81.

Coronel, Sheila S. (ed.). *Pork and Other Perks: Corruption and Governance in the Philippines*. Metro Manila: Philippine Center for Investigative Journalism, 1998.

Coronel, Sheila S. (ed.). *Investigating Estrada: Millions, Mansions and Mistresses*. Metro Manila: Philippine Center for Investigative Journalism, 2000.

De Dios, Emmanuel S. and Ricardo D. Ferrer. "Corruption in the Philippines: Framework and Context". Manila: Transparent and Accountable (TAG) Project, August 2000.

Endriga, Jose N. "Historical Notes on Graft and Corruption in the Philippines". *Philippine Journal of Public Administration*, Vol. 23, Nos. 3 & 4 (July-October 1979), pp. 241-254.

Florentino-Hofilena, Chay. *News for Sale: The Corruption of the Philippine Media*. Metro Manila: Philippine Center for Investigative Journalism and the Center for Media Freedom and Responsibility, 1998.

Garcia, Manuel Buenconsejo. *Social Problems in the Philippine Context*. Metro Manila: National Book Store, 1994. Chapter 7, "Graft and Corruption", pp. 172-186.

Gleeck, Lewis E. Jr. *President Marcos and the Philippine Political Culture*. Manila: Loyal Printing, 1987. Chapter 12, "The Anatomy and Dynamics of Economic and Political Corruption (1979-1981)", pp. 177-201.

Gleeck, Lewis E. Jr. *The Third Philippine Republic 1946-1972*. Quezon City: New Day Publishers, 1993. Chapters 3, 7 and 8.

Hutchcroft, Paul D. "Oligarchs and Cronies in the Philippine State: The Politics of Patrimonial Plunder". *World Politics*, Vol. 43, No. 3 (1991), pp. 414-450.

Hutchcroft, Paul D. "Obstructive Corruption: The Politics of Privilege in the Philippines". In Mushtaq H. Khan and Jomo K.S. (eds.), *Rents, Rent-seeking and Economic Development: Theory and Evidence in Asia*. Cambridge: Cambridge University Press, 2000. Chapter 5, pp. 207-247.

218

Hutchcroft, Paul D. *Booty Capitalism: The Politics of Banking in the Philippines.* Quezon City: Ateneo de Manila University Press, 1998.

Iglesias, Gabriel U. "The Passage of the Anti-Graft Law". In Raul P. de Guzman (ed.), *Patterns in Decision-Making: Case Studies in Philippine Public Administration.* Manila: College of Public Administration, University of the Philippines, 1963, pp. 15-68.

Kintanar, Galileo C. *The Two Billion Dollar Human Rights Uproar: The Controversial Claims Against the Marcos Estate.* Quezon City: Truth and Justice Foundation, 1999.

Kirk, Donald. *Looted: The Philippines after the Bases.* Basingstoke: Macmillan Press, 1998. Chapter 9, "Their Own Worst Enemies", pp. 173-195.

Langston, Richard L. *Bribery and the Bible: Applied to the Philippines.* Singapore: Campus Crusade Asia Limited, 1991.

McDougald, Charles C. *The Marcos File: Was He a Philippine Hero or Corrupt Tyrant?* San Francisco: San Francisco Publishers, 1987.

Mijares, Primitivo. *The Conjugal Dictatorship of Ferdinand and Imelda Marcos.* San Francisco: Union Square Publications, 1976.

Moratalla, Nelson Nogor. "Graft and Corruption: The Philippine Experience". In *Resource Material Series No. 56.* Tokyo: UNAFEI, December 2000, pp. 501-523.

Padilla, Perfecto L. "Low Salary Grades, Income-Augmentation Schemes and the Merit Principle". In Proserpina D. Tapales and Nestor N. Pilar (eds.), *Public Administration by the Year 2000: Looking Back into the Future.* Quezon City: College of Public Administration, University of the Philippines, 1993, pp. 186-214.

Parayno, Guillermo Jr. "Combating Corruption in the Philippine Customs Service". In Peter Larmour and Nick Wolanin (eds.), *Corruption and Anti-Corruption.* Canberra: Asia Pacific Press, 2001. Chapter 12, pp. 204-220.

Ravenholt, Albert. "The Peso Price of Politics in the Philippines". *American Universities Field Staff Reports*, Southeast Asia Series, Vol. 6, No. 4 (May 1958), pp. 1-10.

Rodriguez, Filemon C. *The Marcos Regime: Rape of the Nation.* Quezon City: MOED Press, 1985.

Root, Hilton L. *Small Countries, Big Lessons: Governance and the Rise of East Asia.* Hong Kong: Oxford University Press for the Asian Development Bank, 1996. Chapter 8, "The Philippines: The New State of Patronage", pp. 111-138.

Rosell, Annabelle B. *Corruption Prevention Strategy for the Philippines: Incorporating Ethical Norms in the Performance Appraisal System.* Canberra: Asia Pacific School of Economics and Management Working Papers, Asia Pacific Press, 1999.

Salonga, Jovito R. *Presidential Plunder: The Quest for the Marcos Ill-Gotten Wealth.* Quezon City: Center for Leadership, Citizenship and Democracy, University of the Philippines, 2000.

Santiago, Miriam Defensor. *Cutting Edge: The Politics of Reform in the Philippines.* Mandaluyong City: Woman Today Publications, 1994. Chapter

219

1, "The Culture of Corruption, Commissioner of Immigration and Deportation, 1988-89", pp. 1-146.

Seagrave, Sterling. *The Marcos Dynasty*. New York: Harper and Row Publishers, 1988.

Sidel, J.T. "Coercion, Capital, Corruption, and the Post-Colonial State: Bossism in the Post-War Philippines". Ph.D. dissertation, Cornell University, 1995.

Tampipi, Ruth. "Bureaucratic Corruption: A Philippine Public Sector Reform Perspective". *Development Bulletin* (Canberra), No. 42 (July 1997), pp. 16-18.

Varela, Amelia P. "Different Faces of Filipino Administrative Culture". In Tapales and Pilar (eds.), *Public Administration by the Year 2000*, pp. 161-177.

Venzon, Regina Emily P. "Graft and Corruption and the Institutional Mechanisms Promoting Accountability under the Aquino Administration: Focus on the Office of the Ombudsman and the *Sandiganbayan*". M.A. thesis, University of the Philippines, 1998.

Singapore

Alatas, Syed Hussein. "The Problem of Corruption". In Kernial S. Sandhu and Paul Wheatley (eds.), *Management of Success: The Moulding of Modern Singapore*. Singapore: Institute of Southeast Asian Studies, 1989. Chapter 45, pp. 985-1002.

Chua, Cher Yak. "Good People, Good Laws: Curbing Public Sector Corruption". In *Progress in the Fight Against Corruption in Asia and the Pacific*. Manila: Asian Development Bank, 2001. Chapter 6, pp. 65-66.

Chua, Cher Yak. "Corruption Control: What Works?" Paper presented at the seminar on Promoting Integrity and Fighting Corruption in Guiyang, China, November 19-21, 2002.

The Corrupt Practices Investigation Bureau. Singapore: CPIB, 1990.

Jordan, Peter. "The 'Mr. Clean' of Asia". *Far Eastern Economic Review*, 6 September 1974, p. 23.

Lee, Kuan Yew. *From Third World to First: The Singapore Story, 1965-2000*. Singapore: Times Media, 2000. Chapter 12, "Keeping the Government Clean", pp. 182-198.

Lim, Siong Guan. "Integrity with Empowerment: Challenges Facing Singapore in Combating Corruption in the 21st Century". *Asian Journal of Political Science*, Vol. 6, No. 2 (December 1998), pp. 132-139.

Mohan, S. Chandra. "The Control of Corruption in Singapore". Volumes 1 and 2. Ph.D. thesis, School of Oriental and African Studies, University of London, 1987.

Quah, Jon S.T. *Administrative and Legal Measures for Combating Bureaucratic Corruption in Singapore*. Singapore: Department of Political Science, University of Singapore, Occasional Paper No. 34, 1978.

Quah, Jon S.T. "Police Corruption in Singapore: An Analysis of Its Forms, Extent and Causes". *Singapore Police Journal*, Vol. 10, No. 1 (January 1979), pp. 7-43.

Quah, Jon S.T. "Corruption in Asia with Special Reference to Singapore: Patterns and Consequences". *Asian Journal of Public Administration*, Vol. 10, No. 1 (June 1988), pp. 80-98.

Quah, Jon S.T. "Singapore's Experience in Curbing Corruption". In Arnold J. Heidenheimer *et al.* (eds.), *Political Corruption: A Handbook*. New Brunswick: Transaction Publishers, 1989. Chapter 48, pp. 841-853.

Quah, Jon S.T. "Promoting Accountability in Public Management: The Singapore Case". In Goraksha Bahadur N. Pradhan and Mila A. Reforma (eds.), *Public Management in the 1990s: Challenges and Opportunities*. Manila: EROPA Secretariat General, 1991. Chapter 10, pp. 87-103.

Quah, Jon S.T. "Combating Corruption Singapore Style". Paper presented at the Sixth International Anti-Corruption Conference in Cancun, Mexico, 22-25 November 1993.

Quah, Jon S.T. "Combating Corruption in Singapore: What can be Learned?" *Journal of Contingencies and Crisis Management*, Vol. 9, No. 1 (March 2001), pp. 29-35.

Quah, Jon S.T. "Singapore's Anti-Corruption Strategy: Is this Form of Governance Transferable to Other Countries?" In John B. Kidd and Frank-Jurgen Richter (eds.), *Corruption and Governance in Asia*. Basingstoke: Palgrave Macmillan, 2003, Chapter 10, pp. 180-197.

Quah, Jon S.T. "Paying for the 'Best and Brightest': Rewards for High Public Office in Singapore". In Christopher Hood *et al.* (eds.), *Reward for High Public Office: Asian and Pacific Rim States*. London: Routledge, 2003. Chapter 9, pp. 145-162.

Report of the Commission of Inquiry on Investigations Concerning the Late Mr Teh Cheang Wan. Singapore: Singapore National Printers, 1988.

Republic of Singapore. *Public Accountability: The Work of the Public Accounts Committee and the Auditor General's Office*. Singapore: Auditor General's Office, 1988.

Tan, Ah Leak. "The Experience of Singapore in Combating Corruption". In Rick Stapenhurst and Sahr J. Kpundeh (eds.), *Curbing Corruption: Toward a Model for Building National Integrity*. Washington, D.C.: The World Bank, 1999. Chapter 4, pp. 59-66.

Tien, Albert. "How Singapore Stops Corruption". *Insight*, (January 1973), pp. 16-19.

White Paper on Competitive Salaries for Competent and Honest Government: Benchmarks for Ministers and Senior Public Officers. Singapore: Presented to Parliament by the President on 21 October 1994, Command 13 of 1994.

Yoong, Siew Wah. "Some Aspects of Corruption". *National Youth Leadership Training Institute Journal*, (January 1973), pp. 54-59.

South Korea

Blechinger, Verena. *Report on Recent Bribery Scandals, 1996-2000*. Berlin: Transparency International Working Paper, October 2000.

Boettcher, Robert. *Gifts of Deceit: Sun Myung Moon, Tongsun Park, and the Korean Scandal*. New York: Holt, Rinehart and Winston, 1980.

Breen, Michael. *The Koreans: Who They are, What They want, Where Their Future Lies*. London: Orion Business, 1998. Chapter 19, "The Korean Disease", pp. 233-242.

Caiden, Gerald E. and Jung H. Kim. "A New Anti-Corruption Strategy for Korea". *Asian Journal of Political Science*, Vol. 1, No. 1 (June 1993), pp. 133-151.

Chang, C.S., N. J. Chang and B.T. Freese. "Offering Gifts or Offering Bribes? Code of Ethics in South Korea". *Journal of Third World Studies*, Vol. 18, No. 1 (2001), pp. 125-139.

Chang, Ha-Joon. "State, Capital, and Investments in Korea". In J. Edgardo Campos (ed.), *Corruption: The Boom and Bust of East Asia*. Quezon City: Ateneo de Manila University Press, 2001. Chapter 3, pp. 45-68.

Clifford, Mark L. *Troubled Tiger: Businessmen, Bureaucrats, and Generals in South Korea*. Rev. edition. Armonk: M.E. Sharpe, 1998.

Combating Corruption in Korea. Seoul: Office of the Prime Minister, Republic of Korea, October 2001.

Croissant, Aurel. "Electoral Politics in South Korea". In Aurel Croissant, Gabriele Bruns and Marei John (eds.), *Electoral Politics in Southeast and East Asia*. Singapore: Friedrich Ebert Stiftung, 2002, pp. 233-276.

Goh, Kun. "A Systematic Approach to Anti-Corruption: The Case of Seoul Metropolitan Government". *Korea NewsWorld*, Vol. 7, No. 80 (October 1999), pp. 16-17.

Hwang, Kee-Chul. "Administrative Corruption in the Republic of Korea". Ph.D. dissertation, School of Public Administration, University of Southern California, 1996.

Kim, Byong Seob. "Corruption and Anti-Corruption Policies in Korea". *Korea Journal*, Vol. 38, No. 1 (Spring 1998), pp. 46-69.

Kim, Joongi and Jong Bum Kim. "Cultural Differences in the Crusade against International Bribery: Rice-cake Expenses in Korea and the Foreign Corrupt Practices Act". *Pacific Rim Law and Policy Journal*, Vol. 6, No. 3 (1997), pp. 549-580.

Kim, Myoung-Soo. "Regulation and Corruption". In Yong Hyo Cho and H. George Frederickson (eds.), *The White House and the Blue House: Government Reform in the United States and Korea*. Lanham: University Press of America, 1997. Chapter 12, pp. 253-269.

Kim, Myoung-Soo. "Causes of Corruption and Irregularities". *Korea Focus*, Vol. 8, No. 1 (January-February 2000), pp. 1-8.

Kim, Young Jong. *Bureaucratic Corruption: The Case of Korea*. 4th ed. Seoul: The Chomyung Press, 1994.

Kim, Young Jong. *Korean Public Administration and Corruption Studies*. 2nd rev. ed. Seoul: Hak Mun Publishing, 1996.

Kong, Tat Yan. "Corruption and its Institutional Foundations: The Experience of South Korea". *IDS Bulletin*, Vol. 27, No. 2 (1996), pp. 48-55.

Korea's Comprehensive Anti-Corruption Programs. Seoul: Office of the Prime Minister, Republic of Korea, 1999.

Moon, Chung-in and Jongryn Mo (eds.). *Corruption in South Korea: Its Costs and Countermeasures.* Seoul: Oruem Publishing House, 1999.

Moon, Yong-Lin and Gary N. McLean. "The Nature of Corruption Hidden in Culture: The Case of Korea". In John Kidd and Frank-Jurgen Richter (eds.), *Fighting Corruption in Asia: Causes, Effects and Remedies.* Singapore: World Scientific Publishing, 2003. Chapter 12, pp. 297-315.

Moran, Jonathan. "Corruption and NIC Development: A Case Study of South Korea". *Crime, Law and Social Change,* Vol. 29 (1998), pp. 161-177.

Oh, John C.H. and Bruce Wiegand, "Democracy, Development and Corruption: The Case of Korea". *Korean Observer,* Vol. 26, No. 4 (Winter 1996), pp. 499-500.

Oh, John Kie-Chiang. *Korean Politics: The Quest for Democratization and Economic Development.* Ithaca: Cornell University Press, 1999. Chapter 8, "Corruption, the Trial, and the National Assembly, 1995-1996", pp. 164-193.

Oh, Suek Hong. "The Board of Audit and Inspection of the Republic of Korea: Some Structural Aspects". *Korean Journal of Public Administration,* Vol. 9, No. 2 (1971), pp. 164-190.

Oh, Suek Hong. "The Counter-Corruption Campaign of the Korean Government (1975-1977): Administrative Anti-Corruption measures of the *Seojungshaesih*". In Bun Woong Kim and Wha Joon Rho (eds.), *Korean Public Bureaucracy.* Seoul: Kyobo Publishing, 1982. Chapter 14, pp. 322-344.

Park, Byeong-Seog. "Political Corruption in South Korea: Concentrating on the Dynamics of Party Politics". *Asian Perspective,* Vol. 19, No. 1 (Spring-Summer 1995), pp. 138-193.

Park, Key-Chong. "Korea's Anti-Corruption Programs and Implementation Plan". *Korea NewsWorld,* Vol. 8, No. 85 (March 2000), pp. 28-30.

Quah, Jon S.T. "Singapore's Anti-Corruption Strategy: Some Lessons for South Korea". *Korean Corruption Studies Review,* Vol. 4 (December 1999), pp. 173-193.

Wad, Peter. "The Political Business of Development in South Korea". In Edmund Terence Gomez (ed.), *Political Business in East Asia.* London: Routledge, 2002. Chapter 6, pp. 182-215.

Yoon, Sangchul. "Anti-Corruption Movement in Korea: Focusing on International Influence and Internal Political Context". *Korea Journal,* Vol. 40, no. 3 (Autumn 2000), pp. 185-216.

Thailand

Abbott, Jason. *Developmentalism and Dependency in Southeast Asia: The Case of the Automotive Industry.* London: Routledge, 2003. Chapter 5, "Thailand: From a Bureaucratic Polity to the Politics of Corruption", pp. 98-118.

Amara, Raksasataya. "Bureaucracy vs. Bureaucracy: Anti-Corrupt Practice Measures in Thailand". In Ramesh K. Arora (ed.), *Politics and Administration in*

Changing Societies. New Delhi: Associated Publishing House, 1992. Chapter 15, pp. 220-244.

Asian Development Bank. *Governance in Thailand: Challenges, Issues and Prospects.* Manila: ADB, April 1999. See: http://www.adb.org/Documents/Papers/ Governance_Thailand/default.asp?p=govpub.

Bidhya, Bowornwathana. "Thailand in 1999: A Royal Jubilee, Economic Recovery, and Political Reform". *Asian Survey,* Vol. 40, No. 1 (January/February 2000), pp. 87-97.

Borwornsak, Uwanno. "Depoliticising Key Institutions for Combating Corruption: The New Thai Constitution". In Peter Larmour and Nick Wolanin (eds.), *Corruption and Anti-Corruption.* Canberra: Asia Pacific Press, 2001. Chapter 11, pp. 177-203.

Callahan, William A. and D. McCargo. "Vote-buying in Thailand's Northeast". *Asian Survey,* Vol. 36, No. 4 (April 1996), pp. 376-392.

Chai-Anan, Samudavanija. "Problems of Bureaucratic Corruption in Thailand: A Study of Legal Codes, Administrative and Institutional Arrangements". Paper presented at the Bureaucratic Behaviour in Asia Project in Pattaya, January 1977.

Chai-Anan, Samudavanija. "The Bureaucracy". In Somsakdi Xuto (ed.), *Government and Politics of Thailand.* Singapore: Oxford University Press, 1987. Chapter 3, pp. 75-109.

Chotana, Duangkamol and Frank Flatters. *Corruption and the Thai Media.* Bangkok: Thai Development Research Institute Working Papers, 2000.

Dalpino, Catharin E. "Thailand's Search for Accountability". *Journal of Democracy,* Vol. 2, No. 4 (Fall 1991), pp. 61-71.

Doner, Richard F. and Ansil Ramsay. "Rent-seeking and Economic Development in Thailand". In Mushtaq H. Khan and K.S. Jomo (eds.), *Rents, Rent-seeking and Economic Development: Theory and Evidence in Asia.* Cambridge: Cambridge University Press, 2000. Chapter 3, pp. 145-181.

Funston, John. "Political Reform in Thailand: Real or Imagined?" *Asian Journal of Political Science,* Vol. 8, No. 2 (December 2000), pp. 89-108.

Hicken, Allen. "Governance and Growth in Thailand". In J. Edgardo Campos (ed.), *Corruption: The Boom and Bust of East Asia.* Quezon City: Ateneo de Manila University Press, 2001. Chapter 7, pp. 163-182.

Laird, John. *Money Politics, Globalisation, and Crisis: The Case of Thailand.* Singapore: Graham Brash, 2000.

Maneewan, Chat-uthai and Gary N. McLean. "Combating Corruption in Thailand: A Call to an End of the 'White Buffet'". In John Kidd and Frank-Jurgen Richter (eds.), *Fighting Corruption in Asia: Causes, Effects and Remedies.* Singapore: World Scientific Publishing, 2003. Chapter 13, pp. 317-348.

McVey, Ruth (ed.). *Money and Power in Provincial Thailand.* Singapore: Institute of Southeast Asian Studies, 2000.

Morell, David. "The Functions of Corruption in Thai Politics". *Asian Affairs*, Vol. 3, No. 3 (1976), pp. 151-184.

Neher, Clark D. "Political Corruption in a Thai Province". *Journal of Developing Areas*, Vol. 11, No. 4 (July 1977), pp. 479-492.

Nontophon, Nimsomboon. "Administrative and Financial Accountability in Thailand". In Sirajuddin H. Salleh and Arabinda Kar (eds.), *Administrative and Financial Accountability: The ASEAN-SAARC Experience.* Kuala Lumpur: Asian and Pacific Development Centre, 1995. Chapter 8, pp. 2-3-225.

Nualnoi, Treerat. "Thailand: Fight Against Corruption". See http://www.fes.or.kr/Corruption/papers/Thailand.htm

Ockey, James. "Political Parties, Factions, and Corruption in Thailand". *Modern Asian Studies*, Vol. 28, No. 2 (May 1994), pp. 251-277.

Orapin, Sopchokchai. "Good Local Governance and Anti-Corruption Through People's Participation: A Case of Thailand". Bangkok: Public Sector Reform Project, Office of the Civil Service Commission, October 2001.

Orathai, Kokpol. "Electoral Politics in Thailand". In Aurel Croissant, Gabriele Bruns and Marei John (eds.), *Electoral Politics in Southeast and East Asia.* Singapore: Friedrich Ebert Stiftung, 2002, pp. 277-320.

Pasuk, Phongpaichit and Sungsidh Piriyarangsan. *Corruption and Democracy in Thailand* 2nd edition. Bangkok: Silkworm Books, 1996.

Pasuk, Phongpaichit, Sungsidh Piriyarangsan, and Nualnol Treerat. *Guns, Girls, Gambling, Ganja: Thailand's Illegal Economy and Public Policy.* Chiang Mai: Silkworm Books, 1998.

Prasit, Damrongchai. "Good Governance and Counter Corruption in Thailand". Paper presented at the seminar on International Experiences on Good Governance and Fighting Corruption in Bangkok, Thailand, 17 February 2000.

Scott, James C. *Comparative Political Corruption.* Englewood Cliffs: Prentice-Hall, 1972. Chapter 4, "Corruption in Thailand", pp. 57-75.

Sheridan, Greg. *Asian Values Western Dreams: Understanding the New Asia.* St. Leonards: Allen and Unwin, 1999. Chapter 9, "Culture, Consumers and Corruption in Buddhist Thailand", pp. 174-190.

Thinapan, Nakata. *Bureaucratic Corruption in Thailand: Incongruities between Legal Codes and Social Norms.* Bangkok: School of Public Administration, National Institute of Development Administration, 1977.

Thinapan, Nakata. "Corruption in the Thai Bureaucracy: A Survey of Public Officials and General Citizenry's Attitudes". *Thai Journal of Development Administration*, Vol. 17 (July 1977), pp. 355-405.

Thinapan, Nakata. "Corruption in the Thai Bureaucracy: Who Gets What, How and Why in its Public Expenditures". *Thai Journal of Development Administration*, Vol. 18, No. 1 (January 1978), pp. 102-128.

Wescott, Clay G. (ed.). *Key Governance Issues in Cambodia, Lao PDR, Thailand, and Viet Nam.* Manila: Asian Development Bank, 2001. Chapter 4, "Summary of Thailand Governance Assessment", pp. 37-52.

Wingfield, Tom. "Democratization and Economic Crisis in Thailand: Political Business and the Changing Dynamic of the Thai State". In Edmund Terence Gomez (ed.), *Political Business in East Asia.* London: Routledge, 2002. Chapter 8, pp. 250-300.

Vietnam

Gillespie, John. "The Political-Legal Culture of Anti-Corruption Reforms in Vietnam". In Tim Lindsey and Howard Dick (eds.), *Corruption in Asia: Rethinking the Governance Paradigm.* Annandale: The Federation Press, 2002. Chapter 10, pp. 167-200.

Maitland, Elizabeth. "Corruption and the Outsider: Multinational Enterprises in Vietnam". In Lindsey and Dick (eds.), *Corruption in Asia,* Chapter 9, pp. 147-166.

Nicholson, Pip. "The Vietnamese Courts and Corruption". In Lindsey and Dick (eds.), *Corruption in Asia,* Chapter 11, pp. 201-218.

Wescott, Clay G. (ed.). *Key Governance Issues in Cambodia, Lao PDR, Thailand, and Viet Nam.* Manila: Asian Development Bank, 2001. Chapter 5, "Summary of Viet Nam Governance Assessment", pp. 53-65.

World Bank. *Viet Nam: Combating Corruption.* Washington D.C.: World Bank, 2000.

COMPARATIVE STUDIES

Alatas, Syed Hussein. *Corruption and the Destiny of Asia.* Petaling Jaya: Prentice-Hall Malaysia, 1999.

Arvis, Jean-Francois and Ronald Berenbeim. *Implementing Anti-Corruption Programs in the Private Sector: Lessons from East Asia.* Washington, D.C.: World Bank, 2002.

Bloodworth, Dennis. *An Eye for the Dragon: South-East Asia Observed 1954-73.* Harmondsworth: Penguin Books, 1975. Chapter 14, "The Sweet Smell of Corruption", pp. 159-170.

Bolongaita, Emil. "Southeast Asia". In Robin Hodess (ed.), *Global Corruption Report 2003.* Berlin: Transparency International, 2003, pp. 140-152.

Caiden, Gerald E. "Towards a General Theory of Official Corruption". *Asian Journal of Public Administration,* Vol. 10, No. 1 (June 1988), pp. 3-26.

Caiden, Gerald E. "Undermining Good Governance: Corruption and Democracy". *Asian Journal of Political Science,* Vol. 5, No. 2 (December 1997), pp. 1-22.

Callahan, William A. *Pollwatching, Elections and Civil Society in Southeast Asia.* Aldershot: Ashgate, 2000. Chapter 9, "Addressing Political Corruption in Southeast Asia", pp. 143-164.

Callahan, William A. "Political Corruption in Southeast Asia". In Robert Williams (ed.), *Party Finance and Political Corruption*. Basingstoke: Macmillan Press, 2000. Chapter 7, pp. 163-198.

Callick, Rowan. "East Asia and the Pacific". In Robin Hodess (ed.), *Global Corruption Report 2001*. Berlin: Transparency International, 2001, pp. 10-22.

Campos, J. Edgardo (ed.). *Corruption: The Boom and Bust of East Asia*. Quezon City: Ateneo de Manila University Press, 2001.

Carino, Ledivina V. (ed.). *Bureaucratic Corruption in Asia: Causes, Consequences and Controls*. Quezon City: JMC Press, 1986.

Djalal, Dini. "Southeast Asia". In Hodess (ed.), *Global Corruption Report 2001*, pp. 23-38.

Dwivedi, O.P. "Bureaucratic Corruption in Developing Countries". *Asian Survey*, Vol. 7, No. 1 (January 1967), pp. 18-36.

Goh, Keng Swee. "Business Morality in Less Developed Countries". *Petir* (Singapore), Vol. 7 (1980), pp. 4-13.

Goh, Keng Swee. "Public Administration and Economic Development in Less Developed Countries". Fourth Harry G. Johnson Memorial Lecture delivered at the Royal Society in London on 28 July 1983. Reprinted in Linda Low (ed.), *Wealth of East Asian Nations: Speeches and Writings by Goh Keng Swee*. Singapore: Federal Publications, 1995, pp. 126-144.

Haggard, Stephan. *The Political Economy of the Asian Financial Crisis*. Washington, D.C.: Institute for International Economics, 2000. Chapter 1. "Business-Government Relations and Economic Vulnerability", pp. 15-46.

Hors, Irene. *Fighting Corruption in Customs Administration: What Can We Learn From Recent Experiences?* Paris: OECD Development Centre Technical Papers No. 175, April 2001. (See http://www.oecd.org/dev/publication/tp1a.htm)

Kang, David C. *Crony Capitalism: Corruption and Development in South Korea and The Philippines*. Cambridge: Cambridge University Press, 2002.

Khan, Mustaq H. "Patron-Client Networks and the Economic Effects of Corruption in Asia". In Mark Robinson (ed.), *Corruption and Development*. London: Frank Cass Publishers, 1998, pp. 15-39.

Khan, Mushtaq H. and K.S. Jomo (eds.), *Rents, Rent-Seeking and Economic Development: Theory and Evidence in Asia*. Cambridge: Cambridge University Press, 2000.

Kidd, John B. and Frank-Jurgen Richter (eds.). *Corruption and Governance in Asia*. Basingstoke: Palgrave Macmillan, 2003.

Kidd, John and Frank-Jurgen Richter (eds.), *Fighting Corruption in Asia: Causes, Effects and Remedies*. Singapore: World Scientific Publishing, 2003.

Kim, Taek. "Comparative Study of Anti-Corruption Systems, Efforts and Strategies in Asian Countries: Focusing on Hong Kong, Singapore, Malaysia, and Korea". In John B. Kidd and Frank-Jurgen Richter (eds.), *Fighting Corruption in Asia: Causes, Effects and Remedies*. Singapore: World Scientific Publishing, 2003. Chapter 14, pp. 349-375.

Kim, Young Jong. "Corruption in Socialist and Capitalist Countries", In Charles Sampford and Noel Preston (eds.), *Public Sector Ethics: Finding and Implementing Values*. London: Routledge, 1998. Chapter 7, pp. 91-101.

Kunio, Yoshihara. *The Rise of Ersatz Capitalism in Southeast Asia*. Singapore: Oxford University Press, 1988. Chapter 4, "Rent-seekers and Speculators", pp. 68-98.

Kunio, Yoshihara. *The Nation and Economic Growth: The Philippines and Thailand*. Kuala Lumpur: Oxford University Press, 1994. Chapter 15, "Crime", pp. 188-200.

Law, Joseph King-Hea. "A Comparative Study of the Anti-Corruption Measures of Hong Kong and Singapore Since 1945". M.Soc.Sc. (Public Administration) dissertation, University of Hong Kong, 1985.

Lindsey, Tim and Howard Dick (eds.). *Corruption in Asia: Rethinking the Governance Paradigm*. Annandale: The Federation Press, 2002.

Lipset, Seymour Martin and Gabriel Salman Lenz. "Corruption, Culture, and Markets". In Lawrence E. Harrison and Samuel P. Huntington (eds.), *Culture Matters: How Values Shape Human Progress*. New York: Basic Books, 2000. Chapter 9, pp. 112-124.

Lo, T. Wing. *Corruption and Politics in Hong Kong and China*. Buckingham: Open University Press, 1993.

Lu, Xiaobo. "East Asia". In Robin Hodess (ed.), *Global Corruption Report 2003*. Berlin: Transparency International, 2003, pp. 128-139.

Moran, Jon. "Patterns of Corruption and Development in East Asia". *Third World Quarterly*, Vol. 20, No. 3 (June 1999), pp. 576-582.

O'uchi, Minoru. "A Study of Corruption: A Paradigm for Analysis". *The Yachiyo Journal of International Studies*, Vol. 9, No. 4 (January 1997), pp. 1-50.

Palmier, Leslie. "The Control of Corruption in the Developing World". *India International Centre Quarterly*, Vol. 10, No. 1 (March 1982), pp. 3-12.

Palmier, Leslie. "Bureaucratic Corruption and its Remedies". In Michael Clarke (ed.), *Corruption: Causes, Consequences and Control*. London: Frances Pinter Publishers, 1983. Chapter 12, pp. 207-219.

Palmier, Leslie. *The Control of Bureaucratic Corruption: Case Studies in Asia*. New Delhi: Allied Publishers. 1985.

Palmier, Leslie. "Corruption in the West Pacific". *The Pacific Review*, Vol. 2, No. 1 (1989), pp. 11-23.

Pedro, Antonio C. Jr. (ed.). *Combating Corruption in East Asia*. Manila: Yuchengo Center for East Asia, De La Salle University, 2001.

Political and Economic Risk Consultancy. "Corruption in Asia in 2001". Hong Kong: PERC, March 7, 2001. See http://www.asiarisk.com/lib10.html

Pye, Lucian W. "Money Politics and Transitions to Democracy in East Asia". *Asian Survey*, Vol. 37, No. 3 (March 1997), pp. 213-228.

Quah, Jon S.T. "Bureaucratic Corruption in the ASEAN Countries: A Comparative Analysis of Their Anti-Corruption Strategies". *Journal of Southeast Asian Studies*, Vol. 13, No. 1 (March 1982), pp. 153-177.

Quah, Jon S.T. "Tackling Bureaucratic Corruption: The ASEAN Experience". In Gerald E. Caiden and Heinrich Siedentopf (eds.), *Strategies for Administrative Reform*. Lexington: Lexington Books, 1982. Chapter 9, pp. 109-121.

Quah, Jon S.T. "Controlling Corruption in City-States: A Comparative Study of Hong Kong and Singapore". *Crime, Law and Social Change*, Vol. 22 (1995), pp. 391-414.

Quah, Jon S.T. "Combating Corruption in Asia: Comparing Anti-Corruption Agencies in South Korea, Taiwan and Thailand". Paper presented at the conference on "Institutionalizing Horizontal Accountability: How Democracies can fight Corruption and the Abuse of Power" organised by the Institute for Advanced Studies and the International Forum for Democratic Studies in Vienna, Austria, 26-29 June 1997.

Quah, Jon S.T. "Combating Corruption in South Korea and Thailand". In Andreas Schedler *et al.* (eds.), *The Self-Restraining State: Power and Accountability in New Democracies*. Boulder: Lynne Rienner Publishers, 1999. Chapter 15, pp. 245-256.

Quah, Jon S.T. *Comparing Anti-Corruption Measures in Asian Countries*. Singapore: Centre for Advanced Studies, National University of Singapore, CAS Research Papers Series No. 13, November 1999.

Quah, Jon S.T. "Corruption in Asian Countries: Can it be Minimized?" *Public Administration Review*, Vol. 59, No. 6 (November/December 1999), pp. 483-494.

Quah, Jon S.T. "Accountability and Anti-Corruption Agencies in the Asia-Pacific Region". In *Combating Corruption in Asian and Pacific Economies*. Manila: Asian Development Bank, 2000, pp. 101-124.

Quah, Jon S.T. "Democratisation and Political Corruption in the Philippines and South Korea: A Comparative Analysis". Paper presented at the International Studies Association Conference in Hong Kong, 26-28 July 2001.

Quah, Jon S.T. "Globalization and Corruption Control in Asian Countries: The Case for Divergence". *Public Management Review*, Vol. 3, No. 4 (December 2001), pp. 453-470.

Quah, Jon S.T. "Combating Corruption in the Asia Pacific Region". In Gerald E. Caiden *et al.* (eds.), *Where Corruption Lives*. Bloomfield: Kumarian Press, 2001. Chapter 10, pp. 131-144.

Quah, Jon S.T. "Responses to Corruption in Asian Societies". In Arnold J. Heidenheimer and Michael Johnson (eds.), *Political Corruption: Concepts and Contexts* 3rd edition. New Brunswick: Transaction Publishers, 2002. Chapter 28, pp. 513-532.

Quah, Jon S.T. "Corruption". In David Levinson and Karen Christensen (eds.), *Encyclopedia of Modern Asia*, Vol. 2. New York: Charles Scribner's Sons, 2002, pp. 175-180.

229

Quah, Jon S.T. "Controlling Corruption". In Colin Kirkpatrick, Ron Clarke and Charles Polidano (eds.), *Handbook on Development Policy and Management*. Cheltenham: Edward Elgar, 2002. Chapter 34, pp. 333-341.

Quah, Jon S.T. "Causes and Consequences of Corruption in Southeast Asia: A Comparative Analysis of Indonesia, Philippines and Thailand". Paper presented at the 64th National Conference of the American Society for Public Administration on "The Power of Public Service" in Washington, D.C., U.S.A., 15-18 March 2003.

Rahman, A.T. Rafique. "Legal and Administrative Measures Against Bureaucratic Corruption in Asia". In Ledivina V. Carino (ed.), *Bureaucratic Corruption in Asia: Causes, Consequences and Control*. Quezon City: JMC Press and College of Public Administration, University of the Philippines, 1986. Chapter 4, pp. 109-162.

Ramos, Fidel V. "Good Governance Against Corruption". *The Fletcher Forum of World Affairs*, Vol. 25, No. 2 (Summer 2001), pp. 9-17.

Scott, James C. *Comparative Political Corruption*. Englewood Cliffs: Prentice-Hall, 1972.

Searle, Peter. "Coping with Corruption and Cronyism". In Gerald Segal and David S.G. Goodman (eds.), *Towards Recovery in Pacific Asia*. London: Routledge, 2000. Chapter 6, pp. 69-84.

Segal, Philip. "Dealing with the Devil: The Hell of Corruption"v *Impact* (Spring 1999). See: http://www.ifc.org/publications/pubs/impact/impsp99/s9corruption.html

Shah, Aqil. "South Asia". In Hodess (ed.), *Global Corruption Report 2001*, pp. 39-52.

Singh, Gurharpal. "South Asia". In Hodess (ed.), *Global Corruption Report 2003*, pp. 153-164.

Thompson, Nicholas and Scott Thompson. *The Baobab and the Mango Tree: Lessons About Development, African and Asian Contrasts*. London: Zed Books, 2000. Chapter 7, "Corruption: From Nibble to Gulp", pp. 119-138.

Wedeman, Andrew. "Looters, Rent-Scrappers, and Dividend-Collectors: Corruption and Growth in Zaire, South Korea, and the Philippines". *Journal of Developing Areas*, Vol. 31 (Summer 1997), pp. 457-478.

Wedeman, Andrew. "Development and Corruption: The East Asian Paradox". In Edmund Terence Gomez (ed.), *Political Business in East Asia*. London: Routledge, 2002. Chapter 1, pp. 34-61.

Weder, Beatrice. *Model, Myth, or Miracle? Reassessing the Role of Governments in the East Asian Experience*. Tokyo: United Nations University Press, 1999. Chapter 5, "Causes and Consequences of Corruption", pp. 89-117.

Wertheim, W.F. "Sociological Aspects of Corruption in Southeast Asia"v In Arnold J. Heidenheimer (ed.), *Political Corruption: Readings in Comparative Analysis*. New York: Holt, Rinehart and Winston, 1970. Chapter 19, pp. 195-211.

Wescott, Clay. "Combating Corruption in Southeast Asia". In John Kidd and Frank-Jurgen Richter (eds.), *Fighting Corruption in Asia: Causes, Effects and Remedies*. Singapore: World Scientific Publishing, 2003. Chapter 10, pp. 237-269.

SOME USEFUL WEB SITES

1. See Transparency International's web site: http://www.transparency.org for details of the Corruption Perceptions Index from 1995-2002. For Transparency International's Daily Corruption News, see http://www.transparency.org/press_moni.html. To subscribe send an e-mail to dcn@transparency.org.

2. For Political and Economic Risk Consultancy's surveys on corruption from 1995-2001 see: http://www.asiarisk.com/lib10.html.

3. Asian Development Bank's web site: http://www.adb.org.

4. For Governance World Watch and Governance Asia-Pacific Watch, see: http://www.unpan.org/whatsnew.asp#reports.

5. Organisation for Economic Co-operation and Development Anti-Corruption Unit. See http://www.oecd.org/daf/nocorruption/index.htm.

6. Anti-Corruption Ring Online, AnCorr Web: http://www1.oecd.org/def/ASIAcom/countries/index.htm.

7. Fraud and Corruption News Alerts, Institute of Public Finance, United Kingdom. See: http://www.ipf.co.uk/Governance/alerts/HTML/FraudNews.htm.

8. Bangkok Post's website on corruption scandals in Thailand: http://www.bangkokpost.net/issues/scandals/news.html.

9. Anti-Corruption Agency, Malaysia: http://www.jaring.my/bpr/.

10. Central Bureau of Investigation, India: http://www.cbi.nic.in.

11. Central Vigilance Commission, India: http://www.cvc.nic.in.

12. Corrupt Practices Investigation Bureau, Singapore: http://www.gov.sg/pmo/cpib.

13. Independent Commission Against Corruption, Hong Kong: http://www.icac.org.hk.

14. Independent Commission Against Corruption, New South Wales, Australia: http://www.icac.nsw.gov.au.

15. Korean Independent Commission Against Corruption, South Korea: http://www.kicac.gov.kr.

16. Seoul Metropolitan Government's OPEN system: http://open.metro.seoul.kr.

17. United Nations Development Programme's web site: http://www.undp.org.

18. World Bank's web site: http://www.worldbank.org.

List of Abbreviations

ACA	Anti-Corruption Act (South Korea)
ACA	Anti-Corruption Agency (Malaysia)
ACB	Anti-Corruption Branch (Hong Kong, Singapore)
ACB	Anti-Corruption Bureau (India)
ACO	Anti-Corruption Office (Hong Kong)
AVD	Administrative Vigilance Division (India)
BAI	Board of Audit and Inspection (South Korea)
BJP	Bharatiya Janata Party (India)
CBI	Central Bureau of Investigation (India)
CCC	Counter Corruption Commission (Thailand)
CID	Criminal Investigation Department (Hong Kong, Singapore)
CIO	Complaints and Investigations Office (Philippines)
CPC	Commission for the Prevention of Corruption (South Korea)
CPD	Corruption Prevention Department (Hong Kong)
CPD	Criminal Police Department (Mongolia)
CPI	Corruption Perceptions Index
CPIB	Corrupt Practices Investigation Bureau (Singapore)
CRD	Community Relations Department (Hong Kong)
CVC	Central Vigilance Commission (India)
CVO	Chief Vigilance Officer (India)
DECS	Department of Education, Culture and Sports (Philippines)
DJP	Democratic Justice Party (South Korea)
DSPE	Delhi Special Police Establishment (India)
ECD	Economic Crime Division (Mongolia)
ICAC	Independent Commission Against Corruption (Hong Kong)
ID	Investigation Department (Mongolia)
GDP	Gross Domestic Product
GPO	General Prosecutor's Office (Mongolia)
IAS	Indian Administrative Service
KICAC	Korean Independent Commission Against Corruption (South Korea)

LAC	Law on Anti-Corruption (Mongolia)
MDU	Mongolian Democratic Union
MHA	Ministry of Home Affairs (India)
MP	Member of Parliament
MPO	Misdemeanours Punishment Ordinance (Hong Kong)
MPP	Mongolian People's Party
MPRP	Mongolian People's Revolutionary Party
NCCC	National Counter Corruption Commission (Thailand)
NDP	National Democratic Party (Mongolia)
OCD	Organised Crime Division (Mongolia)
OPEN	Online Procedure Enhancement for Civil Applications (South Korea)
PAGCOM	Presidential Anti-Graft Committee (Philippines)
PAP	People's Action Party (Singapore)
PARGO	Presidential Agency on Reforms and Government Operations (Philippines)
PCAC	Presidential Complaints and Action Commission (Philippines)
PCAGC	Presidential Commission Against Graft and Corruption (Philippines)
PCAO	Presidential Complaints and Action Office (Philippines)
PCAPE	Presidential Committee on Administrative Performance Efficiency (Philippines)
PCGG	Presidential Commission on Good Government (Philippines)
PCPEA	Presidential Committee on Public Ethics and Accountability (Philippines)
PD	Presidential Decree (Philippines)
PERC	Political and Economic Risk Consultancy (Hong Kong)
PFFC	Presidential Fact-Finding Committee (Philippines)
PMO	Prime Minister's Office (Singapore)
POBO	Prevention of Bribery Ordinance (Hong Kong)
POCA	Prevention of Corruption Act (India, Malaysia, Singapore)
POCO	Prevention of Corruption Ordinance (Hong Kong, Singapore)
RA	Republic Act (Philippines)
RHKPF	Royal Hong Kong Police Force
RRC	Regulatory Reform Committee (South Korea)
SCS	Singapore Civil Service
SDP	Social Democratic Party (Mongolia)

SPF	Singapore Police Force
TI	Transparency International (Berlin)
UNDP	United Nations Development Programme

Index

235

Indonesia
  bureaucracy, 187-8, 189
  civil service salaries, 9
  Income Tax Law, 12
  media, 188-9
  Opacity Index, 3
  opportunities for corruption,
    11-12, 15, 189
  Political Economic Risk
    Consultancy ranking, 3, 59
  political system, 183, 184
  population, 182, 183
  TI Corruption Perceptions
    Index, 1, 52, 183
Inter-American Development Bank,
  193
International Development Research
  Centre (IDRC), ix
international community, 18-19, 20, 193

Japan
  civil service salaries, 160
  Opacity Index, 4
  Political Economic Risk
    Consultancy ranking, 3
  political system, 183, 184
  politician's salaries, 65
  population, 182, 183
  prime minister's salary, 65
  TI Corruption Perceptions
    Index, 2, 183

Kim Dae Jung, President, 18, 152,
  155, 165-6, 168-9, 169, 170, 179
Kim Young Sam, President, 18, 151,
  155, 163-4, 166-8, 169, 174n, 179
Korean War, 154

Lee Hsien Loong, 122
Lee Kuan Yew, 15, 99, 115, 120, 125-6,
  186, 187, 188
Lim Yew Hock, 114-15

Macapagal, President Diosado, 92
Malaysia
  Anti-Corruption Agency (ACA),
    17
  anti-corruption laws, 19
  Political Economic Risk
    Consultancy ranking, 3

political system, 183, 184
population, 182, 183
Prevention of Corruption Act
  1961, 17
TI Corruption Perceptions
  Index, 2, 183
Marcos, Imelda, 90
Marcos, President Ferdinand, 82, 87,
  89-90, 92, 93, 94, 99, 180, 184,
  185, 187
media, deterrent against corruption,
  15, 188
  coverage of Estrada trial,
    Philippines, 96
  media poll, Mongolia, 38-9
  public awareness campaign,
    South Korea, 165
  reporting of police corruption,
    Singapore, 110
Mongolia, 26-57
  anti-corruption agencies, 19
  anti-corruption laws, 19
  anti-corruption strategy, 44-7
    evaluation, 47-51
  banking scandals, 33, 39-40
  bureaucracy, 36-44, 48-9
  China influence, 32
  civil service salaries, 31-2, 42-4,
    56n, 190
  communist state, 26, 29, 34, 36,
    37, 180
  corruption extent, 35-44
  Criminal Code, 16, 44, 46, 46-7, 49
  Criminal Police Department
    (CPD), 47
  demography, 31-2
  economy, 27, 28-31
  Erdenet ore-dressing plant, 40-1
  Friendship and Mutual
    Assistance Treaty (with
    Soviet Union), 29
  General Prosecutor's Office
    (GPO), 47, 49
  geography, 27-8
  hunger strike, 37
  infrastructure, 27
  judiciary system, 49, 50
  Law on Anti-Corruption, 16,
    44-6, 180
    effectiveness, 47-9